American Indian
BASKETS

American Indian
BASKETS

BUILDING AND CARING FOR A COLLECTION

William A. Turnbaugh and Sarah Peabody Turnbaugh

Schiffer Publishing Ltd

4880 Lower Valley Road • Atglen, PA 19310

Other Schiffer Books by the authors:
Indian Baskets, 3rd edition, ISBN: 0-7643-1900-0. $29.95
Indian Jewelry of the American Southwest, 3rd edition, ISBN: 0-7643-2577-9. $12.95

Library of Congress Control Number: 2013930054
ISBN: 978-0-7643-4404-6

Library of Congress Cataloging-in-Publication Data

American Indian baskets: building and caring for a collection / William A. Turnbaugh ; Sarah Peabody Turnbaugh.
   p. ; cm.
Includes bibliographical references and index.
1. Indian baskets – North America – History. 2. Basket making – North America. 3. Indians of North America – Crafts. 4. Indian baskets – Collectors and Collecting. 5. Arts and Crafts Movement – American – Indian baskets.
I. Turnbaugh, William A. II. Turnbaugh, Sarah Peabody, joint author. III. Title.

Printed in China
Published by Schiffer Publishing, Ltd.
4880 Lower Valley Road
Atglen, PA 19310
Phone: (610) 593-1777; Fax: (610) 593-2002
E-mail: Info@schifferbooks.com

For the largest selection of fine reference books on this and related subjects, please visit our website at **www.schifferbooks.com.** You may also write for a free catalog.

This book may be purchased from the publisher.
Please try your bookstore first.
We are always looking for people to write books on new and related subjects. If you have an idea for a book, please contact us at proposals@schifferbooks.com
Schiffer Books are available at special discounts for bulk purchases for sales promotions or premiums. Special editions, including personalized covers, corporate imprints, and excerpts can be created in large quantities for special needs. For more information contact the publisher.

In Europe, Schiffer books are distributed by
Bushwood Books
6 Marksbury Ave.
Kew Gardens
Surrey TW9 4JF England
Phone: 44 (0) 20 8392 8585; Fax: 44 (0) 20 8392 9876
E-mail: info@bushwoodbooks.co.uk
Website: www.bushwoodbooks.co.uk

Dedication

We dedicate this book to basket makers
and basket collectors everywhere.

Fashioning baskets has been a standard human activity since time immemorial. Constructed from locally available materials using one of just several common weaving techniques, baskets have served the same essential functions in nearly every society, no matter when, no matter where. How curious that people should become so fascinated with other cultures' baskets that more than a few individuals would take on the effort and expense of procuring examples that somehow appeal to them. But such is the collector's passion.

Because they are handmade, no two baskets are ever precisely the same. And, into each is woven a kind of cultural DNA that challenges those with an interest in such matters to analyze, identify, and compare. Studied at this level, a basket may reveal much about a people's lifeways, environment, or world view. *By their baskets we shall know them.* Discerning creatures that we are, human beings place a value on fine distinctions, and we often express our admiration most directly by seeking to acquire what we truly appreciate. In a very real sense, then, basket collecting–as does basket making–reflects and affirms our shared humanity.

THE PIMA BASKET

I am the Pima basket.
    I was made of nature's materials.
I was once a willow standing
    by the running water with the arrowweed.
I was once a cattail waving
    in the river with the fishes.
I was once a devil's claw growing
    in the field with the squash plants.
I was once a pattern woven
    in a legend of my tribe.
Now I am all these things
    woven into one, woven long years ago.

–from a poem by Uretta Thomas, an Akimel O'odham (Pima)
    student at the Phoenix Indian School, 1941

Above: Pima (Akimel O'odham) or Maricopa woman at her hearth, with a fine coiled basket rimmed with glass trade beads, Arizona, c. 1900; *right*: European basketmaker depicted on an 18th- or early 19th-century glazed tile.

THE BASKET-MAKER

From the osier by the brook,
    From the weeping willow's head,
Pliant, drooping boughs I took,
    Of my spoils these baskets made.
Plaited, twin'd, and closely wove,
    All their diff'rent uses try;
With their price my wants remove,
    Gentle friends, my baskets buy.

Angler, this can hold thy fish,
    Silk-made flies, and baits, and hooks;
Pretty girl, this, to thy wish,
    Holds thy dinner, work, and books.
Mother, here can sleep thy babe,
    Of its tender griefs beguil'd;
From cold winds and frost to save,
    Buy a cradle for thy child.

–from *Little Jack of All Trades*, by William Darton,
    London, 1814

Contents

Section Two:
Collector Showcase

Section Three:
Caution Corner

Preface

Schiffer Publishing released our first book on this topic, *Indian Baskets,* in 1986. It has remained in print and available to new collectors ever since. That volume emerged out of an interest that both authors developed while working with museum collections as far back as the 1960s. Writing that book and preparing its manuscript for publication was a labor of love, especially for its primary author, who patiently typed draft after draft on her manual typewriter.

Getting the earlier book into print was an uncertain prospect. No publisher we approached in the late 1970s was confident that enough readers would be interested to warrant a general work covering the Native basketry of all North American regions. The manuscript slowly circulated through a succession of commercial publishers and academic presses. It had languished at Harvard for several years before our friend and colleague Ann McMullen (now at the Smithsonian Institution) alerted Peter and Nancy Schiffer to our work. Schiffer Publishing was planning a Native American arts series that was to include a book specifically on Indian baskets. A few months after we delivered our manuscript to the Schiffers, *Indian Baskets* emerged, published in collaboration with the Peabody Museum of Archaeology and Ethnology, Harvard University.

At the time, our book joined only several other broad studies of Native American basketry to appear since the Smithsonian's publication of Otis T. Mason's *Aboriginal American Basketry* and George Wharton James's self-published *Indian Basketry* at the opening of the 20th century. Building on Mason's approach, we systematically considered basketry region by region. Our keys to identification, based on technical aspects of construction, form, material, and decoration, enabled those interested in basketry to see and compare Native examples from throughout North America in a single volume. For the first time, many readers found they were able to attribute an unfamiliar basket to a region or possibly even a specific tribe.

The accessibility of this approach, in turn, helped foster a wider collector interest in Native American basketry at a time when general enthusiasm for Indian culture was already blossoming. Collector interest spurred a growing market for vintage Indian baskets, including those from areas previously bypassed in favor of Southwest or California baskets (which had never lost their appeal among Old West collectors and decorators). Antiques dealers, Indian arts galleries, auction houses and, soon, on-line auction services such as eBay began to offer Indian baskets more regularly, often referencing our *Indian Baskets* to support their identifications.

Scholarly research, too, has intensified during the years since our earlier publication. By now, many focused studies on individual regions and specific tribes—and even individual basketmakers—are available. As the attention afforded to basketry expands, more people have become much better informed about the topic. While it is true that Indian baskets have become more valuable as *marketplace commodities* in this time, they are also better appreciated as *cultural documents.*

Perhaps most significantly, the amplified interest in—and market for—American Indian basketwork has inspired pride among Native crafters, some of whom have responded by producing baskets in the traditional style of their elders, while others experiment with new forms and materials.

Schiffer Publishing released the authors' first book on this topic in 1986.

The authors around the time *Indian Baskets* first appeared.

Introduction

We have written this book especially for the "typical" American Indian basket collector. We assume that our reader may already have some interest in this topic, perhaps even a passion for Native American crafts such as basketry. We hope that this enthusiasm has at least occasionally prompted a responsive action, so that our reader may actually possess some nice baskets—or maybe more than a few. We don't expect that our audience will include the most advanced basketry connoisseurs, nor all the major dealers in the antique basketry trade, nor the most eminent scholars in the field. This book is not intended for them, though we should be glad if they happen to see it.

Our hope in writing this book is that it may provide that "typical" collector with a few new and helpful ways of looking at and understanding Native American basketry. We begin with some background on Indian basketmaking and Indian basket collecting. We believe this historical context can only add to the interest and pleasure one derives from the hobby. We especially want to explore the so-called "basket craze" of a century ago, when popular enthusiasm for Native American basketry reached a crescendo. Some of the same baskets woven and collected during this period are still circulating today, and they form the basis for many collections.

Basket collectors, especially those who occasionally buy or sell baskets when the opportunity arises, will find our in-depth look at "Wannabe" and "Maybe" Indian baskets to be particularly valuable. Here, we examine many categories of non-Indian baskets that can be (and so often are) confused with those actually made by Native Americans. A case of mistaken identity could prove very costly! Detailed comparison photographs prepared especially for this book point out diagnostic differences that will help the reader to distinguish between authentic Indian-made baskets and some of their foreign-made imitators.

Another of the book's most significant contributions is its attention to Northeast Indian basketry, a topic that until now has received little regard in most general studies. Our discussion puts New England's native basketmaking tradition into its historical setting and argues that it deserves more collector interest and respect. The generous photo gallery selections for this region should allow collectors, perhaps for the first time, to more readily identify these frequently overlooked works of American Indian handicraft.

The hundreds of baskets, from Abenaki to Zuni, pictured in full color in our regional Collector Showcase (Section Two) and throughout the book, are exactly the kinds of baskets a collector can most likely expect to come upon. They represent the full range of baskets that one currently finds in antique shops, flea markets, local auctions, or even garage sales. The photos and captions should help one in evaluating a potential purchase or assessing a personal collection.

This book offers the collector access to many other resources with, for example, an extensive bibliography of general works on Indian basketry, plus citations for focused studies of individual tribal styles. We provide Internet addresses for useful websites and also list one hundred North American public and tribal museums with notable collections of Native American baskets.

Section One

Indian Basketmaking and Collecting

Havasupai basketmaker and her materials, Arizona, c. 1900.

chapter 1
Basketry Background

Basketmaking is arguably one of humankind's oldest handicrafts. In many regions of the world, basketry preceded such arts as metallurgy or pottery making by many centuries. Although for most of us the term "basketry" would probably call to mind a fairly standard class of woven vessel, the term generally applies to an array of "hard textile" containers constructed from a selection of various kinds of plant or occasionally other materials. The definition might even extend to softer bags or pouches woven from twisted fibers or flexible strips, as well as rigid buckets or boxes of sewn bark, for examples.

Like most organic products, basketry ordinarily decays and disappears soon after being discarded or buried. Nevertheless, traces of what appear to be a woven textile—possibly a twined basket fragment—survive as impressions in hardened clay at a 25,000 to 27,000-year-old archaeological site in the Czech Republic. In several parts of North America, archaeological textiles specialists have identified twined impressions and tiny basketry fragments from sites of the so-called Archaic period of roaming hunters and gatherers that are about 10,000 years old. A bit of carbonized bark from Meadowcroft Rockshelter near Pittsburgh, Pennsylvania, radiocarbon-dated to 19,600 years ago, may represent a birchbark container in the opinion of the archaeologist who discovered it. At this point, it appears that coiled and plaited basketry technology followed twining by several millennia.

Better-preserved pieces and, rarely, entire ancient baskets have survived at a few sites in the American deserts. Southwestern rockshelters and caves protected some fine examples made by the ancestors of the Puebloan people who still occupy the region. In fact, archaeologists once called the earliest of these ancestral cultures "the Basketmaker People." That name—not so often used today—was bestowed decades ago when researchers knew little about the *people* of the culture, other than the fact that they used basketry extensively because they had not yet learned to make pottery. Their 2,000-year-old sites preserve both coarse utilitarian baskets of plain design and fine decorated examples that they perhaps reserved for special ceremonial use, much as their Puebloan descendants did in later centuries. Other woven artifacts survive from these early time periods. For example, a brace of reed-bundle duck decoys, once deployed in seasonal lakes, came to light at Lovelock Cave in northern Nevada, and little wrapped-stick effigies of quadrupeds (perhaps deer or mountain sheep) have been found in and around the Grand Canyon.

Fig. 1. Pueblo III two-rod-and-bundle double coiled cylindrical basket from northwestern New Mexico, about 800 years old, is well-preserved and rather contemporary in appearance, 9" high.

Fig. 2. Pueblo III two-rod-and-bundle double coiled tray has complex polychrome design, from the Four Corners area, c. 1200 A.D., 15" diameter.

Fig. 3. Coarsely coiled utilitarian basket from Mug House, Mesa Verde National Park, southwestern Colorado, c. A.D. 1100-1300.

Although moist environmental conditions in the eastern United States less often allow for good organic preservation, archaeologists did recover a large section of an ancient bark container at the late prehistoric Sheeprock Shelter site in southwestern Pennsylvania. Also included among the oldest surviving Indian baskets from the Northeast are several small twined sacks. Algonquian natives typically used such pouches to carry corn meal for preparing their jonny ("journey") cake, but Narragansett and Mohegan makers in the mid-17th century gifted these particular examples to European neighbors who then carefully preserved them.

Collectible basketry from archaeological sites and the early settlement period is extremely rare. Today, most ancient sites are protected by state or federal law, and artifacts removed from them are safeguarded in museums or returned to descendant tribes as part of their cultural heritage. Collectors, though, do enjoy access to a much more bountiful crop of baskets dating from the 19th and 20th centuries.

Fig. 4. Prehistoric quadruped effigy formed by splitting and wrapping a single twig, from a site sheltered within the Grand Canyon, Arizona, 3,000 to 5,000 years old.

Fig. 5. Sewn bark container recovered from the late prehistoric Sheep Rock Shelter in southwestern Pennsylvania.

Fig. 6. Mohegan (Connecticut) twined "yokeag" bag for parched corn meal, c. 1650, decorated with three bands of diamond-shaped "stockades," a layout that persisted into 18th- to 20th-century southern New England basketry, despite a technological turn from twining to plaited splintwork.

chapter 2
Weaving a Tradition, Past to Present

The Enduring Craft

Of all the principal Native American craft arts–basketry, jewelry, pottery, weaving, painting, carving–traditional basketmaking is arguably the most precarious today. Basketry's demise has been predicted prematurely more than once, however. Frontier travelers throughout the 18th and 19th centuries (and even earlier in eastern regions), almost as though scripted, ruefully observed that iron kettles, pails, tin plates, and cups were rapidly replacing their Native counterparts. Old women, they said, wove the few baskets still being made, while younger women generally seemed to possess neither the skills nor the inclination to take up the craft.

Despite the dire forecasts, Indian basketmaking remains a living craft tradition today, though with a changing visage. A few centers of Native basket production flourish where artisans old and young maintain their own tribal heritage, sometimes alongside others who reach beyond the customary boundaries to create innovative forms of fiber art. But in some other once-vibrant basketmaking communities hardly any baskets are now being made.

Traditional Basketmaking

Making a traditional Native basket requires much more than simply a desire to carry on a noble and ancient heritage. Any basket that is completely true to its tradition must have woven into its form an entire body of cultural knowledge and practical expertise. This *wisdom*—for that is what it is—is based on generations of experience, transmitted to and through the craftsperson, her family, and her community. A basket might be readily woven to closely resemble a traditional form. (As we shall see, ladies in the American Arts & Crafts Movement did it all the time with the aid of printed instructions and commercial materials.) But when completed, such a basket shares only a superficial relationship with the authentic model that it mimics.

Cultural Concerns

A traditional Native basketmaker has had to master more than weaving techniques. Though twining or plaiting or coiling can be exacting processes, they are soon mastered through practice and finally perfected through experience. Any competent weaver may acquire an eye for shape or form. But a traditional basketmaker bears heavy responsibilities to generations of her family and community to make a basket that is proper in all regards. Her work may be constrained by cultural standards that extend even to the proportions of the form or the direction she takes in her weaving. Incorporating acceptable design elements into the basket's fabric can actually be a most demanding task. The design layout that will grace a basket's surface often carries special significance, so the maker may have very little latitude in choosing it. At least for her most conventional work, her selection of appropriate motifs also can be governed by tribal or family custom or belief rather than by her individual preference.

Likewise, *when* or even *where* a basket may be woven could be matters for cautious consideration. Cultural taboos may restrict a woman from crafting a basket at critical times of the month or in the presence of certain individuals. As an example, early-20th-century Navajo basketmakers felt themselves so restricted by the ritual prohibitions related to their activity that continuing to weave the sacred baskets might endanger themselves and their clan. So the Navajo turned to their Paiute neighbors, who did not share the same basketmaking taboos, and thus "out-sourced" the basketmaking along with all the attendant risks. If one encounters a vintage "Navajo" wedding basket, the odds are great that it was probably crafted by a Paiute.

Knowing Nature

A traditional basketmaker's knowledge encompasses both the cultural and the natural realms. Basketry materials do not necessarily grow on trees, though some may! A basketmaker must command almost encyclopedic botanical information. What plants can be used? Where do they grow? In a given region, many species may offer potentially suitable elements for basketmaking, but only a few are likely to grow conveniently close at hand or be available at just the right time. Each plant may yield only one useful kind of material: perhaps a strip of inner bark or a fine root, or maybe a grass or fern stem, or possibly a fiber twisted from seed fluff or pulled from a long leaf. Basketmaking resources can be all but invisible to the uninitiated. The bark or vines or stalks that one assumes might readily be made into a serviceable basket will not necessarily work.

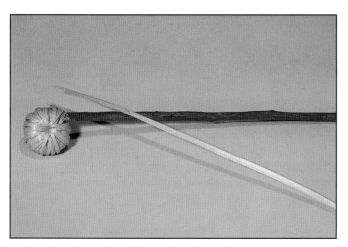

Fig. 7. Contemporary Navajo "wedding basket" starts with a tight dime-sized coil and a single rod of sumac, which is inserted butt end first to simulate the "growing outward" of the plant and the basket that is made from it.

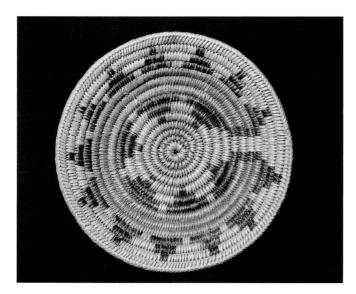

Fig. 8. Older traditional Navajo-style "wedding basket," probably Paiute-woven.

Fig. 9. Also known as sourberry or skunkbush, three-leaf sumac was a favorite material of Navajo and Paiute basketmakers.

Finding the right plant for the task is but one part of the problem. Properly harvesting and preparing the materials are also major concerns. Certain materials can be gathered during just a brief period each year. Is this willow taken while it still retains its springtime suppleness, or should one wait until it has toughened? Should these grass stems be cut or pulled? Will this vine remain pliable if coiled and stored away, or must it be kept soaking in water until used? Is this outer bark layer to be peeled off? For how long must one bury these reed stems in mud to turn them black without rotting? How soon will these yucca strips be properly bleached in the sun?

The craftsperson who combines a number of different materials into a strong and beautiful basket must precisely schedule the right times to gather each one. She must know how to prepare them all. Then she must carefully preserve her materials under just the right conditions. Only when everything aligns perfectly can a basket be created that will conform satisfactorily to all the established cultural norms.

Traditional basketmaking embodies the natural realm's rhythmic cycles in harmony with an abiding faith in social continuities. A disturbance from any source can shove the craft toward an uncertain future.

Fig. 10. Edward S. Curtis photographed this woman gathering round-stemmed tule reeds at Lake Pomo, California, in 1924. Though such large grasses as these might be used to build a shelter, basketmaking materials would have been collected in a similar manner.

Fig. 11. Bundle of red willow collected for basketmaking.

Fig. 12. Split yucca leaves prepared for basketmaking, with dried yucca seed pod.

Native Basketmaking in Transition

Not one, but several interrelated factors—technological, economic, social, ecological—contributed to the decline and near disappearance of traditional Native American basketmaking in many areas by the mid-19th century. Most of these influences stemmed either directly or indirectly from Euramerican contact, which brought about cataclysmic changes in Native society that are too many and too familiar to be enumerated here. Certainly, the course of these interactions severely disrupted longstanding Indian lifeways in most regions.

Trade Goods

One of the greatest change agents was the importation of European commercial goods. The new commodities that were dispersed into Indian societies nearly always diminished both the role and perceived value of comparable Native products, including handwoven containers. Metal kettles and pails, glass bottles, sturdy canvas, and other goods rapidly supplanted their indigenous counterparts. Whether or not they might be regarded as superior, such trade goods put many a Native craftsperson out of work.

In view of the readily available and often more durable Euramerican products, the time-consuming demands of traditional basket weaving became difficult to sustain or justify. The dissolution of familiar lifeways and an ever greater dependence on manufactured guns and ammunition, tools, cloth, and even necessities like food that had to be purchased, forced Indian women and men alike to find ways to engage in the new economic order, where a cash economy prevailed.

Handmade baskets found a new role in a few of these ravaged societies. Some Native craftspersons—still primarily women—found customers willing to pay for their handiwork. Useful Indian baskets were readily accepted in places where their makers were not always welcome. The town houses and farmsteads of New England took in Algonquian-made splintwork storage containers and laundry baskets, feather and pie baskets, hat boxes and baby rattles, as well as novel forms devised by the weavers. The incorporation of Native basketry into Euramerican lifeways began very early in this region. Similar exchanges followed in the wake of expanding settlements across other parts of the Northeast and into the Southeast, where practical Cherokee double-weave rivercane basketry likewise earned the approval of white settlers. Their useful products gave certain basketmaking individuals and groups a portal through which they might engage with the newly prevailing society.

New Directions

By the mid-19th century in the Northeast, factories began turning out utility baskets that largely replaced the products of Native hands. Many Indian craftpersons soon shifted to making baskets that appealed to tourists and curio seekers but departed markedly from customary wares.

Elsewhere, too, traditional basketmaking was in decline and, in many regions, becoming a nonessential and nearly lost art. Conservative elements in some western tribes carefully preserved their irreplaceable older baskets for ritual use, for no replacements were being made.

By the 1880s, private collectors and museum ethnologists, concerned over the doubtful future of the craft, were becoming motivated to acquire Native American basket specimens wherever they could still be found. Few genuinely old examples remained, but in places like California, the Southwest, and the Pacific Northwest, as well as New England, those basketmakers who were yet able to practice or recall their craft or who could learn it anew might find an economic opening that still eluded most Native people. In certain areas, basketmaking actually revived in response to collector interest. Baskets—whether curios or not, even when sold too inexpensively when compared to the time put into them—afforded industrious Indian women a way to earn at least a little money for themselves and their families. Basketmaking also helped affirm their identity as Native Americans, though that was not always considered an advantage in the new order.

Fig. 13. Tohono O'odham basketmaking materials include harvested devil's claw (*Proboscidea* sp.) seed pods gathered into a "hat" for storage (*rear*) and split for weaving (*left foreground*); metal tipped awl with wooden handle; split red banana root (*Yucca* sp., *right foreground*); coils of split willow (*Salix* sp.).

Fig. 15. Hopi matron repairs a traditional plaited ring basket sifter in this 1899 photo.

Fig. 14. Completed Tohono O'odham "Man in the Maze" or "Elder Brother" basket, with yucca, willow, and devil's claw.

Fig. 16. Rosie Skuki and her mother Mary Roberts offer baskets in southern British Columbia, 1923, a region with a long history of selling to tourists and collectors.

By the 20th century, virtually everywhere across the American continent, baskets had gone from playing a functional role in nearly every aspect of traditional Native life to becoming a commercial commodity in an alien culture.

Survival and Revival, 1900-1940

Basketmaking skills comprising the experience of countless lifespans could be lost in as little as a single generation once the continuity was broken. That accumulated wisdom—the intimacy with nature's resources, an aptitude for rigorous techniques, an inherent fluency in cultural meaning—would not be readily retrieved once lost. The survival of Native American basketmaking through the 20th century did not happen without assistance. What is currently a bright craft activity in a few places today often persisted not long ago only as dying coals.

Certain individuals actively fanned these flickering embers before they might be forever extinguished. In southern California, George Wharton James, an admirer and major booster of Indian basketry in the early 1900s, was one of them. He viewed the basketmaking craft as a noble undertaking in its own right, and also as a marketable enterprise that had the potential to lift its practitioners out of poverty. To that end, James and the network of fellow enthusiasts with whom he was in contact sought to encourage the craft. Long anticipating several modern Native basketmaker associations, James's "Basket Fraternity" saw the preservation and promotion of American Indian basketry as a positive goal. James himself, always an energetic and imaginative salesman who knew how to capitalize on the next "good thing," underwrote and edited the group's short-lived (1903–1904) periodical, *The Basket*, while using its advertising pages to market his own basketmaking patterns and craft supplies through his East Coast agent. The organization's mission included the study and appreciation of Indian baskets as well as the active promotion and support of traditional Native basketmaking. One stated goal was to encourage Native makers to continue using traditional practices, materials, and designs in preference to turning out cheapened commercial products. Another urged that basketry skills be taught to every female enrolled in the government-run Indian schools.

Fig. 17. Important Native American basketry periodicals. Final issues of *The Basket* (July, October 1904), edited by George Wharton James for "The Basket Fraternity;" inaugural issue of John Gogol's *American Indian Basketry Magazine* (1979), beginning a five-year run; and first issue (Autumn1975), two special Basketry Issues (Autumn 1979, Summer 1999), and recent article in *American Indian Art Magazine*.

Promoters and Patrons

In a more immediate and practical way, James and fellow Indian basketry promoters were already accomplishing some of these goals on a limited scale. In the early years of the 20th century, Grace Nicholson, Dr. John Hudson, and Rev. Henry Meredith, three other California basket merchants, were encouraging and even commissioning Native weavers, like Elizabeth Hickox and her daughter Louise (Wiyot-Karuk) and the husband and wife team of Mary and William Benson (Pomo), to make the best baskets possible for resale to their favored private and institutional clients. In Carson City, Nevada, Abe and Amy Cohn exploited the considerable talents of Washoe basketmaker Louisa Keyser (more famously known in her time as Dat-so-la-lee) and several other weavers who produced fine baskets for sale at the Cohns' Emporium. Anthropologists who worked among the California basketmaking groups—including, for examples, Roland Dixon among the Maidu, Alfred Kroeber among the Mission and Pomo, Samuel Barrett among the Pomo, and Lila O'Neale among the Yurok/Karuk—likewise encouraged the craft through the approving expressions of admiration in their writings as well as through their own professional collecting activities.

Fig. 19. Washoe *degikup*, coiled in the one-rod gap-stitched technique developed by Dat-so-la-lee.

Most of the "better" baskets produced in the West during this period were woven specifically for non-Indian customers, whether museums or collectors. Basketry scholar Dorothy Washburn has aptly described these productions as "neo-traditional," suggesting that they were consciously woven to comply with prescribed cultural standards. With prompting from James and other patrons who demanded that baskets be "pure Indian" in form and design, some weavers abandoned commercial dyes and novelty shapes, but then proceeded to devise innovative styles (such as the Washoe *degikup*) and decorate them with supposedly symbolic motifs (which dealers like Amy Cohn might then "translate" for an appreciative customer).

As considered in the next chapter, a Golden Age of Indian basket collecting endured until the First World War, then quickly faded. Indian arts actively sought new audiences as the 20th century lengthened. In 1922, the Museum of New Mexico sponsored an "Indian Fair" in Santa Fe that featured ethnological exhibits from the area. An outgrowth of that event is today's Santa Fe Indian Market, hosted annually by the Southwestern Association for Indian Arts (SWAIA) to bring together Native artisans and crowds of enthusiastic collectors. But in most areas, including the Southwest, the basketmaking craft was once again waning. Young Native American women, forcibly enrolled in government boarding schools such as those at Carlisle (Pennsylvania) or Phoenix (Arizona), lost any opportunity they might have had to learn the skills necessary to continue the Native craft. In any event, few continued to hold the craft in high regard.

Government Programs

During the Depression years in upstate New York, Arthur C. Parker, an archaeologist of Iroquois descent and the director of the Rochester Museum and Science Center, devised a WPA-sponsored government program to employ his Seneca neighbors.

Fig. 18. Washoe basketmaker Dat-so-la-lee (Louisa Keyser) poses with a selection of *degikup* baskets in this photo by Amy Cohn, c. 1900.

Between 1935 and 1941, men and women worked at home for 50 cents an hour to produce nearly 6,000 "typically Seneca" objects, including splint baskets and cornhusk items. These crafts were not sold, but were instead used in museum displays to document Seneca material culture. Parker's program was at once an attempt to salvage Native skills, foster renewed pride, and generate income.

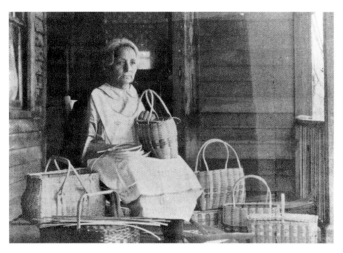

Fig. 20. Seneca Iroquois woman plaits splint baskets on the porch of her home, c. 1930s.

Around the same time, in 1935, the United States Congress acceded to John Collier, the Commissioner of Indian Affairs under Franklin D. Roosevelt, who had urged the establishment of an Indian Arts and Crafts Board. The Board's expressed purpose was to advance the economic development of American Indians and Alaska Natives through promoting their handcrafted products. Its efforts soon brought Native arts some much-deserved attention. The Board's second general manager, Rene d'Harnoncourt, assembled a popular exhibit of Indian art for the San Francisco Golden Gate International Exposition in 1939. Then, in 1940–1941, as a guest curator, d'Harnoncourt installed a much-expanded version of his display at New York's Museum of Modern Art.

The highly-acclaimed MoMA exhibition, "Indian Art of the United States," and the attendant publicity it garnered, put Native American arts on the map. An accompanying book of the same title further popularized the topic. Among the over 200 objects pictured was an array of basket works representing several regions: a Basketmaker Culture burden basket from 500–600 A.D., Tlingit open berry basket, large old Pomo burden basket, Pomo feathered gift basket, Yurok lidded basket, Washoe bowl by Dat-so-la-lee, Western Apache olla and tray, Hopi wicker tray, two contemporary O'odham geometric plaques and a playful

duck basket, an Iroquois cornhusk mask, two Canadian birchbark boxes, and a modern Cherokee wastepaper basket.

Contemporary Indian Baskets

Native American basketry remains a tenuous craft even now. We have seen that traditional basketmaking flourished within specific natural and cultural environments. For better or worse, the old lifeways that nurtured the craft disappeared long ago. Today's basketmakers work in very different situations. What they manage to accomplish is done against the odds. Understandably, when compared with vintage baskets, contemporary Indian baskets generally reveal some significant distinctions.

Fig. 21. Co-author with Melissa Darden, granddaughter of Chitimacha basketmaker Lydia Darden, who holds award ribbons for her double-weave rivercane lidded basket and her miniature basket at SWAIA's 2002 Indian Market in Santa Fe.

Art or Craft?

For instance, the individual maker's name is more commonly connected with her baskets nowadays. Today's consumer tends to look for the *brand* as much as the *product*. At present, name recognition is the primary driver in the market for *art* and, to an increasing degree, *craft*. Traders and merchants recognize that customers expect to learn a basketmaker's name and perhaps to see her picture when they purchase her basket. The savvy basketmaker accepts the need for this exposure. Modern weavers soon acquire an individual reputation if their work is of both superior technical quality and sufficient volume to sustain a market.

Ever since baskets first became a consumer commodity, well before the basket craze of the early 1900s, the basketmaker's skills have been an important gauge of her product's market value. The same is true today. Many contemporary basketmakers have attained a high level of proficiency in their pursuit. Some approach or possibly match or even exceed the technical mastery of such legends as Louisa Keyser (Washoe), Elizabeth Hickox (Wiyot-Karuk), or Susie White (Akimel O'odham). Their modern talents may be showcased in the extremely fine workmanship displayed in miniature or, alternatively, exhibited in oversized and ostentatious forms. Or they can magically enhance even a simple basket of ordinary dimensions.

Most basket weavers realize that their handiwork is destined to enter a fickle and competitive marketplace. Products that consciously adhere to traditional forms or designs appeal to certain collectors, while highly innovative departures from the old traditions excite others. Anticipating the buyer's preferences can be tricky. Every modern weaver faces a dilemma. Is she expected to represent a particular *craft* tradition, perhaps the one most closely associated with her proclaimed ethnic identity? Or is she producing *art*, and therefore freed (or maybe expected) to express herself through more experimental creations, liberated from tribal strictures? The basket that falls somewhere between, perhaps a familiar form woven from non-traditional materials, may be the most difficult to sell.

Marketing Baskets

The relative scarcity of authentic, contemporary Indian basketry has resulted in more limited, controlled outlets for these products. It is still possible for an independent basketmaker to vend her creations in her own village or perhaps take her wares to a nearby tourist spot. But life for most women is too busy and complex to allow for basket-marketing in addition to basketmaking, given other obligations. Many weavers today appreciate the advantages of affiliating with a regional or tribal basketmakers' association. These cooperatives offer instruction, encouragement, and sales opportunities. Some artisans do personally represent themselves at periodic gatherings like the Santa Fe Indian Market or the Heard Museum's annual Indian Fair and Market in Phoenix. Others enjoy an established relationship with a particular gallery or trader that will represent and advocate for them. The patron who promotes a promising

Fig. 22. Susie White, virtuoso Akimel O'odham (Pima) basketweaver and one of her award-winning miniature coiled willow lidded baskets. The same basket appears in the midst of a cluster of tiny examples in this late 1940s photograph.

Fig. 23. Striving for more attention and higher prices, early 20th-century Indian basketweavers created novel products, such as this California basket large enough to accommodate two 1920s "flappers," each displaying a miniature coiled basket.

basketmaker naturally expects to share in the benefits as her prestige and the prices for her work increase.

Collectors must be prepared to pay relatively more for a finer, recently made Native American basket than for a standard antique Indian basket. While the vintage basket will be priced according to its scarcity, condition, and overall collector appeal, the modern basket represents the creative output of a living person. The maker's talent for converting simple raw materials into an appealing product should be acknowledged and rewarded. That person's time, which includes the preparation of materials required to fashion the basket, has to be factored into the retail price. Any merchants involved in the transaction will surely tack on some additional overhead costs. In fairness, there ought to be some profit to share as well! The collector who purchases a modern American Indian basket not only helps to assure its maker a living wage, but also fosters a tradition in need of as much support as it can get.

Today's basketmakers often have alternative opportunities for gaining a livelihood, yet a few have chosen to continue their craft. These days, for example, Indian gaming operations on many reservations across the United States appeal to Native employees with the incentives of regular wages and benefits. Younger people are especially attracted to the excitement and experiences they can anticipate while working at the casinos. By contrast, the prospect of trying to make ends meet through the tedious and time-consuming process of handweaving baskets from a mass of sharp and resistant filaments demands a prudent woman's careful evaluation. Most of those who choose to continue basketmaking are doing so in order to remain true to their own heritage and thereby pass along their craft as a legacy to following generations.

Fig. 25. Eastern Cherokee basketmakers of North Carolina are among those who market their handicrafts at roadside tourist attractions.

Fig. 24. This miniature White Mountain Apache leather-trimmed burden basket, woven with non-traditional fiber, won a prize ribbon at the 1995 Gallup Inter-tribal Indian Ceremonial.

Fig. 26. Tohono O'odham (Papago) basketmakers have offered their wares through the commercial Gila River Arts & Crafts outlet in Arizona for decades.

Fig. 27. Co-author with basketweaver Sally Black, eldest daughter of Mary Holiday Black, the matriarch of one of contemporary Navajo basketry's most prominent families, widely considered responsible for the craft's revival.

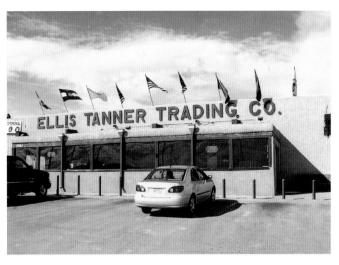

Fig. 28. Indian trading posts on or near reservations can be good sources of baskets produced by local tribes.

Indian Basketmaker Associations

Both the confinement of once mobile people to a reservation and the destruction of their cultural and natural environments contributed to the decline of the basketmaking craft. As we have noted, basketry closely mirrors the local ecology. Many materials grow only in specific habitats. In the past century or so, the extensive ecological changes associated with farming, lumbering, mining, development, road building, and other land clearing operations have destroyed many habitats altogether. Altering a stream by damming it, polluting it, or pumping too much water from it may do likewise. Burning an area too often, or too little, may have consequences that affect plants used in the craft. Extended droughts in the Southwest and elsewhere impact natural basketry materials as well as other resources. The result is that today many of the specific plants required for traditional basketmaking are hard to find. Even the once-abundant sweetgrass and brown ash favored by Native New England basketmakers are threatened now as coastal development limits access to the grass and as emerald ash-borers and Asian longhorned beetles invade the northern forests. As further examples, rivercane is similarly threatened in the South, as are stands of rushes such as juncus in southern California.

Fig. 29. Terry DeWald, long-time Native American arts trader featured here in a 1997 article, has fostered Tohono O'odham (Papago) basketmaking by encouraging individual weavers and marketing their products through his wholesale/retail business. His informative book, *The Papago Indians and Their Basketry*, attracts new collectors, as it has since 1979.

Global environmental concerns since the mid-1970s have led some Americans to reflect on what they perceive to be the Indians' more harmonious relationship with nature. One outgrowth of this admiration has been the renewed notice given to Indian craft arts, including basketry. Many Native American basketmakers, also concerned about their craft's future as well as the earth's, have stepped to the forefront of the environmental or "green" movement. Since 1991, for example, the California Indian Basketweaver's Association (CIBA) has raised concerns over the future of traditional basketmaking materials. They actively oppose non-selective herbicide spraying to eliminate "weeds," a word often applied to their important basket plants such as beargrass, white root, juncus, and others. CIBA advocates for access to and preservation of plant habitats (for example, through controlled burns), with the ultimate goal of maintaining the resources through sustainable harvests.

The California group is not alone. A much earlier basketmaker alliance dates to just after World War II, when a Native arts and crafts cooperative (now the Qualla Arts and Crafts Mutual) was organized on the North Carolina reservation of the Eastern Band of Cherokee. Its purpose was to market baskets and other craft products to tourists. Under the tutelage of an accomplished Cherokee basketweaver and teacher, Lottie Stamper, and Gertrude Flanagan, a non-Cherokee U.S. Indian Arts and Crafts Board employee, the co-op set tight guidelines with regard to basket forms, materials, and dyes. This structured approach proved its worth as Cherokee products achieved and even today maintain a respected place in well-rounded collections of Native American basketry.

Following CIBA in the early 1990s, Native basketmakers in several other regions organized themselves in quick succession in order to promote, perpetuate, and preserve all aspects of the Native American basketry tradition: Maine Indian Basketmakers Alliance (MIBA, 1992), Tohono O'odham Basketweavers Organization (TOBO, 1996), Northwest Native American Basketweavers Association (NNABA, 1996), and Great Lakes Indian Basket and Box Makers (GLIBBA, 1997–1998), among others.

Fig. 30. Modern Southwest basketmakers prefer cultivated hybrid devil's claw (*Proboscidea* sp., *background*) over the wild variety that grows on weedy vines in the desert environment.

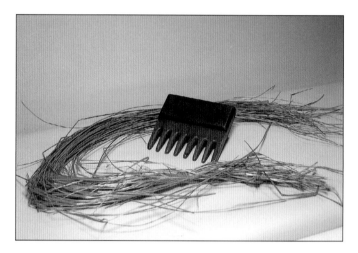

Fig. 31. Northeastern sweetgrass (*Hierochloe odorata*) and a traditional wooden comb from Maine that a Wabanaki basketmaker uses to clean and straighten the stems.

Fig. 32. Beargrass (*Xerophyllum tenax*), a standard basketmaking material in California and elsewhere in the West, can again be lawfully harvested by Native weavers on public lands, due to the efforts of CIBA.

Whether of long standing or more recently organized, basketmaker organizations are serving important roles today. W. Richard West, Jr., founding director of the National Museum of the American Indian in Washington, D.C., summarized the mission of these groups in his foreword to Bernstein's *The Language of Native American Baskets from the Weavers' View* (2003:6):

> The community of American Indian weavers, in fact, has been growing since the early 1990s, when a number of Native individuals and organizations, inspired by the basketry groups of the early 20th century, founded several new tribal or regional weaving associations. Through these associations, weavers are addressing such challenges as the scarcity of raw materials or their limited access to them on public and private lands, health risks from the use of pesticides and herbicides at plant-gathering sites, and the issue of non-Native people making and selling baskets as "Indian-made." These groups also encourage young people to learn basketmaking. Some associations have combined basketry classes with Native language lessons and workshops in other traditional skills, helping to preserve the rich heritage of their cultures and to keep the spiritual aspect, as well as the technical craft, of basketmaking vibrant.

Fig. 33. Contemporary ash splint and braided sweetgrass vase, made by covering a small jelly jar with plaiting, was sold through the Maine Indian basketmakers' cooperative organized by five Wabanaki tribes.

Fig. 34. Tohono O'odham Basketweavers Organization (TOBO) represents many individual weavers at popular events such as the Heard Museum's annual Indian Fair and Market in Phoenix.

chapter 3
Indian Basket Collecting

Where Are the "Old" Indian Baskets?

Most Indian baskets are not as old as many collectors may assume them to be. We have noted that truly ancient baskets, those of archaeological antiquity, only rarely survive. Very few of them remain intact when found. Made primarily of organic materials and relatively fragile, ordinary basketry utensils were intended for service, and most wore out and were eventually discarded. Even those baskets reserved for special purposes, such as ceremonies or grave offerings, did not long endure once they were finally abandoned to the elements. And some cultures routinely disposed of all personal possessions, including baskets, by burying or burning them when they were used up or immediately upon their owner's death.

Though very old baskets are seldom available to collectors, a few have survived. On the East Coast, rare specimens of 17th-century Native American handiwork were preserved as heirlooms, including the previously mentioned Mohegan and Narragansett "jonny cake" bags from New England. By the later 18th century, however, Indians in that region were making baskets specifically for sale to their Euramerican neighbors. At first their wares adhered closely to basic functional forms—generally practical containers of various sizes and shapes. But by the second half of the 19th century, as we shall see, some Northeast Indian craftspersons were creating entirely new kinds of whimsical baskets to be sold as souvenirs or decorations.

Pioneering travelers in other regions of the country also sometimes acquired samples of Native handiwork through interaction and exchange. For example, as Indians accepted European containers they might discard or barter away some of their old baskets to interested parties. Early 19th-century Russian traders on the northern California coast and Spanish settlers in southern California appreciated the handsome baskets woven by local Indians. Some venerable examples from this period are still prized in European and American collections. In all, though, fewer than 150 surviving California baskets are known to pre-date the Gold Rush of 1849.

The Rise of Museums

The rise of formal museums in the United States in the mid-19th century, soon followed by the developing science of anthropology—the study of human cultural and biological adaptations—provided an incentive for formally collecting every class of cultural product for comparative research and display. Among the categories routinely carted back to late19th-century museum storerooms and galleries were specimens of basketwork from all regions.

The Peabody Museum, established in 1866 at Harvard University in Cambridge, Massachusetts, is one of the nation's oldest. Its collections house some fairly early American Indian baskets, including a Wasco-style twined, root-digging bag collected along the Columbia River by the explorers Meriwether Lewis and William Clark in 1805 or 1806, as well as some of the older New England specimens. But the Peabody Museum, like every other repository, has many more baskets representing the period after about 1875.

Late 19th-Century Collectors

Indian basketry was among the many categories of cultural and natural objects that also attracted individual Victorian-era curio collectors. We tend to think of those times as the "good old days" for accumulating the best examples. More than a few private buyers amassed impressive assemblages of baskets. What few of these collectors—institutions as well as individuals—fully realized was the extent to which Native weavers viewed their interest as a commercial opportunity, and so responded by making more baskets that were specifically tailored to Euramerican preferences. Sometimes they abandoned traditional forms, materials, weaving techniques, and designs altogether in favor of expedient alternatives that would enable them to more readily meet the demand. They recognized that collectors especially coveted heavily-decorated and oversized ollas, trays, and bowls, along with whimsical creations that showcased a weaver's skills.

Fig. 35. Indian baskets, sometimes in profusion, graced many homes at the turn of the 20th century, as seen in this vintage postcard.

Fig. 36. Varied and decorative baskets, like these mostly California examples, attracted early 20th-century collectors.

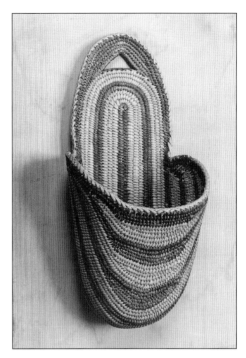

Fig. 37. Non-traditional forms, like this c. 1930 Akimel O'odham (Pima) wall pocket, appealed to tourists as practical and interesting souvenirs.

Already by the 1880s in the West, a few astute basket buyers, perhaps anticipating the craft's supposedly imminent demise in the wake of the challenges that so adversely affected Native lifeways, were actively seeking out particularly fine basketry specimens. Helen Hunt Jackson, reformer and author of *A Century of Dishonor* (1881) and *Ramona* (1884), a fictionalized account of a southern California Indian woman's life, had called attention to the Native basketry of that region in several magazine articles detailing the plight of the Mission tribes. Jackson, herself a collector, fueled the growing frenzy for Indian baskets by purchasing so many of them during her tour. A consequent rise in value took baskets to ten times their previous price, according to a September 1894 *Harper's Bazaar* article. Tiffany & Co. in New York City struggled to keep a few Indian baskets stocked, even at the princely sum of 30 to 40 dollars each. Collectors especially developed a penchant for baskets made by certain California and Pacific coast tribes and by Indians living in the Southwest, considering them to be somehow more "authentic."

It may be understood, then, why the majority of the Indian baskets generally available to today's collectors were made after about 1875, and most of those after 1900. It follows that relatively few of the vintage baskets available for purchase today were actually used or even intended for use by Native people. Most were crafted in direct response to consumer demand and made expressly for sale to non-Indian buyers. Consequently, many non-traditional forms are represented, some of which are essentially Native-made versions of standard Euramerican household items such as vases and calling-card trays.

A Brief Look at a Long Tradition: Northeast Indian Basketry

Some of the oldest Indian baskets in today's market come from the Northeast. Baskets from this region are also among the most readily available and inexpensive, yet collectors tend to more often overlook and less fully appreciate them. The older sweetgrass and woodsplint baskets, and the occasional birchbark items, made by Indians of New England and adjacent areas are still routine finds at yard sales, flea markets, and antique shops in many parts of the country. Though by-passed by some collectors in search of more showy Apache trays or bright Hupa caps, many of these more humble northeastern products are of equal or greater age than their western counterparts.

Fig. 38. Examples like this standard woodsplint and sweetgrass sewing basket, made by a Native in the Northeast more than a century ago, often go unrecognized or unappreciated as Indian work.

Fig. 39. Canadian artist Cornelius Krieghoff (1815-1872) portrayed itinerant northeastern Indian basket sellers in a number of paintings dating to the mid-19th century.

Utility Baskets

Those vintage sweetgrass and woodsplint souvenirs were by no means the earliest Native American baskets acquired by New Englanders. As noted above, northeastern Indians have had a long history of selling baskets to their Yankee neighbors. By at least the late 18th century, Native basketmakers were making their rounds from town to town each year as they peddled the products of their winter labors. Villagers and farmers alike found many uses for the durable woodsplint containers as storage boxes, harvest baskets, egg carriers, and the like. Some of these itinerant Natives bartered with several generations of customers. A few, like the Paugusset maker Molly Hatchett (died 1829) of western Connecticut, enjoyed almost legendary status, and her baskets remain highly prized today.

A story has long circulated in Connecticut about the plaited wares made by another well known basketmaker, "Jim Pan" Harris, a later 19th-century Schaghticoke craftsman. He reputedly wagered the local miller that his woodsplint baskets could transport gallons of apple cider without leaking a drop. And Harris proved just that, though only after first quickly dipping his baskets into a stream and pulling them out to freeze during a cold late autumn night, thereby coating and sealing the closely interlaced splints!

Researchers have not fully resolved the origin of New England woodsplint technology. Some historians insist the Indians learned the craft from Europeans, while others maintain that the technique preceded the settlers. It is noteworthy that the tools historically employed in making splint baskets—the metal "crooked knives," spokeshaves, gauges, and planes—are all of European form and have no obvious Native antecedents in the region. Fragments of splintwork corn sifters excavated from two mid-17th-century Seneca Iroquois sites in western New York supply the earliest direct evidence so far for the antiquity of Native American woodsplint technology. Moreover, iron crooked-knife blades accompanied other European trade goods found in Narragansett Indian burials that also date to the mid-1600s in southern Rhode Island. Significantly, during the next two centuries woodsplint plaiting seems to have all but supplanted the indigenous birchbark technology in the Northeast.

Whatever their lineage, some of these dour and unassuming New England splint containers are among the very earliest Indian-crafted baskets a collector can hope to find.

Fig. 40. Indian-made products like these southern New England plaited woodsplint boxes, decorated with Native motifs, were used by Yankee households for storage. Upper right example, missing its cover, c. 1820, is 11" long.

Fig. 41. European basketmakers, like the weaver seen in this mid-19th-century English lithograph, used specialized tools and techniques to produce plaited baskets.

Fig. 42. Northeastern Indians also employed metal-bladed tools, like these crooked knives and splint cutter (*foreground*) and splint gauges (*background*), to aid production of ash splint strips (*center*) for their plaited baskets.

Fig. 43. Old Town, Maine, Penobscot basketmaker's toolkit consisting of crooked knives, splint gauges, splint cutters, and extra blades.

Beginning around the mid-19th century, in turn, the New England tradition of Native-made woodsplint utility baskets gradually yielded to substitutes that were being mass-produced in Yankee factories. These manufactured baskets generally had nailed rims but were otherwise similar in form and overall appearance to the Indian handmade versions.

Fig. 44. Factory production of utility baskets in New England rapidly replaced Native handiwork after the mid-19th century.

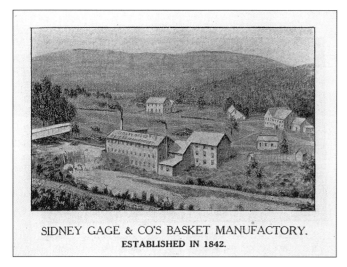

Fig. 45. Gage began basketmaking at this sawmill along the Connecticut River in southern Vermont in 1842. The company produced 600 baskets a day in the 1880s and has continued since 1942 under the name "Basketville."

Fig. 46. Most baskets turned out by Gage and other basket factories featured nailed rims. Note that the prices quoted in this late 19th-century catalog are for a dozen baskets.

Curio Baskets

Forced to seek economic opportunities in a different direction, Wabanaki and other Native basketmakers of northern New England and the Canadian Maritimes looked to the seasonal influx of moneyed tourists. They began selling considerable quantities of their handicrafts in the summer resort communities of coastal Maine, New Hampshire, and Massachusetts more than a century ago. Indian handmade sewing and knitting baskets, glove and handkerchief boxes, pie baskets, wastepaper receptacles, shopper baskets, basketry-covered jars and vases, collar boxes, purses, trays, and other Victorian whimseys, such as fans and bookmarks and doll cradles, were just a few of the many basketry items the vacationers carried home as souvenirs.

Fig. 47. Native basket sellers pose at their camp at a coastal Maine vacation spot in this c. 1900 postcard image.

Fig. 48. In 1934, Penobscot basketmaker Camilla Sockalexis, also known by her Indian name "Sipsis" (Bird), was offering a wide array of basketry at The Flume, a popular destination in the White Mountains of New Hampshire.

Fig. 50. Selling on a commercial scale through its catalogs, St. Regis Indian Basket Company utilized the talents of Mohawk weavers to turn out basketry and other curios for tourists and collectors.

Fig. 49. Maine splint and sweetgrass baskets, made for the market, c. 1890-1930, include flat work or sewing baskets, button baskets, and novelty miniatures.

The popularity of these curios has never abated completely. Basketmakers of these northeastern Native groups (including those around the Great Lakes) plied their craft throughout the 20th century and continue to produce similar basketry products even now. Temporary roadside camps set up at the tourist resorts closed forever during the sad years of the Great Depression. But by the mid-20th century, modern tourist shops and art galleries sited along northern New England's coastal thoroughfares replaced those rustic predecessors. For several decades, familiar locations such as Chief Poolaw's Tepee at Old Town, and Leslie and Christina Francis' Indian Store in Searsport, Maine, gave regional craftspersons reliable access to the traveling public.

Today, the Maine Indian Basketmakers' Alliance, centered at Old Town under Theresa Secord's direction, is a Native artisans' cooperative that actively supports and promotes both customary and innovative basketwork in the 21st century. Unfortunately, the group's handsome retail outlet became victim to another economic downturn and tourism decline when it closed in late 2008.

Anyone, who for some reason missed the opportunities to buy directly, could purchase by mail order many of the same kinds of Indian basketry products supplied by the Abenaki, as well as Huron, Iroquois, and other northern Indian crafters. In business during the early 1900s, the St. Regis Indian Basketry Company was one of several retailers whose illustrated catalogs offered many of the specialty baskets so well-represented in today's collections. Operating out of Hogansport, New York, the firm capitalized on talented Mohawk basketmakers on the St. Regis (now Akwesasne) reservation straddling both sides of the St. Lawrence River on the international border with Canada.

Fig. 51. Maine Indian basketmakers have had a presence on Main Street in Old Town for generations.

Fig. 52. "Chief" Bruce Poolaw, a Kiowa from Oklahoma, and his wife, Princess Watahwaso (Lucy Nicolar Poolaw), a basketweaver and singer known as the "Bright Star of the Penobscot," attracted tourists to their establishment at Indian Island, Maine, with entertainment and craft demonstrations.

Fig. 53, Fig. 54. Chief Poolaw's Tepee, established in 1947, was an outlet for many local Native American basketmakers. Family members maintain a museum at the location today.

Fig. 55. Co-author at the Maine Indian Basketmakers Alliance retail outlet in Old Town, Maine, prior to its 2008 closure.

Fig. 56. Native basketmakers sometimes sell from their private residences, as here in coastal Maine.

Indian Baskets in the American Arts & Crafts Movement

Over 100 years ago, at the opening of the 20th century, the fascination with Indian baskets expanded tremendously with the timely publication of two popular books on the subject. Otis Tufton Mason, a curator at the National Museum in Washington, D.C., prepared a comprehensive and heavily-illustrated survey of Native American basketry that first appeared as part of the Smithsonian Institution's official annual report for 1902. His *Aboriginal American Basketry: Studies in a Textile Art without Machinery* (also issued commercially in 1904 as two volumes with the title *Indian Basketry: Studies in a Textile Art without Machinery*) described the range and function of Indian baskets and compared the traits of each tribe's work. At the time of its release, Mason's opus coincided perfectly with an already heightened public interest in the topic. Over the long term, his monumental work became the foundation upon which nearly all subsequent American Indian basketry research has built.

Also popular with early 20th-century basket collectors were the books written and published by George Wharton James. The California basketry enthusiast (and son of a basketmaking father) boosted collecting by encouraging his readers to appreciate and buy—and even try their own hand at making—Indian baskets. James' first publication on the subject, *Indian Basketry* (1901), drew freely from previous writers on the subject, including Mason, to whom the book was dedicated. James featured photo illustrations of private collections stocked with gorgeous specimens and even portrayed some Native basketmakers with their creations. Within the year, he had enlarged his initial book into a combined volume, *Indian Basketry and How to Make Baskets*. By adding his own precise drawings as well as patterns that were easy to follow, James enticed readers to reproduce Indian-style baskets that could be used for decorating the home or given as gifts.

For a while, the modest pastime of basket collecting ignited into something of a craze. Mason even coined a word for it—"canastromania" ("basket madness," from the Latin *canistra*, basket). In retrospect, this phenomenon may be understood as a minor aspect of a widening and deepening appreciation at that time for skilled, handcrafted workmanship. Essentially a rejection of Victorian norms that condoned fussy furnishings and mechanically mass-produced goods, this new ethic reached deep into everyday life. It expressed itself, among other ways, through a nostalgic regard for well-made domestic products that combined good form with useful function. In England, trend setters such as John Ruskin and William Morris advocated a return to strong design and quality hand craftmanship that emulated an idealized pre-industrial era.

Fig. 57. Tiffany Studios created this leaded glass and bronze chandelier resembling a northern California basketry cap. One of only a few made during the height of the American Arts & Crafts Movement, this example sold for $151,000 in a 1995 auction.

This philosophy (including social dimensions not considered here) soon took root in America as well. Under the guidance of Louis Comfort Tiffany, Gustav Stickley, Elbert Hubbard and the Roycrofters, among others, it became known as the Arts & Crafts Movement. The guiding principles—strong, spare design along with skillful hand-finishing—translated into distinctive homes that showcased harmonious decorative arts: bold oak furniture that glorified the beauty of natural wood grain; art glass and pottery with innovative yet understated glazes; hand-hammered and patinated copper or iron metalwork; and fabrics enhanced with embroidered or hand-printed motifs abstracted from the natural world. Emanating from centers like Boston, New York, Chicago, New Orleans, and Pasadena, the Arts & Crafts fervor filtered into other communities and homes across America through publications, lectures, and vigorous merchandizing.

The movement's basic tenets strongly encouraged individual participation in craft work. The hands-on application and practice of these ideals became a form of recreation (especially for well-off ladies) by which one could personally create some of the practical and beautiful objects required to enhance the home. Classes offered formal instruction, and published plans provided guidance in making Arts & Crafts style furniture, pottery, textiles, jewelry, toleware, book bindings, and basketry at home.

But how, specifically, did *Indian* baskets become part of the Arts & Crafts agenda?

Fig. 59. While "playing Indian" in a New England backyard, c. 1905, these boys used bows and arrows while the girls tended to the baskets.

Fig. 58. Edward S. Curtis's elegantly framed sepia-toned prints, some of which romanticized "the vanishing American," became popular accents in the American Arts & Crafts home.

The movement's emphasis on craftsmanship and nature soon brought some of its devotees to an appreciative reconsideration of Native American lifeways. By that point not much was going well for the Indians. A generation of conflicts with the U.S. Army, starting with the defeat of Custer's troops at the Little Bighorn in 1876 and ending in 1890 with the massacre of Sioux families at Wounded Knee, had reduced the Plains Indians to a sad existence on a few bleak reservations. Native peoples in other regions of the country were faring no better, most having become wards of the government decades earlier. But now that the Native tribes were no longer adversaries, a new generation of Americans became increasingly aware of them, sharing a concern for their welfare with admiration for their former lifeways.

The enthusiasm for all things Indian included particularly a nostalgic appreciation for their handicrafts. As cross-country railroad routes carried more and more easterners into western Indian country, face-to-face commercial encounters at depots, tourist attractions, and recently designated national parks afforded the visitors with opportunities to purchase gifts and mementos directly from the people who had made them. Quantities of Native American wool blankets, silver and turquoise jewelry, pottery, baskets, and other artifacts rode home with the travelers.

Fig. 60. Unique electrified table lamp dating from the Arts & Crafts period with an Akimel O'odham (Pima) bowl for its base and matching 18-inch diameter tray for its shade.

Baskets, which were relatively inexpensive and light to carry, yet both functional and attractive, proved especially popular. Intriguing symbolic designs woven into their textured surfaces often complemented the pleasing shapes, and the presence of such baskets in the Arts & Crafts home contributed an exotic and sophisticated quality to the living space. From this appreciation developed an indigenous style, as embodied in basketry and other Native crafts, that became a hallmark of the new American aesthetic.

A "Basket Craze"

Not surprisingly in this climate, George Wharton James' popular how-to books soon inspired a flock of imitative basketmaking guides that featured designs drawn from many different tribes. Standard women's magazines of the period, including several numbers of *Harper's Bazaar* and *The Ladies Home Journal*, followed James in depicting Indian and other baskets serving as mantle decorations, flowerpot containers, wastepaper receptacles, and pencil holders. A casually placed Indian basket or two was almost *de rigueur* in any well-appointed parlor. Decorating with baskets became yet another art for the homemaker to master.

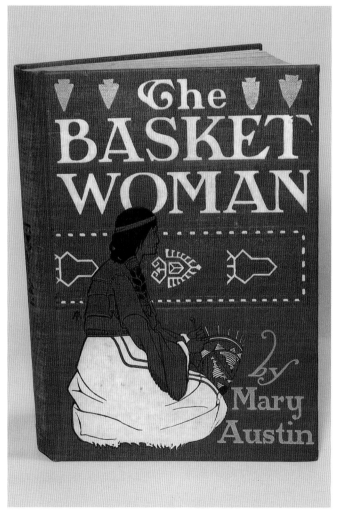

Fig. 61. Decorative cover on 1904 edition of *The Basket Woman*, a collection of California Indian legends, brightened a book shelf in an Arts & Crafts home. In the century from Helen Hunt Jackson's *Ramona* (1884) to Lynn Andrews's *Medicine Woman* (1983), Indian baskets have sometimes played a supporting role in popular literature.

Everybody's Baskets

Basket lovers who wanted to develop their own skill might learn the craft at a local extension school, such as the Manchester Institute in New Hampshire or Boston's Museum of Fine Arts. A routine U.S. agriculture department technical bulletin on willow propagation found unanticipated demand from basketmakers who wished to grow their own weaving material. Those who lacked a moist meadow might turn to a number of commercial firms eager to supply hobbyists with willow withes, ash splints, bundled raffia, coiled rattan, aniline chemical dyes, and other basketmaking resources. Or one could now enroll through the mail in any of several competing correspondence courses on Indian basketmaking. Individual participation in these craft projects further reinforced the American Arts & Crafts mission and strengthened its representation of Native American ideals. The Los Angeles-based Navajo School of Indian Basketry circulated a promotional brochure for its home-instruction course that may have only just slightly overstated the excitement of the times:

> The interest taken by all true Americans and lovers of ancient art in the basket made and used for centuries by the American Indians has grown and expanded until Indian Basketry has been revived and popularized, and now it has taken on the proportions of a great industry.

Fig. 63. With her splint basket for handiwork resting on a rustic stand made of twigs, a Worcester, Massachusetts, grandmother gives a knitting lesson, c. 1900.

Geraniums are an Unusual and Attractive Decoration

Fig. 62. Scrapbooked illustration from *The Ladies Home Journal* of the Arts & Crafts period suggests using an Indian basket to hold potted flowers or vases.

Fig. 64. Northeast Indian woodsplint and sweetgrass basket with an added Arts & Crafts embroidered top with drawstring closure.

Fig. 65. Young women fashion baskets in a course offered by the Museum of Fine Arts, Boston, c. 1910.

Fig. 66. American Arts & Crafts Movement basketmakers could order supplies and instructions from the convenience of their homes.

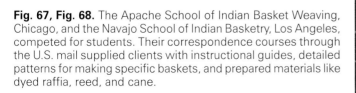

Fig. 67, Fig. 68. The Apache School of Indian Basket Weaving, Chicago, and the Navajo School of Indian Basketry, Los Angeles, competed for students. Their correspondence courses through the U.S. mail supplied clients with instructional guides, detailed patterns for making specific baskets, and prepared materials like dyed raffia, reed, and cane.

Fig. 69. Early 20th-century American Arts & Crafts basket of dyed and undyed raffia, 10" high. Many Arts & Crafts enthusiasts admired what they conceived as an Indian ethos. Their devotion often led to a strong urge to possess Indian-themed products. The raffia bowl at center was the result of a craft project obviously inspired by a Native American basketry design. It recalls the story of a Boston society lady who showed off her "Indian basket collection" at tea one afternoon. "But those aren't real Indian baskets," one guest murmured. "Of course they are, dear, for I made them myself," the hostess retorted. Such baskets sometimes appear for sale today.

Fig. 70. Eye-catching display of northern California twined baskets, dance regalia, and stone implements at Alexander Brizard's emporium, Arcata, California, c. 1900. Photographer A.W. Ericson occasionally acquired baskets from California collectors and shipped them east for sale. Examples from these shelves are undoubtedly preserved in some present-day collections.

By that point, the interest in Indian baskets clearly had ballooned into something of a fad. More than a few avid collectors had already accumulated hundreds of "authentic" Native American baskets. Some buyers sought out representative examples from many tribes. Others acquired every basket they could locate from a particular culture or region. They competed with each other and with public museums that were also actively adding specimens to their display cases.

Economic Impact

Many Native women directly or indirectly benefitted from the basket craze. For example, in Olympia, Washington, Saturday became "Indian Day," when steamships brought Native women and their basket creations from nearby Squaxin Island for a day of selling to eager buyers. Though surely under-compensated for the many hours needed to make a basket, women were able to earn a little money that would afford them at least limited participation in the modern cash economy.

Ultimately, a considerable amount of money did exchange hands over Indian baskets. West Coast visitors who did not connect with the ladies from Squaxin Island might prefer the convenience of selecting from an extensive array of baskets and other ethnographic artifacts displayed in showrooms such as Ye Olde Curiosity Shop, a fixture on the Seattle waterfront since 1899. Collectors who could not personally travel to the West in search of Indian baskets might still discover something appealing in one of the East Coast specialty shops, including Tiffany's, that offered Indian goods for sale. Others could purchase from the mail-order catalogs issued by a number of Indian curio merchants.

By July 1904, the anonymous author of "The Story of the Indian Basket," writing in *The Hill-Top*, a periodical for the Poland Spring, Maine, summer resort community, informed vacationers that:

> The Campbell collection in Los Angeles comprises 138 specimens and is very complete. It has cost upward of $8,000, and besides, it was made before the vogue made the weaves so costly. The more enthusiastic collectors seldom have dealings with the sellers of baskets in the curio stores of th[at] region, preferring to go themselves out among the tribes and to bargain for specimens that suit their fancy.

He went on to add that:

> baskets valued at no less than $5,000,000 have been taken from California and Arizona alone in the last two years. To be sure the makers

received but a small proportion of that sum, the greater profit going to the Eastern dealer. So heavy has been the demand that the Southwest has been nearly denuded of the finer baskets, and hundreds of dealers and agents of museums are vying with one another to get fine specimens of work of the different tribes.

C132. Native Women Weaving Baskets, Alaska

Fig. 71, Fig. 72. The authors discovered several faded photographs taken by George Wharton James around 1900 tucked into one of his books. These two depict southern California basketmakers selling their wares in a store and outdoors. Note the rattlesnake skin hanging at the right of the indoor photo.

Fig. 73, Fig. 74. Postcard views of Northwest Coast basketweavers, c. 1900, suggest the industrious effort devoted to turning out baskets for the tourist trade.

Fig. 77. Ye Olde Curiosity Shop on the Seattle waterfront has been supplying Indian baskets to tourists and collectors for generations.

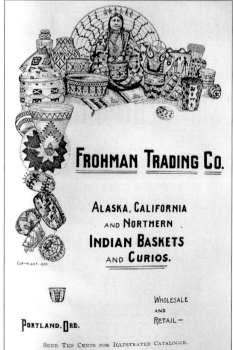

Fig. 75, Fig. 76. Aggressive marketing in the early 20th century stimulated American Indian basketry production to reach commercial levels in some regions.

Fig. 78. Victorian lithographed trade card, c. 1880s, for the Indian Basket Store in Philadelphia advertises one of the earliest eastern retail outlets devoted to the Native craft.

Poland Spring happened to be one of the seasonal tourist retreats where Maine Indians regularly set up camps to display and sell their own sweetgrass and woodsplint baskets. One might hope that the writer was perhaps subtly reminding affluent visitors to purchase some of the local craftspeople's modest souvenirs before going home. Many other northeastern resort locations, such as Bar Harbor, Maine, and the White Mountains of New Hampshire, also hosted seasonal basketmakers-in-residence. Some northern New England Indians traveled further, going south into the eastern urban centers to market their wares.

Despite (or perhaps because of) this focused attention among serious collectors, the fervor for Indian baskets within the general populace dwindled considerably by the First World War (1914–1918). American homemakers were updating their interiors, and the old baskets were retired. Museum curators decided that most contemporary Native American handicrafts were debased, overpriced, and unworthy of adding to their collections. And, in fact, too many basketmakers had allowed their work to become overly commercialized with non-traditional materials, hasty weaving techniques, artificial dyes, and frivolous forms and designs. Yet the most avid of the individual collectors continued to vie for especially fine older specimens whenever and wherever they came available.

A Basket Bias?

A parenthetical comment or two may be added here regarding the predilection many collectors have had for Indian basketry from western North America. That this basketry still tends to be ranked above that of other regions might be explained in a number of ways, quite aside from any judgments based on technological or aesthetic grounds. For one, southern California, particularly the Pasadena area, was the home base for two of the most eminent dealers and promoters of Indian basketry, namely George Wharton James and Grace Nicholson. James's popular books prominently featured basketmakers and collectors from California and the surrounding area. Nicholson's regular clients included many eastern society ladies who wintered in Pasadena. To the north in Ukiah, California, Dr. John Hudson and his talented artist wife Grace Carpenter Hudson were the primary promoters and suppliers of Pomoan baskets. These and other motivated individuals, conveniently situated close to so many California basketmaking groups, were able to foster and guide the craft and directly benefit from its success.

Early anthropologists at the University of California also focused on the Native people of this region and their material culture, particularly their basketry, in scholarly publications. Other ethnologists systematically scoured the Southwest and the Pacific Northwest for basketry of those regions to exhibit in their museums, stimulating even more attention and collector demand.

Fig. 79. Coastal Maine and the White Mountains of New Hampshire were favorite New England vacation spots that put potential buyers into the proper frame of mind for purchasing rustic souvenirs and Native American crafts, including baskets.

Perhaps as a result of all this enthusiasm, the basketry of the western tribes seemed more interesting and alluring. Collectors came to consider it more "authentic" than the "debased" products of Indian handiwork found in the eastern United States, where the Native basketry craft had for so long accommodated itself to Yankee practicality and marketing opportunities. Consequently, to this day a general perception persists that favors western American Indian baskets as the "gold standard." To address this imbalance, we have offered a brief overview of Indian basketmaking in New England on the preceding pages. The reader will also discover that a generous portion of the Collector Showcase (Section Two) highlights the basketry of this region.

Fig. 81. Most collectors a century ago sought out baskets produced by western tribes, like those featured in this c. 1900 magazine layout, in preference to baskets from other regions.

Before leaving San Gabriel, there are two places you should not fail to visit—the Historic Old San Gabriel Mission across from the playhouse, and the Mission Curio Art Shop adjoining the theatre, devoted to the display of the arts and handicrafts of the native tribes from the early period depicted in the Mission Play down to the present time.

Fig. 80. Conveniently located just south of Pasadena, California, the western epicenter of both the American Arts & Crafts Movement and the Indian "basket craze," San Gabriel appealed to visitors with this colorful c. 1905 circular.

chapter 4
What Collectors Should Know

Caveat emptor!

Old baskets are not uncommon. They lurk in an attic's cobwebbed corner. They dangle from exposed beams or peer down from a high book shelf. They tumble across the lawn at yard sales or pile together on a porch. Some might command a reserved spot in the consignment shop's display case. Others compete for space on—or under—a flea market table brimming with might-be treasures. A country auctioneer holds one aloft, awaiting the bid that will confirm his consignor's high hopes. A mellow, glowing orb stares from the computer monitor, seducing an on-line bidder. Suffused light in an exclusive gallery bathes yet another fiber goddess enthroned on a pedestal.

Fig. 82. New England basketry displayed in a corner cupboard tempts early arrivals at an estate sale.

Fig. 83. Two Great Lakes baskets and other vintage knick-knacks on showcase shelves await buyers at a large midwestern antique mall.

Each of these venues affords opportunities to see and study baskets of many kinds. Any one of them may yield the collector a fine old Indian basket. But, which one is it? Given all the places where baskets are offered for sale, you cannot expect every item to be correctly identified or fairly priced. If your interest is specifically American Indian baskets, how do you know which to scoop up and which to pass up?

Asking-prices and prices-realized at auctions and other sales vary widely, even for baskets that appear to be otherwise comparable. So those figures provide little indication of actual value. Is it advisable to take a chance on buying even an inexpensive basket if you don't really know what you are looking at? And you could be risking very serious money on a pricier example.

An Expanding Universe

Say you recently spent $85 at a nice antique mall on that pretty little lidded basket with mellow brown and green designs. Yes, it was clearly labeled "Old Northwest Coast Indian basket." But now you realize that it was made with raffia stitches over a reed foundation, so it is not the Nuu-chah-nulth covered basket you were convinced it was. Instead, you have just bought a fine example of Arts & Crafts handiwork, perhaps made by a follower of George Wharton James's "basket fraternity." Don't pout; at least it wasn't one of the more commonly found and similar-looking grass baskets imported a few years ago from—you guessed it!—China. Oh, and don't bother going back to the antique mall for a refund. They're really serious about that "All Sales Final" sign at the front desk.

Fig. 85. Twined grass lidded baskets of several styles have been common imports from China since the early 1970s. Some of them may resemble American Indian handiwork like the Nuu-chah-nulth basket (Figure 84).

Fig. 84. A typical twined Nuu-chah-nulth covered basket with aniline-dyed design elements, made about a century ago.

Fig. 86. This "Navajo wedding basket" originated in Pakistan and is one of thousands of American Indian-style baskets imported to the United States over the past several decades.

44

If you feel bad (or mad), you are not alone. Many basket sellers don't know any more than their buyers, and some know even less. (That is why, on the one hand, you can be misled, but on the other, it *is* possible for you to come out ahead once in a while.) Novices get fooled all the time. Experts get fooled, too, though probably a little less often than the rest of us. We have known third-generation Indian traders in the Southwest who were candid enough to admit that they hadn't recognized the copies of Navajo-style "wedding baskets" from Pakistan when their Navajo customers began pawning them for cash. Who knows whether those deceptive baskets may have first fooled some of the Navajo themselves?

While writing this book, we have seen scores of baskets, possibly more, that have been misrepresented as authentic

Fig. 87, Fig. 88. Early 20th-century Northeast American Indian sweetgrass basket (*left*) and recently imported Chinese grass basket (*right*). Comparison of the bases reveals the American basket's woodsplint framework, while the Chinese basket is twined entirely from grass. Fortunately, the paper import label remains attached to the foreign basket, but such is not always the case.

American Indian products. They routinely show up in the antique co-ops where multiple dealers offer their goods for sale. Some of these folks are probably making an honest attempt to identify a basket they have turned up at a tag sale somewhere. If it looks even remotely like an Indian basket, or at least what they think one could look like, then it gets labeled as such. After all, here in the United States, authentic Native American artifacts command a premium price.

Very commonly seen these days are delicate lidded baskets of oval, round, or octagonal form, neatly twined of fine grass. Some are sold singly, but they also come in "nests" or stacks of multiple baskets. They may be undecorated, though many have simple geometric designs usually woven in red or green, or brown and red. They are showing up on eBay and at flea markets and antique shops described as "Old Native American sweetgrass baskets" or as "Micmac baskets." They are anything but that. Reportedly still being made by Chinese prisoners, these grass baskets were among the first items exported from mainland China to America after President Nixon's visit in 1972 reopened trade relations. Given the active market for them today, they continue to arrive in quantity, with an attached paper label indicating their foreign origin. It seems that small label can sometimes be really easy to lose!

Just yesterday we spotted a good-sized cylindrical basket with a round bottom and a rim reinforced inside with a twig hoop. It was twill-plaited in a checkerboard pattern of thin, alternating black and white splints. Though we didn't remove it from the display case to look more closely, we are confident that it was made not long ago for tourists visiting the Amazon region of Brazil or Venezuela. Yet, the label confidently proclaimed it to be an "Old Plains Indian Burden Basket—$220." Perhaps it did superficially resemble rare mid-19th-century Indian burden baskets from the Upper Missouri River valley, as illustrated on page 179. There aren't many of them available! A couple of hundred bucks would be a cheap price to pay for the real thing. But in today's market, it is probably too much for someone to pay for the more recent South American souvenir basket we saw.

This experience was not unusual. In fact, it is becoming all too commonplace. Last summer we attended a well-regarded western antique show. Reputable dealers predominate there, and the well-heeled customers feel confident in buying from them. But our shuffle through the many display booths turned up a couple of wildly misidentified "Indian baskets," including another "basket fraternity" raffia production that was labeled "Fine old Pima plaque" on a price tag asking $850. It reminded us that several years ago at the great Brimfield outdoor flea market in Massachusetts, soon after the field opened, we spotted from a distance a truly wonderful and large rattle-top basket of classic Tlingit form. Both of us hurried to it, admiring its muted colors and typical spiral design motif. The tag price of $350 seemed very reasonable for this "Old Indian basket," until we got even closer and saw the whole thing was another Arts & Crafts raffia confection. Some of those folks got very good at replicating Indian baskets, and this one was truly a beauty.

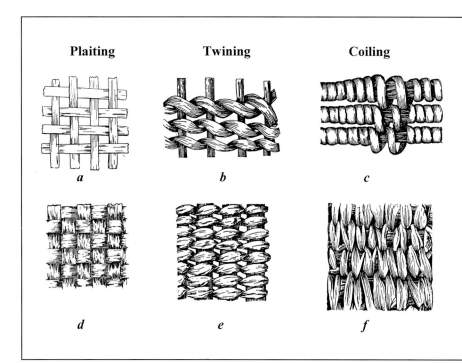

Plaiting   Twining   Coiling

a   *b*   *c*

d   *e*   *f*

Fig. 89. Basic basketmaking techniques–plaiting, twining, and coiling–include many variations, such as open plain plaiting (*a*), plain twining (*b*), bundle coiling (*c*), closed plain plaiting (*d*), closed plain twining (*e*), and bundle coiling with irregularly split interlocking stitches (*f*).

Now, you might think more highly of us if we told you that after each of these episodes we transformed ourselves into a pair of basket ninjas to avenge all those who had been or soon would be defrauded by such misinformation or chicanery. But, alas, we simply walked away, shaking our heads and muttering a fervent hope that the next person to come along would not be duped. Still, such experiences have given us a further nudge toward writing this book. In the meantime, at least until you have read on, *caveat emptor*!

Fig. 91. Detail of plaiting, with a twill plaited over-three-under-three interval.

Basket Anatomy 101

Form

Traditional cultures everywhere tackled mostly the same basic tasks. If form follows function, then it may be expected that one people's baskets might be confused with the baskets made elsewhere by others. The natural tendency to rely too heavily on shape similarities for basketry recognition and identification will very often lead one astray. It is never sufficient to consider an undocumented basket's *form* alone, or even primarily, when assigning it to a particular source. Food trays, gathering baskets, storage containers, trinket boxes, fish traps, and many other forms were similar around the world.

Frank S. Thayer, Publisher, Denver.

Fig. 90. Hopi basketmaker plaits a work basket from yucca strips.

Fig. 92. Havasupai weaver twines a small basket at her camp, c. 1900. Her capacious gathering basket is also twined work.

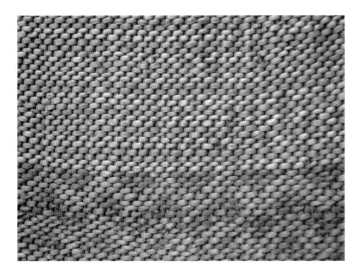

Fig. 93. Detail of twining shows weft strands (horizontal) wrapped around warp elements.

Fig. 94. Hopi woman coiling a basket in front of her home has at least seven unfinished coiled plaques displayed on a blanket. A completed coiled plaque stands behind her, and a twill-plaited yucca ring basket perches beside her, at left.

Technique

Details of *technique*—observing precisely how a basket was woven or stitched—can be much more useful for narrowing or attributing the work to a region or an individual group. Basketmakers relied on just a few primary techniques: plaiting, twining, or coiling, plus some important variations. These construction details may require an expert eye to distinguish but can be important. Given the limited range of construction techniques, it should not be surprising that some non-American Indian baskets may happen to closely resemble those made by certain Native American groups. In the Philippines, for instance, a preferred technique for basketwork trays and lidded boxes was one-rod coiling. Northern Athabascan Indians sometimes employed the same technique for making very similar forms, though other attributes differ, including materials. The shared resemblance between these Asian and American baskets has led to inadvertent misidentifications and confusion.

Decoration

Decoration can be just as misleading as form when overemphasized for basketry identification purposes. Inspired by nature yet somewhat constrained by their medium's technical limitations, basketmakers in widely separated areas independently settled on a narrow repertoire of similar design elements and layouts. Geometric and even representational compositions from region to region can seem to closely parallel each other. The palette of natural colors available to the artisan was likewise limited, confined as it was to local mineral or vegetal dyes.

Materials

Although form, technique, and decoration must be evaluated, most often the key to establishing a basket's origin will be the *materials* used in its construction. Traditional basketmakers relied on natural materials from their local habitats. So recognizing a basket's materials and knowing something about the native plant resources and ecology of a given region will help one to narrow the possibilities. Correctly identifying the actual plant species

Fig. 95. Two Hopi coiled basket starts. Galleta grass strands are continually added into the bundle as the coil is stitched tightly with yucca of varied colors to form the design.

incorporated into a basket can be difficult, but clues may be found by noting how the weaving elements appear to the naked eye or under low magnification. Is the color dyed or natural? Is the material smooth or rough, papery or coarse, stiff or flexible? Is it bark, stem, or fiber? Split or whole? Does it have a particular odor or an unusual gloss? Are any irregularities, nodes, pores, or growth layers visible on its surface or in its cross-sections?

Of course, fine ethnic baskets from anywhere in the world merit scholarly attention and can excite collector interest in their own right. But if North American Indian baskets are your focus, then a passing familiarity with *bamboo* (a woody grass), *rattan* (a woody vine), and *raffia* (strips of palm leaf membrane with a papery feel)—none of which was used in older traditional Native American basketwork—will go a long way toward helping you to avoid some mistakes. Also unfamiliar to most basketmakers in temperate America were the tough, flexible *palm leaf* strips favored by basketweavers throughout the Pacific, Asia, and Africa—and for those modern Pakistani copies of North American Indian baskets that we will examine more closely. Only some Southeast groups, like Florida's Seminole Indians and the African-American Gullah people of coastal South Carolina, regularly incorporated local Sabal palmetto leaves into their crafts.

The ability to recognize commercial *rush*, *reed*, and *cane* will also prove helpful. Popular with earlier and contemporary crafters, these materials tend to be lighter in weight than most Native American basketry materials and of more consistent dimensions. The end products may have a lighter "heft" and perhaps appear more "bland" than a vintage basket, even though an applied stain may mimic an antique patina. These standardized commercial filaments, along with "Hong Kong" twisted *paper cord* or even *plastic* strands and coated *wire*, are extensively used for all kinds of "wicker" products, ranging from baskets to furniture. By contrast, natural wicker materials found in traditional Native American work generally taper in thickness from base to tip and may look nubby—as do the thin, mostly unpeeled, red willow switches seen in old Pueblo utility baskets.

Fig. 97. "Hong Kong cord," commercially prepared twine of twisted paper or grass, was adopted by northeastern Native basketmakers in the 1920s but abandoned as buyers objected. Detail of Hong Kong cord embellishment on tall woodsplint yarn basket, including its braided strap handle.

Fig. 98. Comparison of natural, aromatic braided sweetgrass (*left*) and commercial Hong Kong cord (*right*) on sewing baskets. Unbraided natural sweetgrass covers the center of each lid.

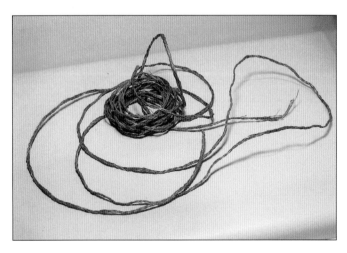

Fig. 96. Vintage coil of natural sweetgrass, braided in preparation for weaving into a Northeast woodsplint basket.

Fig. 99. Two Hopi *piiki* trays used to hold sacred blue corn bread. In the smaller example (*left*), the light colored plaiting material is commercial reed, which substitutes for the traditional scrub sumac shoots or fragrant dunebroom stems used in earlier trays (*right*). Yucca bindings finish the rims of both.

Native American basketmakers have not altogether ignored the commercial products, however. Many Northeast basketweavers began substituting Hong Kong cord for natural braided sweetgrass around the 1920s and 1930s because it was stronger and convenient to use. Some modern groups, including Hopi and Oklahoma Cherokee weavers, have accepted commercial reed for their plaques and baskets, even though it folds or bends more sharply than buckbrush or the honeysuckle vine adopted a few decades earlier. As a final example, several Native American weavers are now including waxed linen fiber and even artificial "sinew" among their basketmaking supplies.

What Wear Means

This seems like a good place to remind ourselves that the appearance of some baskets that look ancient can be deceptive. A basket that simply has been abused may have aged prematurely. It could be tattered or torn or misshapen. It may lack an original handle or lid. Perhaps it was casually mended with old thread or yarn. In the course of its existence, many a fine Indian basket has been employed inaptly as a flowerpot holder, a toddler's plaything, a painter's brush caddy, or a carryall tote, with unfortunate consequences. Ironically, some baskets were intentionally made and sold for such unlikely purposes, but the sad fact remains that fragile baskets cannot long withstand hard use. Other serious, though inadvertent, damage may result from displaying a basket in direct sunlight or placing it too near a woodstove or perhaps from heedlessly holding it by the rim.

Typical damage very commonly includes broken or missing stitches, warping, water stains, fading, mildew, brittleness, paint spots, and so on. Whatever the excuse, baskets that are incomplete or in poor condition due to mishandling hold little collector interest and have less value.

Damaged Goods

Sadly, even very minor damage may significantly diminish a basket's monetary worth. Experienced collectors generally require that a basket be in nearly perfect condition with no major problems to distract from its appearance. Just a few broken or missing stitches can greatly reduce a basket's appeal and price.

As a case in point, we came across a handsome old Western Apache olla many years ago and were delighted to find that its modest price matched our budget. In our excitement over the basket's many fine features, including its generous size and the many figures that graced its surface, we blissfully ignored several bite-sized chunks missing from its rim. We brought it home with us. Over time, however, as we admired our basket its flaws only became more apparent. Soon our gaze was drawn irresistibly to the voids. We had to find a way to correct them.

Fig. 100. Western Apache basket with obvious damage, visible even when viewed from its "best" side.

Fig. 101. Pomo twined mortar basket or hopper, 20" diameter, was set over a stone mortar cavity for processing acorns.

We visited a skilled and respected Indian basket conservator. His California workshop was cluttered with stoic "patients," wounded Native American baskets in need of his curative powers. With an artist's eye and a surgeon's skill he could re-weave a tear or re-sew a coil one delicate stitch at a time, using all the appropriate materials and techniques. The restored basket would once again make a collector proud.

We begged him to make our Apache olla whole again. To our disappointment, he said no. He explained that he had to charge by the stitch and our basket was so finely woven that it counted more stitches per inch than most. Besides, in a couple of spots our basket was missing sections of two or three coils, each of which would have to be rebuilt and then re-sewn with the thinnest of willow strands. Altogether, he estimated, the cost of the repair would exceed by several times the then-current market value of a similar basket in decent shape. Besides, he said, he already had so many projects lined up that he would not get to ours for several years!

It was a hard lesson. Eventually we let our basket go through an auction in "as is" condition, where someone else bought it for a "bargain" price.

Fig. 102. Large southern California (Mission) cooking basket, showing evidence of hard use and Native repairs to keep it in service.

Native Use

On the other hand, a basket exhibiting damage or wear that confirms its genuine Native use may intrigue serious collectors. With such examples, look for wear patterns or repairs that are consistent with a basket's history and role within Native culture. For instance, interior scorch marks in a large California twined bowl may testify to the ingenious practice of cooking acorn soup in a basket by dropping fire-heated stones into the liquid until it boils. Another big California basket with its bottom apparently missing—a ragged gap where its base would be—might have been a basket hopper attached to a mortar in which the acorns were crushed into meal for the soup. A Southwest basket with musty powder caked between its stitches may have held the corn meal offered in a Navajo ceremony. An old, seemingly warped burden basket may have been distorted in use against an Apache woman's strong back.

Other baskets confirm their cultural connections through the Native repairs made to extend their useful life. Basket bottoms were at times mended by expertly re-weaving a replacement section with natural materials or by more hastily sewing a hide or cloth patch over the hole. A split basket might have been sutured several times before being finally retired from service. The savvy collector learns to recognize and evaluate wear and tear resulting from a basket's traditional function, versus the unwanted deterioration caused by careless handling. This ability contributes to building a more interesting and worthwhile collection.

Take a Second Look

When contemplating an "American Indian" basket, a collector should be certain to consider whether it could possibly be something else. If scrutinized both independently and collectively, the components of a basket's anatomy—form, technique, decoration, material—should move a collector in the right direction for deducing its proper identity. With the aid of a checklist "key," such as the one included in our earlier book, *Indian Baskets*, the recognition of an American Indian basket may be further refined in some cases to the regional or tribal level.

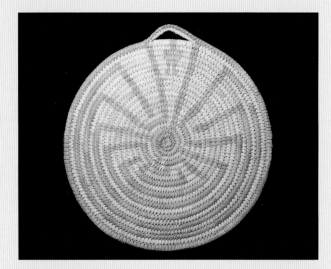

Fig. 103. "Good" Tohono O'odham "Man in the Maze" plaque.

Fig. 104. "Better" Tohono O'odham plaque is generously sized.

Fig. 105. "Best" Tohono O'odham basket has additional features.

What Makes a Basket Good, Better, or Best?

Indian basket dealers encourage collectors to buy the best they can, which is wise advice. Many find it is better to have a few nicer baskets than a larger number of mediocre pieces. One finer basket also is likely to increase in value more quickly than a shelf full of lesser examples. So, what typifies "quality" in better baskets?

Indisputably, the basketry of certain regions or tribes tends to be more highly valued than others, and certain styles of baskets find favor among collectors at any given time. But even allowing for similar age, tribal origin, form, technique, design, and material, not all baskets are equal.

Consider three comparable late 20th-century coiled Tohono O'odham baskets, each depicting the "Man in the Maze" motif that represents one's path through life from birth to death. While all are collectible baskets, each has characteristics that separate the three as "Good," "Better," and "Best."

The "Good" plaque (*top*), coiled entirely in low-contrast bleached and unbleached yucca, made by an unknown maker, has an anatomically simple figure and is comparatively small at 8" diameter.

The "Better" plaque (*center*), by known maker Sophie Stevens, is coiled of yucca and black devil's claw with a simple figure but a carefully planned and executed maze. Stitching is fairly even, given its generous 17" diameter.

The "Best" basket (*bottom*), woven by Marian Cruz of Sells, Arizona, in 1997, is more desirable in nearly every way. An intricate high-contrast polychrome squash blossom design encircles its maze. Fine coils are evenly stitched in natural yucca, black devil's claw, and rare red yucca root that is hard to collect and prepare. The figure is more anatomically detailed and possesses a neck—missing from the other two figures. These qualities outweigh its smaller 13.5" diameter and distinguish this premium basket. Its asking price is likely to be considerably higher.

chapter 5
The Business of Baskets

How Much Is That Old Basket? (And What Is It Worth?)

A basket's asking price and its value are really two separate matters. In the general marketplace, cost and worth usually tend to be linked. They may often approximate one another quite closely, yet sometimes they do not. Let us explain how it works with reference to Indian baskets.

Indian baskets are a bit different from most other commodities. They are handmade by individual makers, they come in a wide range of forms, and they vary in both quality and condition. No two are exactly alike. While automobiles arrive at the dealership with MSRP stickers attached, older baskets do not. Generally, a seller needs some experience to determine what the market will bear—that is, what a buyer might be willing to pay—and then charge accordingly. So, if a basket's price is set arbitrarily, it could be "high," "low," or even "fair."

Setting prices and determining values for baskets are each imprecise and rather subjective processes. That statement brings to mind a comment by the editor/publisher of the now-defunct *New Hampshire Antiques Monthly* as he held out this promise to his readers some years ago:

> [S]ooner or later we will do a piece on *woven baskets*. We are always amazed at the prices paid for a bunch of weeds when they are old and woven together to make a basket, so we shall investigate this field together sometime.

Evaluating Baskets

We have to acknowledge that worth, like beauty, is largely in the eye of the beholder. For instance, a basket's overall aesthetic appeal may be primary with art-oriented collectors and decorators, while those with an anthropological interest may seek out baskets with a well-documented cultural connection. In either case, value is being determined on an individual, subjective basis. Nevertheless, Indian basketry enthusiasts generally agree that some or most of the following criteria would rank high in calculating a basket's worth:

- *Form*, including symmetry and balance
- *Construction*, evidencing a mastery of weaving technology
- *Decoration*, when culturally appropriate and contributing to overall aesthetic appeal
- *Dimension*, properly scaled to large, average, or miniature size
- *Quality materials*, well-selected and carefully prepared
- *Function*, whether utilitarian, decorative, or ceremonial
- *Cultural relevance*, or "authenticity," rooted in tribal tradition
- *Provenance*, documenting origins and history
- *Condition*, only minimal or no breakage, missing stitches, warping, fading, or restoration

Collectors sometimes encode all this information in the concept of "rarity," a word that implies the result of some comparative consideration of a basket's aesthetic characteristics (form, decoration, size, etc.), condition (age, preservation), significance (cultural importance, provenance), and/or other factors in order to assess its value or worth. Higher rarity often correlates with higher prices, though not always, since seller and buyer may each perceive the same basket differently. Thus a basket's worth to the collector might be more or less than the seller's asking price.

Buying Indian Baskets

These days, an active basket collector might insist that the hobby presents two major challenges. The first is: *how to buy a nice basket at a good price,* and the second is: *how to sell a good basket at a nice price.* Both transactions have become seemingly more difficult in recent years.

Visualizing a Collection

Practical collectors plan ahead, trying to visualize ideally what they want their collection eventually to become. A collector can take many directions with baskets. Will the goal be to gather a comprehensive assemblage representing all regions and tribes, or only a few, or even just one? Are particular forms—ollas, trays, cradles, hats, Plateau bags—to be the focus? Baskets by named makers, like Dat-so-la-lee and some others, are of very limited availability and extremely expensive but would make an impressive collection. Sources and resources—what is "out there" and what is in your pocket—both have to be considered when starting a collection.

The most important point is to be selective: 1) buy only what you really like, and 2) buy only the best quality that you can afford. Regardless of what you choose to collect, aim for a standard level of value that you can maintain. A single basket of exceptional worth may be lost among a lot of average specimens, just as even a few sub-standard baskets can diminish an otherwise high-quality collection. In time, the numbers of baskets can add up. A collector who has been too undiscriminating may discover how difficult it can be to unload the overburden. Mediocre baskets are much easier to buy than to re-sell.

American Indian basketry has become another commercial product in the marketplace. Purchasing a basket requires due diligence on the buyer's part. We have previously considered that in today's global bazaar one has to be alert to the likelihood of honest mistakes as well as the possibility of intentional deception. Even Native Americans have occasionally been known to pass along knock-off baskets as their own creations. Hoping to garner a higher return, some Internet sellers are notorious for their practice of misattributing foreign-made products as American Indian. It is not just an issue of trust—or lack thereof; it is also a matter of knowledge—or lack thereof. The fault can lie with either party, buyer or seller, or with both.

Auctions, On-Line and On-Site

By now, most of the established "brick-and-mortar" auction houses, even the smaller regional firms, sell simultaneously on-line. That practice potentially makes any offering available to a worldwide bidding pool. Competition on a global scale for desirable items like fine old Indian baskets can drive up prices and make it harder for a local, on-the-scene bidder to prevail. On the other hand, of course, the advent of the Internet-aided market has opened up once-remote sales locations and even individually-offered personal possessions to nearly everyone. Some real treasures occasionally surface through the Internet auction sites.

Along with the increased accessibility and attention that on-line auctions have generated has come a deluge of stuff to be sold, including items that were once considered rare. A winning high bid for one example will often shake others loose, which can sometimes depress prices as the market makes a "correction." It is certainly possible to be on the right or the wrong side of such corrections, whether you are buying or selling. You could buy in a rising market and sell into a falling market just as readily as doing the opposite. This fact, plus a severe global recession in recent years, has destabilized prices for most categories of collectibles, including Indian baskets. For too many economic and sociological reasons to be considered here, no one can predict when or if the commercial value of non-essentials, such as antiques and art objects, will fully recover. (An exception may be made for those truly exquisite rarities that always seem to drive appreciative gazillionaires into frenzied competition.)

Fig. 106. Apache-style basket, sold at auction for $190–plus buyer's premium–was actually made in Pakistan. How much would you have wanted to pay for this attractive, non-Native American decorator item?

When attending an auction in person, one should fully inspect any intricate, one-of-a-kind, handcrafted item such as a basket before placing a bid. Buying a basket without first closely examining it carries a high degree of risk. Indian baskets, unlike baseball cards, coins or comics, are not mass-produced, so their condition is not easily ranked by any standard grading system. Most Internet sellers and major auction houses with an on-line presence do provide images, and sometimes many images, in lieu of an on-site auction preview. Multiple views, plus enlargement capabilities, enable one to remotely inspect certain details, including construction techniques and any obvious damage. It may be more difficult, however, to determine what materials were used in the basket or to detect hidden repairs. A basket's true colors or dimensions are not always easy to judge from an on-screen image, either.

Many auctioneers will try to assist potential Internet bidders by answering questions prior to the sale, but ultimately it comes down to a decision on whether to bid on an item without personally

Fig. 107. Sotheby's, Skinner, and Allard are among the established auction houses that host catalogued American Indian and ethnographic art sales on a regular basis. Most auctioneers try to represent their merchandise honestly, but buyers must understand that auction lots usually are sold "as is."

All things considered, it may be less risky and more satisfying to buy baskets in-person. Many country auctioneers come up with an occasional Indian basket or two that may warrant inspection and bidding. In addition to the large firms, like Sotheby's, Christies, Bonhams, and Heritage, regional auction houses, like Skinner's in New England or Cowan's in the Midwest, hold one or two sales a year in their galleries that feature ethnographic arts, often including a selection of Native American baskets. Other auctioneers specialize primarily in Indian arts and related material. For example, Allard auctions coincide with the Santa Fe Indian Market each August and also take place in the Phoenix area each spring and fall. Munn auctions in New Mexico and Seahawk auctions in British Columbia offer quantities of baskets in their periodic American Indian auctions, as does Old Barn in Ohio. On-site auctions offer an excellent opportunity to personally study—and perhaps bid on—an array of baskets, while mingling with other knowledgeable collectors and prominent dealers. Of course, these auctions are now also regularly on-line for those who cannot attend in person.

handling or studying it close-up. Most auction lots are not sent off "on approval" after the sale, so attempting to return an item once it has been purchased can be difficult and unpleasant. Unless intentional misrepresentation on the seller's part can be proven, the disappointed buyer may just have to live with his or her remorse.

The key is to ask questions before placing a bid. If you plan to participate as an absentee bidder, carefully preview the auction catalog or on-line descriptions and illustrations for any lots that interest you. Allow yourself time—generally at least three days—to request from the auctioneer a "full condition report" on any basket you might be considering. If, after purchasing a basket you were unable to examine in person, you then discover a problem that was not mentioned in the condition report, you should have recourse to return your purchase for a refund.

Fig. 108. New Mexico's Gallup Inter-tribal Indian Ceremonial has celebrated Native American culture and arts since 1922, giving attendees an opportunity to buy directly from the source.

Dealer Shows

Specialized shows where invited dealers sell American Indian arts and antiques offer other buying opportunities that many collectors anticipate each year. The Whitehawk antique ethnographic and Indian arts shows are the foremost of those held in conjunction with the (mid-August) Santa Fe Indian Market. Several other fine shows immediately precede, follow, or overlap this market. Also, in early August, the Gallup Inter-tribal Indian Ceremonial in western New Mexico, which has been running since 1922, includes craft vendors as well as live demonstrations and dance exhibitions. Each February, for many years now, Martindale's "Marin show" and seminar on vintage Indian arts has brought collectors to San Rafael, California, north of San Francisco. Two "Old West" shows—Lebel's in Denver, Colorado, in late June and High Noon's in the Phoenix, Arizona, area each January—include some Indian arts among the cowboy trappings. The respected dealers who participate in these shows are well known to one another and their merchandise is of the highest quality available.

Speaking face-to-face with a knowledgeable dealer can be a mutually rewarding experience, since most enjoy "talking baskets" with avid collectors and even novices. These conversations provide a chance to ask questions and learn from people who probably have seen and handled many more baskets than one can even imagine.

Fig. 109. Natalie Linn and Elaine Tucker, of Linn-Tucker Indian Baskets, regularly display an enticing selection of high-quality vintage baskets for sale at major ethnographic and antique Indian arts shows. Reputable dealers are the most reliable source of fine collector baskets.

And, in the course of chatting, if you should happen to spot a basket you think you cannot live without, be sure to find out everything about it, too. Inquire about its maker, provenance, and documentation, all of which can greatly increase a basket's value (and also usually its price), since Indian baskets ordinarily were unsigned or made by anonymous weavers. Most importantly, do not hesitate to ask if the dealer is aware of any damage, prior repairs, or restoration. An ethical seller should not be put off by your questions. Even the most skillfully done alterations may be revealed with the aid of a good black light (ultraviolet) scan or sometimes by closely examining the basket with just a basic illuminated magnifier. Have more than a few stitches been replaced? Has a faded design been retouched, or have beads or feathers been added? Has oil or stain been used to enhance the color?

Ask if there is anything else you, as a potential buyer, should know about the basket. The dealer may not have all the answers on the spot, but he or she should be willing to find out before you commit to the purchase. Finally, verify that the seller would be willing to refund your money if further condition issues should arise shortly after the sale. As a buyer, you are in control and have the choice to walk away. Comparable (or maybe better) baskets probably are available somewhere else—possibly even in the next shop or booth you enter!

Museum Shops and Galleries

Some museums maintain shops where one may purchase modern Native American baskets and sometimes older ones consigned by collectors. (Be sure to ask questions here, too.) Just a few of the more prominent museum shops can be named here, leaving it for you to discover others. The Heard Museum in Phoenix, Arizona, is near the top of our list for its basket-focused shop, as is the Case Trading Post, in the lower level of Santa Fe, New Mexico's, Wheelwright Museum. The Museum of Northern Arizona at Flagstaff has been a source for treasured collector baskets over the years. The Smithsonian's National Museum of the American Indian, on the Mall in Washington, D.C., offers a fine selection of contemporary Indian arts, including some basketry. Nearby in the nation's capital, the U.S. Department of the Interior headquarters, at 1849 C Street, N.W., houses the Indian Craft Shop with an extensive representation of Native American products.

In cities and towns and at individual shops and even remote trading posts situated on or around the major Indian reservations in the West (as well as some close to reservations in other parts of the country), one can find display cases stocked with Indian arts. Gallup in New Mexico, Phoenix and Scottsdale in Arizona, and the Santa Fe area obviously come to mind. Each has so many fine galleries that one will need several days—and maybe as many bank accounts—to visit them all. Flagstaff, Sedona, and Tucson in Arizona also boast shops well worth visiting, as do Denver, Seattle, San Francisco, and Vancouver. For other parts of the country, be sure to check the local business listings for "Native American" or "Indian" arts whenever you may be planning to visit an unfamiliar destination. You never know what you may turn up.

Nearly all of these specialty stores will have a friendly and well-informed person—often the proprietor—on hand to assist you. What most of these showrooms offer that less formal settings may not is the security of buying with confidence. Estate sales, flea markets, pawn shops, and general antique malls usually do not provide much information with your purchase, nor will most warrant its authenticity. Many individual vendors in such settings do not bother with even a basic sales receipt unless you request one.

Fig. 110. Old Red Lake Trading Post, on the Navajo Reservation in northeastern Arizona, has served the local Native community, travelers, and tourists for generations. Indian arts outlets, both long-established and more recent, are scattered across the Southwest's Four Corners region, offering souvenir goods and collectible crafts, including an occasional "prize."

Fig. 111. Alston and Deborah Neal's Old Territorial Shop in Scottsdale, Arizona, has been a favorite with basket collectors since Alston's mother Rita opened the business in 1969. Long-time Indian arts dealers like the Neals are quite knowledgeable about the varied items they offer.

Fig. 112. Antique Tribal Arts Dealers Association (ATADA) logo displayed by merchants committed to selling authentic ethnographic objects.

ATADA

Since ATADA's founding in 1988, members of the Antique Tribal Arts Dealers Association (see Appendix A) have committed to high ethical standards when buying and selling vintage Indian material. They will provide buyers with all available information on provenance, and they guarantee the authenticity of the objects they sell. ATADA members and other reputable dealers at invitational shows and the major galleries and museum shops will gladly provide itemized receipts that document your purchase. These vouchers should be carefully preserved along with a clear photograph of your purchase, for they help to corroborate the significance of the item.

Selling Indian Baskets

Advanced hobbyists in nearly every collecting field agree that a sure approach to building a great collection is to start early and buy the "best" examples one can afford. For various reasons, many beginners don't heed the advice. Not yet fully committed to their pastime, some are reluctant to plunge in, so they timidly wade around in the shallows. Those of limited means understandably fret about being extravagant in spending on non-essentials. A novice simply may not recognize better quality specimens or even know where to look for them. As a result, many new collectors of Indian baskets, like most other collectors, don't venture far from familiar sources and they stay within a modest price range far too long.

Such beginners tend to acquire many low-end or average examples. Then, one day, they may take an objective look and recognize that they have accumulated an assortment of mediocre baskets. At that point, they may decide to upgrade or to downsize their holdings. Most basket collectors, regardless of whether their baskets are just average or even the very best, will sooner or later decide to winnow their collections. Ultimately, for others, the time may come to dispose of the collection altogether.

Selling Indian baskets, like acquiring them, can be accomplished through a number of venues. We have seen lately that baskets, like most commodities, have fluctuating market values. Within the relatively small field of collectors, any sudden increase or decrease in the quantity of Native American baskets available for sale, or any recent advance in scholarship, publication of a widely circulated article, or new collector trend can magnify price variations. It is unlikely that a basket you added to your collection just a few years ago will have gained substantially in monetary value. Realistically, you should not expect a profit from its sale, nor even necessarily a full return on your "investment" (if we may consider the matter so crassly for the moment). Such would be the case especially if you bought from a retail source, like a gallery or museum shop.

Not surprisingly, a basket's resale value is determined by current collector interest. In turn, the amount of interest a basket generates is a direct factor of its condition and rarity, as well as its provenance record, especially any documentation linking it to a known maker, an important collection or exhibition, or a significant publication.

Private Sales

If you should decide to sell just one or a few baskets from your collection, whether perhaps to upgrade or to downsize, an obvious starting place might be that fellow collector who has openly admired (or secretly coveted) your collection over the years. Maybe a swap would work out satisfactorily for both parties if an outright sale is not possible.

You might also consider revisiting some of the places where you have purchased baskets. If you have bought repeatedly from particular dealers or galleries, they might be good people to contact. Not everyone who once sold a basket to you will be willing to buy, but they may be happy to direct you to a potential prospect. If they are willing to consider repurchasing from you, it would likely be at the wholesale level—a much lower figure that allows for profit and other expenses to be calculated into a new retail price, which could be lower than the price you originally paid.

Consignments

As an alternative to outright purchase, the shop might allow you to consign your basket with them for resale. Some advantages are that your basket will be exposed to lots of potential customers and the merchant has not had to lay out any cash. The details of this arrangement must be established in writing, of course, so that both parties fully understand and agree on pricing structure (including any potential discounts to be offered), commission, and final payoff. The contract should also specify any additional owner or seller responsibilities and set a date for return if the item is unsold.

Another advantage with consignment is that one is able to set the asking price, but commission rates are steep, usually in the 30% to 60% range.

Dispersing a Collection

Dispersing more than a few baskets at a time from your collection requires more careful planning. Take time to develop a strategy for maximizing your returns instead of too quickly dumping your hard-won baskets. You (or perhaps your heirs) likely would be disappointed with the results if your collection were to be sold through a tag sale, even if you were there to personally oversee it. The folks who race around on those Saturday morning outings expect real bargains, and few of them share the specialized knowledge that makes you so deeply appreciate your baskets.

Done correctly, however, selling off a large number of baskets at one time can attract the attention of potential buyers who might be drawn by having a "critical mass" of examples to consider. If your collection is particularly fine, perhaps replete with good representative examples from a group famous for its skilled weavers, or maybe specimens from an older collection, then you might consider contacting a major dealer or gallery that specializes in basketry of that type. As before, you may find that outright purchase is not possible, but perhaps an advantageous consignment agreement could be negotiated. Or a dealer planning to attend a major Indian arts show might consider displaying some of your baskets, or even ask you to share the cost of the exhibit booth rent in exchange for representing your items. Commiting to the important details of such arrangements in writing is advisable.

If one is willing to make the effort, a collection could be sold off, one basket at a time, through eBay or a similar Internet auction service, or perhaps through an on-line "store." Sellers may choose to handle the whole process themselves, or they can seek out a local middleman in most communities who will post the listings, monitor the auction, receive payments, and ship the lots.

Auctions

Selling at any kind of auction entails some of the same advantages and drawbacks that buying at auction does. That local hall where you have picked up some fine baskets for a song is not likely to do much better when it comes to selling yours! And those famous-name auction houses will not give you the time of day unless each lot you offer them can be reasonably expected to fetch at least a couple thousand dollars. So, depending on the quantity and quality of your items, you may have to approach several auctioneers in your region before finding one who is able to provide the services you require. Ideally you would hope to identify someone with previous experience in selling Indian material. The auctioneer you elect to work with should secure your baskets ahead of time until they can be scheduled for a sale that features some comparable items—perhaps other art, home furnishings, or collectibles, not dairy cows and tractor parts. The baskets should be mentioned or even pictured in sale advertising to guarantee that they attract some interest.

For Indian baskets, a final auction sale price may be difficult to estimate in advance, since it necessarily depends on how much enthusiasm at least two or more potential bidders will show for your item. Examples representing a single area, or a particular tribe, or of a certain form may have more appeal. Baskets that are accompanied by provenance documentation (sales/purchase record, photo, description, maker's name where known), and especially any that are traced back to a prominent early collection or that have been previously exhibited or illustrated will usually command higher bids.

Setting a "reserve," a price below which you will not agree to sell, is sometimes an option, though many auction houses discourage the practice or insist on fairly modest minimum bids. Since any unsold property reverts to you following the sale, an unrealistic reserve can defeat your purpose in selling. Auctioneers work on commission, so the "hammer price" you heard as the gavel came down will usually be reduced by a double-digit percentage (commission rate plus any insurance or photography fees) before it goes into the check you receive a month or two after the sale. Auctioneers generally take a commission of between 10% and 20% of the selling price, plus expenses.

Charity Benefits

Some collectors weigh the idea of contributing their items to benefit a worthy cause, such as a charity auction or a fund-raiser for a not-for-profit museum, school, or historical group. Others desire to donate their collection outright to a museum. Under current tax laws, if the organization has federal 501(c)(3) not-for-profit status, then a contribution could qualify the donor for a tax deduction. Strict regulations apply here, and tax codes do change, so anyone considering this strategy should speak first with their own tax adviser and the proposed charitable recipient. The donor, not the recipient museum, is responsible for obtaining an independent appraisal to support the tax claim. Museums and their staffs are ethically constrained from formally evaluating donations. Licensed appraisers may be located through professional organizations (see Appendix A), or through advertisements in publications such as *American Indian Art Magazine*.

Not every museum is willing to accept objects, given their space limitations and curatorial requirements. Others will take only collections that are accompanied by sufficient funds to underwrite the cost of maintaining the new acquisitions. Donors should also realize that museums generally accept items only as unrestricted gifts outright. They have no obligation to exhibit them or even to keep them after a three-year waiting period recommended by the IRS, beyond which the objects may be deaccessioned and transferred or sold to benefit the organization.

Don't Become a Basket Case!

Since its passage by Congress in 1990, the Native American Graves Protection and Repatriation Act (NAGPRA) has introduced some uncertainty to the collecting of American Indian arts, including basketry. Initially, the law's primary objective was to protect Native Americans' exclusive rights to their ancestral human remains and ritual objects found on federal and tribal lands, and to provide a mechanism for the return to tribal custody of any such materials already held by museums and other institutions that receive federal funds. However, since its passage NAGPRA's provisions and definitions have been subject to increasingly broad interpretation, so that by now nearly any tribal object deemed to be culturally significant might arguably be subject to NAGPRA consideration.

The law's widening scope and ambiguities concern many private collectors. Though the law does not specify Indian baskets, any basket removed from a burial or other archaeological context on federal, tribal, or most other public lands would almost certainly fall under NAGPRA's jurisdiction and might be subject to other antiquities laws as well. And because the 1990 law also covers "sacred objects" and "objects of cultural patrimony," which has come to mean pretty much any item having ongoing religious or cultural significance (however defined) to a tribe, certain non-archaeological baskets could also be considered (by some) as inappropriate for collectors to own. Baskets originally intended for ceremonial or ritual use, or those made for some communal purpose, as examples, might be viewed in this way. Having a sales receipt from a basket's Native seller may not always be an adequate defense, since some tribes assert that no individual tribal member ever has ownership privileges to any sacred object, and therefore no right to dispose of it by sale or any other means.

While American Indian basketry has not yet garnered much attention under NAGPRA, and few private Native arts collectors have been subject to federal raids and seizures to this point, it is nonetheless likely that confusion over legal rights to possess specific cultural objects—possibly including certain baskets— could lead to such actions in the future. In the meantime, questions are sometimes triggered when culturally sensitive objects come up for sale or are offered to museums that are themselves subject to NAGPRA. Even if legally held in private possession for a very long time, an item that would currently be covered by NAGPRA or other legislation may now be illegal to buy, sell, trade, or even donate. Unfortunately, no universal guidelines apply; each situation is case-specific.

Some baskets may fall within the scope of other federal laws that were designed to protect endangered wildlife. In recent years federal authorities have alleged that sales even of antique American Indian items that include migratory bird feathers, marine mammal products, or parts of other endangered species are criminal acts. Indian baskets sometimes incorporated such materials. Baleen baskets with whale or walrus ivory bases and finials have been a specialty of Alaskan natives since the mid-20th century. Inuit coiled grass basketry at times displays thin strips of textured birdskin as decorative elements (seal gut and commercial yarn were also used). Tapestries of colorful bird feathers have brightened traditional Pomo gift baskets for generations. Individual bird quills may subtly accent older baskets from a few other western tribes as well. There are exemptions, but a century's worth of overlapping laws make it increasingly challenging to collect these kinds of baskets.

The collector should bear in mind, of course, that the vast majority of Indian baskets are not impacted by these laws. There is no cause for general alarm. But the situation is fluid as legal interpretations evolve, so a collector who has concerns should stay informed about these topics. Consult recent issues of *American Indian Art Magazine* and the ATADA website, or contact an Indian arts dealer who is an ATADA member (see Appendix A).

chapter 6
Caring for Indian Baskets

A Legacy from the Past to the Future

All Native American baskets were woven for a purpose. Some older examples actively participated in everyday life as utilitarian objects, or they may have played a central role in ceremonies. Even those woven specifically for tourists or collectors to purchase were fulfilling an important function just by being sold. And those same Indian baskets usually acquired new uses when they entered an early 20th-century, middle-class home, perhaps serving as a vase for dried flowers, a sewing basket, or a centerpiece. Today, these same old baskets may have retired to a more passive though still meaningful capacity in a modern collector's home or a museum gallery.

A basket's biographical past, as well as its present environment and the continuing care it receives, all factor into its current condition and its prospects for long-term preservation. Despite being brought into a collection, away from an active cultural setting, a basket remains vulnerable. Baskets were expected eventually to wear out from use, and even those that are being preserved can still deteriorate with age or neglect. Proper handling, display, and storage are required to keep them in good condition.

The collector should be aware that environmental factors such as heat, light, humidity, and pollution can adversely affect fragile basketry. Biological agents like insects, rodents, mold, and mildew can, as well. Of course fire, flood, and theft pose significant hazards, too. Careless treatment can cause just as much damage as all the other factors. The basket collector naturally wants to inhibit these processes, or stop them altogether, or possibly even reverse existing damage, if possible. It is definitely time to stop and reconsider if you are still using that old Indian basket as a magazine holder or a child's toy box!

Commonsense Care: Display, Storage, and Maintenance

A Native American basket display can bring much satisfaction and pride to its collector. The exhibit may account for considerable expenditures of time and money. The baskets themselves document other lifeways, so should be regarded as objects of cultural value. It is important that they be preserved. Collectors should be alert to common problems affecting baskets and take steps to prevent or deal with them.

Display

Some decorative baskets, like broad trays or flaring bowls, beg to be viewed vertically with their central designs fully visible. A basket resting upright on its edge should be well supported and either rotated periodically or set back on its bottom after a short time.

Baskets mounted on a wall or a display case backboard look impressive, but their fabric could be stressed, which may result in warping or tearing over time. If you feel your basket really has to be displayed upright, then be sure to hang it in a way that distributes its weight across the largest possible surface area rather than concentrating the "pull" on one part of the basket. Devise a method to secure the basket from the center outward, or from several points of its radius, rather than attaching it at one part of the rim. Metal wire supports, including commercial plate hangers, should be avoided, as should the use of fine nylon monofilament and strong thread as hangers, since these can readily cut into a basket. To minimize this risk, some museums fabricate inert plexiglass supports that cover the back surface and extend outward to gently clasp the basket's rim at several points.

Do not rely on an integral loop or rim coil to suspend a basket, such as those sometimes woven on O'odham or Hopi or other plaques. And, obviously, it is *never* a good idea to nail a basket through its center in order to attach it to a wall or overhead beam, as was formerly the practice in some Old West trading posts!

Lighting

Baskets sitting in an illuminated display case or mounted on a wall that is exposed to natural sunlight may be subject to fading over time. Vegetal or chemical (aniline) dyes used in

Fig. 113, Fig. 114, Fig. 115. Handsome display cases preserve a fine Native American basketry collection in North Carolina. The artful arrangement presents each basket in its own space, with glass-enclosed shelves to reduce dust, and low UV-filtered lighting and window draperies that minimize fading.

certain baskets can be especially fugitive, but even naturally colored elements like black devil's claw can eventually bleach out in sunlight. Light damage is both cumulative and irreversible, so exposure should be minimized. Baskets can be periodically rotated on and off display. When possible, keep direct artificial lighting turned off, and use draperies or shades to darken the room. Sun-control film applied to windows effectively filters out most harmful ultraviolet light. Fluorescent bulbs can be covered with UV-filtering sleeves.

Temperature and Humidity

Baskets should not be exposed to extremes in temperature or humidity. For example, they should not be displayed near fireplaces, stoves, or other heat sources. High temperatures cause fibers to dry out or break and may accelerate other damaging processes. Likewise, rapid fluctuations between hot and cold temperatures or high and low humidity cause swelling or shrinkage that weaken a basket's fabric. High relative humidity encourages mold and mildew growth, while very low humidity allows elements to become brittle. The advisable environmental range is between 35% and 65% relative humidity with a comfortable temperature below 80 degrees Fahrenheit.

If all of that is hard to keep in mind, just think about it this way: Baskets (and most of the other things people collect) like to live in the same environment you enjoy—one that is neither too warm and dry nor too cool and damp. Of course, as you accumulate more and more baskets your own living space could go from cozy to crowded!

Handling

Moving baskets around involves risk, too. Ideally they should be handled with clean or even gloved hands since one's own natural oils can stain fibers or leave residues that promote mold. The temptation to reach for a basket's handle or rim should be resisted. Always lift and carry a basket near its base. Visitors should be politely cautioned *before* they grab.

Storage

Baskets that are not displayed should be stored in a stable environment. A damp basement or an oven-hot attic are both detrimental to a basket's long-term health. Darkness is less of a problem, as long as you turn on the lights periodically to see that vermin have not set up housekeeping inside your favorite Washoe *degikup*. Check seasonally for dust, insect eggs, mold, discoloration, or breakage.

Although we do not advise the following, if you need to accommodate a lot of baskets in a small storage area, consolidate cautiously. Protect fragile stitches from snagging or breaking by loosely wrapping individual baskets in acid-free tissue paper. If you absolutely must stack, place trays upright inside one another, using liners to separate each one, beginning with the largest and heaviest on the bottom. As long as they too are wrapped, smaller baskets can be stored inside archivally-stable cardboard boxes. Especially in humid climates, it is best to avoid sealed vinyl bags and plastic tubs for long-term storage. Realize that a crushed basket is difficult to reshape, so do not crowd them too tightly.

Keep an inventory as you pack each container and then attach a copy as a "finding aid" that will help you to more easily retrieve a basket from its storage place.

Fig. 116. Though its Hopi maker probably expected this integral rim loop would be used for hanging the basket, the loops on Hopi and Tohono O'odham (Papago) and other baskets may eventually stretch or break out when used for suspension, so another display method is recommended.

Fig. 117. Museum curators regularly don thin white cotton gloves to minimize contact before carefully handling baskets and other artifacts.

Fig. 118. Although sunshine may eventually fade baskets, a carefully monitored dose might be effective for drying baskets that have been stored in an area that has attracted dampness.

Dust, Insects, and Mildew

Baskets can be dusted periodically with a very soft, long-bristled brush, as long as you are careful not to snag any stitches. Vacuuming may be done in conjunction with the brushing, though carefully and with the nozzle gauze-covered and held slightly away from the basket's surface.

Fine powder under a basket, or maybe a tiny hole drilled into its coils or splints, can indicate the presence of insects. Insect sprays may discolor a basket. Mothballs can be effective, but the odor and health concerns that come with their use are negatives. We have been told that dog or cat flea collars, cut into several sections and placed close to baskets, can repel insects for a few weeks at a time. If just one or two baskets seem to be affected, it may be possible to forestall an infestation by the simple remedy of putting the basket in your home freezer for several weeks (enclosed in a re-sealable freezer bag to help protect delicate stitches). Remove it for a few days to allow any eggs to hatch, then re-freeze it once more to kill any new larvae. Check to make sure the display or storage area around your baskets is clean and free of attractants.

Signs of potential concern include the musty or sweet/sour odor of mildew. Mold and mildew may appear as a hazy blush on a basket's surface after an extended period of humidity. These fungi will quickly succumb to bright sunshine, but you must weigh the risk of fading. While diluted ammonia or denatured alcohol is usually more effective than bleach solutions for killing fungal spores, no liquids or chemicals of any kind should be casually applied to a basket. They may stain or embrittle the structure. Again, an alternative technique is to seal the basket in a plastic bag, freeze it for a couple of days to disable the mold, then carefully brush off the basket outdoors. If the problem persists, it is time to consult a conservator. And perhaps invest in a dehumidifier!

Minor Repairs

It is almost inevitable that a stitch will eventually loosen or a spot will appear on a basket. Even minor repairs to a basket should be undertaken with concern and care, if they are to be undertaken at all. A highly valued basket should be examined and treated only by a professional conservator. But if a collector decides to go ahead, there are some important "Don't"s and not too many "Do"s to know about. For example, Don't use a hot glue gun! Don't get out the craft glue, either.

In fact, it is best to avoid glues and tape altogether. Most of them leave unsightly shiny residues and, besides, they may be stronger (and less flexible) than the original basket materials, which can lead to more damage.

You really should speak to a conservator first!

Cleaning

Attempting to remove that spot can also create more problems. Colored pigments and dyes that were applied to some baskets (Hopi wicker plaques, for example) may be bright but are completely soluble in water. Avoid these areas. But, if the blemish is elsewhere and you feel compelled to proceed, then begin by spot-testing an inconspicuous area with a moistened Q-tip. See if the stain resists or if distilled water dissolves it. Solvents like naphtha or mineral spirits might work if water fails, but they are toxic and must be handled with caution and with concern for oneself as well as for the basket. Again, do a spot-test first, but in a well-ventilated space. Remember, both water and solvents can leave permanent, unsightly "tide lines" when they dry, so your basket could look worse after this treatment. Soaps and detergents can't be easily rinsed from a basket, so they can leave a dull and tacky surface that just attracts more grime.

If you really care about the basket, get a conservator to look at it before you go too far.

Fig. 119. Co-author's friends scrub sooty Apache baskets after a 1964 museum fire. This approach is definitely not encouraged today.

The very first experience that one of the co-authors had with Indian baskets was in 1964, after a damaging fire at a local museum left a fine, old San Carlos Apache basket collection blackened with soot. Knowing no better, several of us youthful volunteers gathered bath soap, tap water, and brushes. Then we vigorously scrubbed the big ollas and trays until we had scoured away all the soot. In the end, those tough old willow baskets came out looking surprisingly well, though they had lost their original mellow patina and seemed a bit less flexible. We were just dumb-lucky that time. The full-immersion water bath is definitely on the "Don't" list!

Some old-time collectors had a favorite technique for preserving their baskets—varnish. They liked to varnish (or shellac) baseballs signed by heroes like Babe Ruth back then, too. In either case, baskets or baseballs, the long-term results are about the same. The glossy coating impregnates the surface, changes its color, and cannot be removed without practically destroying what it protects. As a result, value plummets. In a word, "Don't."

Professional Conservation

Notwithstanding any anxiety the foregoing paragraphs may have provoked, we admit that basic basketry care is not rocket science. The typical collector is fully capable of keeping baskets from harm or destruction under most normal circumstances. But if a collector has some special concerns, then a conservator might be able to advise or help. One should certainly consult a professional before attempting to repair or aggressively clean a basket, or in the event of serious damage. Staff members at a nearby museum or historical association may be able to suggest a conservation specialist in your area. The Internet has resources like the website of the American Institute for Conservation of Historic and Artistic Works (see Appendix A), which has a "Find a Conservator" feature and other information that may be of assistance.

Fig. 120. Structural repairs, like those needed to restore the lid of this coiled and imbricated Salish trunk, should be left to professional conservators.

Section Two
Collector Showcase

"I wish long life for the woman who always has a basket in her hands." –Hupa informant, 1904

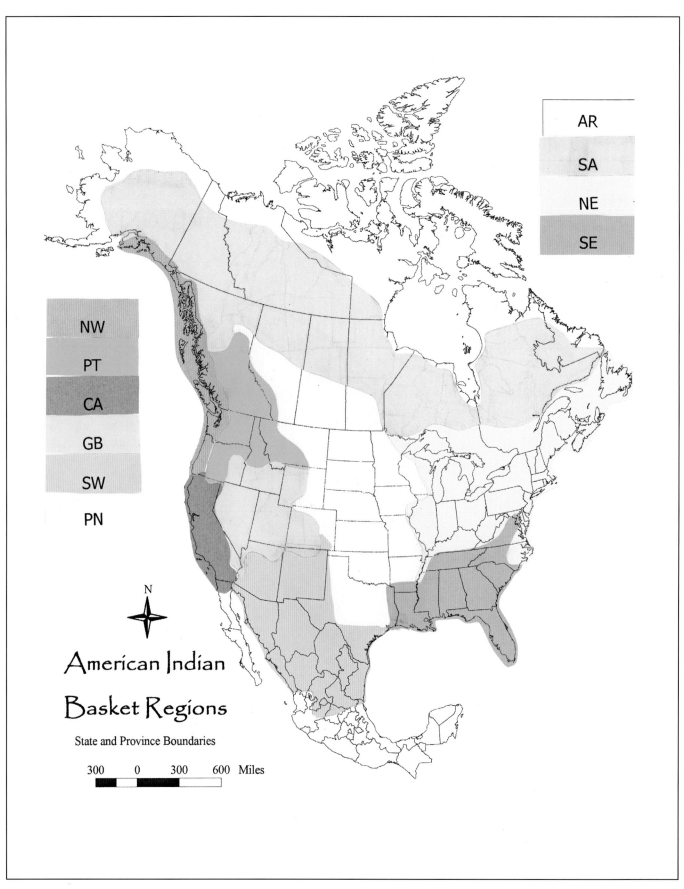

MAP: American Indian Basket Regions.

AR
SA
NE
SE

NW
PT
CA
GB
SW
PN

N

American Indian
Basket Regions

State and Province Boundaries

300   0   300   600 Miles

chapter 7
Basket Regions

American Indian baskets made within certain defined regions of the continent (as shown on our map) tend to share more similarities than differences when compared to baskets produced outside those regions. This observation supports the time-tested "culture area" concept, which anthropologists apply more broadly to include most components of Native culture. The culture area approach provides researchers with one useful way to generally classify or even more specifically identify otherwise undocumented baskets.

Recognizing a few significant traits that might be shared with other, known basketry examples should—in theory, at least—enable one to place an unattributed basket into a cultural region with some confidence. To identify a given basket, one must begin by determining that it is indeed American Indian on the basis of its overall form, construction, designs, and materials. Certain diagnostic traits might then indicate that it originated, let us say, somewhere within the Great Basin region. Even more detailed characteristics might allow us to ascribe it to the Washoe tribe. And, finally, some very precise attributes or perhaps some reliable documentation may link it to its individual maker, say, Tootsie Dick Sam.

In actual practice, unfortunately, not every basket can be so readily identified to a specific maker. And more than a few must inevitably remain ambiguous, even at the tribal level, since a "pure" tribal style was seldom (if ever) followed. The social history of most basketmaking groups, especially over the past two centuries, has involved near decimation, population movements, intermarriage, exchange, commercialization, and individual innovation, among other influencing factors. So perhaps a more realistic approach to identification might be to consider any undocumented basket as having been "made in the style of" a certain tribe or group. Baskets that exhibit a blend of "tribal" traits might still be assigned to a general region, though not in every instance. In fact, as we illustrate elsewhere in this book, it is becoming more challenging these days to determine whether some baskets actually originated in North America.

The Collector Showcase is organized by cultural area, or region. Illustrated baskets are identified—in the sense just discussed—where possible. We have not placed individual tribes on our basket region outline map. For current and historical locations of specific Native groups, readers should consult standard references, including the encyclopedic multi-volume *Handbook of North American Indians* published by the Smithsonian Institution, and other sources.

Southwest

The Southwest is well known for its baskets, which are among the most actively collected and highly prized wares in North America. Basketry has been made here for thousands of years. Today, it continues to be created for Native utilitarian and ritual purposes as well as for sale to tourists and collectors. All three major construction techniques—coiling, twining, and plaiting—are practiced in this region, though individual and tribal preferences vary.

Southwestern basketmakers may be grouped generally into four divisions:

• Puebloans
• Uto-Aztecans like the O'odham (Pima and Papago)
• Southern Athabascans like the Apache and Navajo
• Hokan groups, including Pai peoples (Havasupai, Hualapai, and Yavapai) as well as the Seri of Sonora, Mexico.

Puebloan Baskets

Eastern or Rio Grande Puebloans live in villages like Jemez and Santo Domingo along the Rio Grande River in New Mexico. Western Puebloans like the Zuni and Hopi are likely descended from ancestral Puebloan cultures, also known as Anasazi, of the Four Corners region.

Most Puebloan peoples have fashioned utilitarian bowls and trays, including twill-plaited ring baskets for winnowing and red willow wicker bowls for fruit gathering. Some, like the Zuni, once made a variety of baskets in several techniques, including many water bottles and gathering baskets for their own use, but traded widely for others. Still produced today, highly colorful Hopi wicker plaques and baskets, made only on the westernmost Third Mesa, are eye-catching examples of Native American plaited wicker work.

Hopi residents of middle or Second Mesa are best known for bundle-coiled bowls, plaques, and seed storage jars that have distinctive thick, soft coils. As with designs on plaited wicker plaques from Third Mesa, some coiled motifs may look geometric but their Native names refer to elements of the natural world. Others clearly represent kachinas, whirlwinds, birds, or other life forms. Bundle-coiled examples are created with galleta grass foundations stitched with natural, sun-bleached, or dyed yucca strands.

Uto-Aztecan Baskets

Uto-Aztecans like the Akimel O'odham (Pima) and Tohono O'odham (Papago) and northern Mexico groups like the Huichol and Tarahumara probably are modern-day descendants of the prehistoric Hohokam of southern Arizona and northern Mexico.

Uto-Aztecan speaking O'odham groups are famous for their bundle-coiled baskets stitched with willow or cottonwood and bearing frets and whorls fashioned with naturally colored black devil's claw (*Proboscidea* sp.). Early Akimel O'odham (Pima) and Tohono O'odham (Papago) baskets resemble one another, though basic differences in some foundation materials, forms, and designs have been documented by others. To summarize, Akimel O'odham baskets generally have a rounder, smaller base and more flaring walls than do comparable early Tohono O'odham examples. Tohono O'odham baskets fashioned with willow stitches tend to be more densely decorated with black, because these basket weavers often used more devil's claw than did the Akimel O'odham. Tohono O'odham basketmakers also have favored more static design compositions.

Coiled basketry starts for both groups are sometimes formed with a spiraling self-stitched coil, but more usually they consist of an obvious four-part square knot. A distinctive false-braid rim finish—like that of the Navajo, Jicarilla Apache, and Havasupai—edges some, but not all, Akimel O'odham baskets.

Tohono O'odham basketmaking declined in the early 20th century but rebounded with the establishment in 1938 of the all-Native Papago Arts and Crafts Board and subsequent commercialization of Native craft products. As Tohono O'odham basketmaking revived, weavers moved away from coiling traditional forms and designs with materials like willow and devil's claw. Basketmakers substituted less time-consuming and labor-intensive alternatives. They also more frequently incorporated representational design elements like people, saguaro cacti, and chuckwalla lizards or gila monsters. Their basketry took on different, often smaller or larger, commercially-oriented forms, like bundle-coiled beargrass examples with spaced stitches of yucca, that could be created more quickly. Only a handful of these more recent products have been made using willow and devil's claw or red yucca root for stitching elements.

Many weavers also eventually turned to coiling miniature baskets of willow, yucca, or horsehair earlier in the 20th century. (Miniatures have been a perennial theme with many other groups as well, because collectors adore them.) By the late 20th century, with the encouragement of traders and Native craft associations, Tohono O'odham makers were creating more miniature and regular-sized baskets for sale than any other Native American group. However, the increasing popularity of casinos that offer opportunities for employment and stable compensation, along with the loss of habitat that supported stands of native materials, has severely impacted the craft in recent years.

SW-1. Detail of Western Apache coiled olla or jar.

Southern Athabascan Baskets

The Western Apache are recognized for their finely coiled bowls, trays, and large storage jars or ollas. These baskets are fashioned by stitching together three willow or cottonwood rods in a bunched triangular arrangement to build a narrow, hard coil. Designs stitched with devil's claw often consist of geometrics in vertical, horizontal, or whirling layouts, or of star- or flower-shaped elements.

After about 1900 to 1915, a number of baskets made for sale added new design motifs like crosses and life forms including humans, quadrupeds, and saguaro cacti. Weavers also incorporated dark red yucca root stitching elements in addition to black devil's claw, thus forming polychrome patterns.

All of the Apache peoples have used twined basketry forms as utilitarian vessels for maintaining daily life. Pitch-covered water jars are a significant form of twined Apache work, though they can resemble some made and used in adjacent regions. Burden baskets, often with swaying rawhide fringe and conical tin cones that tinkled merrily, have been employed routinely in Native culture as well as made for collectors.

Coiled basketry of the Eastern Apache, namely the Mescalero Apache and Jicarilla Apache, has wide coils that differ in appearance from Western Apache examples. The Mescalero Apache have generally constructed a two- or three-rod vertical or stacked coil with a thin fiber bundle along the top, while the Jicarilla Apache have used three- or five-rod coiling methods. Stitches of split yucca leaf in natural shades of green, yellow, and white, and occasionally of red yucca root, account for the distinctive appearance of Mescalero Apache trays, bowls, water jars, and lidded baskets. These forms frequently feature all-over, radiating patterns such as the star or petaled design.

The Jicarilla also employ the star or flower device, as well as many other representational and geometric elements, in large trays, bowls, jars, and innovative forms. Their baskets, which are coiled with willow or sumac stitches, are more rigid than Mescalero wares and are often colored with bright aniline dyes that can readily fade. Characteristic Jicarilla rims are finished in the false-braid style, found also on Navajo, Havasupai, and Akimel O'odham baskets.

One of the most widely recognized basket designs is that of the so-called "Navajo wedding basket." Its bold, black-dyed bands of triangles separated with a central red-dyed stripe have made this tray a popular choice for both collectors and interior decorators. Many of these ceremonial baskets actually were coiled by neighboring San Juan Southern Paiute and Southern Ute basketmakers who traded them to the Navajo, as cultural taboos increasingly restricted basketmaking among the early 20th-century Navajo. Genuine old Navajo baskets that were created with a two-rod-and-bundle foundation, not the three- or four-rod foundations of Paiute or Ute workmanship, are scarce. A vibrant Navajo basketmaking revival began in the 1970s and continues today.

Hokan Baskets

The Havasupai, Hualapai (Walapai), and Yavapai have created coiled bowls and trays that collectors can confuse with Western Apache wares. Most Havasupai designs look less complex than Western Apache layouts. The Havasupai prefer horizontal and radiating black bands and simple geometric patterns. The Yavapai also have favored circular banded patterns, but they often have filled the dark areas of their basket designs with light-on-dark "negative" decorative elements and tend to create more exacting, symmetrical design layouts and compositions than in much Western Apache work. The Hualapai made a limited number of coiled baskets in the early 20th century, and their designs generally are even simpler, though more solid and heavy looking than Western Apache designs. Rims of Havasupai baskets often are finished with false-braid stitching, distinguishing them from Western Apache, Yavapai, and Hualapai examples finished with vertical whipstitched self-rims.

Seri coiled baskets of northern coastal Mexico have spare designs that can resemble some Western Apache examples, but they are bundle coiled and share other construction details with O'odham work.

Havasupai and Hualapai basketmakers also have twined utilitarian baskets. Typical Hualapai bowl-shaped baskets, which have been twined especially for sale, are decorated with distinctively simple bands of dyed elements in combinations like red and green or orange and brown. In the mid- to late 20th century, many tourists visiting the Grand Canyon returned home with one or two of these cheerful little bowls tucked in their luggage. Some occasionally appear today on Internet sites and turn up unexpectedly in secondary markets from coast to coast, far from their original source—along with turquoise rings, squash blossom necklaces, Route 66 kachinas, and other collectible examples of Indian baskets, pottery, and rugs.

SW-2. Hopi maiden plaits a yucca ring basket in a c. 1910 Fred Harvey postcard view

SW-3. Three Puebloan ring baskets plaited of yucca: (*left*) Jemez (Rio Grande) Pueblo, 13″ diameter, (*others*) Hopi Pueblo.

SW-4. Jemez Pueblo basketmakers typically treat several yucca strands—four, in this instance—as one unit when plaiting a ring basket. By varying the interval used in twill plaiting, the weaver has created a traditional diamond design element.

SW-7. Old twill-plaited yucca ring basket, Zuni Pueblo.

SW-5. Rio Grande Puebloan basketmaker completes an all-purpose plaited yucca ring basket before trimming the fringe.

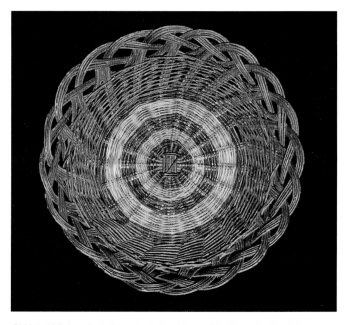

SW-8. Wicker fruit bowl, plaited by a Rio Grande Puebloan man, possibly Thomas Stone, using supple young red willow shoots harvested from local arroyos and waterways near his village, c. 1980s, 12" diameter.

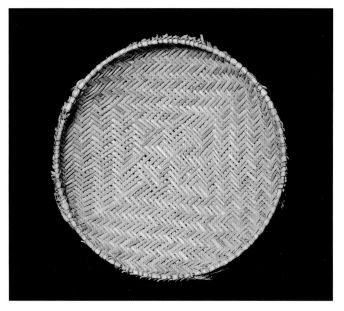

SW-6. Hopi ring basket using single yucca strands as weaving elements. Different parts of the yucca leaf, as well as different curing processes, produce the shades that accent the twill-plaited diamond pattern.

SW-9. Basketry has provided an important source of cash income for generations. Karl Moon's vintage photo, "The Basket Seller," depicts a peddler of Puebloan red willow baskets.

SW-11. Hopi plaque with coiled galleta grass foundation and dyed and natural-colored yucca stitches, early 20th century, 13" diameter.

SW-10. Hopi bundle-coiled seed jars, sometimes with lids, held seed corn for spring sowing, early 20th century, 5" high.

SW-12. Hopi coiled tray has an eleven-petaled design, c. 1940, 14" diameter.

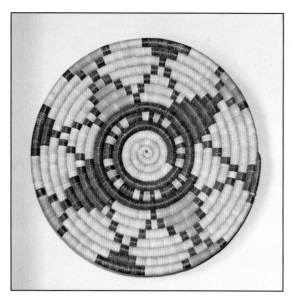

SW-13. Hopi coiled tray with an embellished eight-pointed polychrome element.

SW-15. Detail of Hopi wedding plaque in SW-14, showing the start, courses of bundle coiling, and overstitched rim finish.

SW-14. Hopi bundle-coiled yucca wedding plaque with a five-pointed star or flower in three traditional colors, early 20th century, 16" diameter.

SW-16. Hopi coiled plaque represents Shalako Maiden, one of the most elaborate and beautiful women's dance figures, mid-20th century, 9.75" diameter.

SW-17. Hopi coiled tray depicting Crow Mother, coiled by Sitak-pu of Shungopavi, c. 1900, 11" diameter.

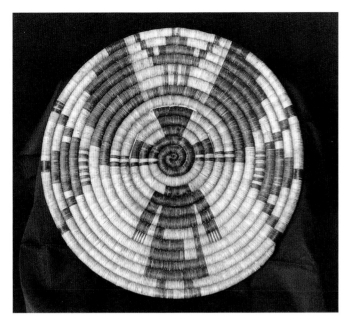

SW-18. Hopi coiled tray featuring stylized rain clouds and Crow Mother, 14.25" diameter, whom many Hopi consider the matriarch of all kachinas. During the Bean Dance in February, marking the coming growing season, Crow Mother assists in the initiation into the Kachina Society of eligible children upon their reaching adulthood.

SW-19. Another colorful Hopi kachina plaque dates to the 1990s.

SW-20. Hopi deep bowl, more challenging to make and thus less commonly found than trays, features a kachina mask as the central element with a band of rain cloud symbols, above, and mesas, below, 20th century, 15.5" high.

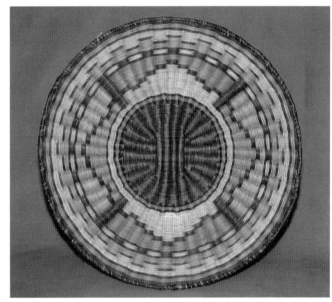

SW-21. Hopi Third or Western Mesa plaited wicker tray with a cloud design, c. 1910, 13" diameter.

SW-22. Two Hopi Third or Western Mesa plaited wicker trays feature rain clouds, expressing the perennial prayer for rain and successful crops in this semi-desert region, early to mid-20th century, (*left*) 13" diameter.

SW-23. Three Hopi plaited wicker trays with a distinctive start forming a diagonal line at the center, sometimes called a Grand Canyon start, seldom made after 1930, *(left)* 10.25" diameter.

SW-25. Rainbow-like colors remain bright in the black-bordered, banded "thread" pattern resembling bobbins moving up and down on this Hopi plaited wicker tray, c. 1985, 13.5" diameter.

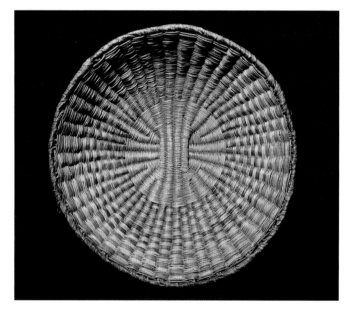

SW-24. Early Hopi plaited wicker bowl has a faded appearance due to the transient nature of applied white kaolin clay pigment and fugitive dyes.

SW-26. A butterfly spreads its wings on this Hopi plaited wicker plaque by Jennie Horace, 1937, 12" diameter.

SW-27. Detail of Hopi butterfly plaque. In an ideal world, collection data would accompany every basket. This string tag succinctly identifies the plaque, gives its maker's name and village location, and the date. The "B90" tag is a catalog number added by an earlier owner.

78

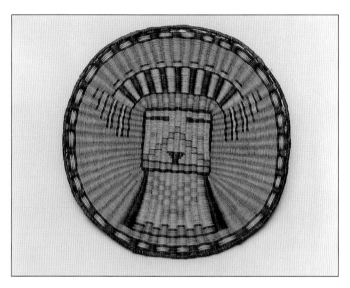

SW-28. Kachinas are a perennial theme on both bundle-coiled and plaited wicker trays like this example, c. 1910.

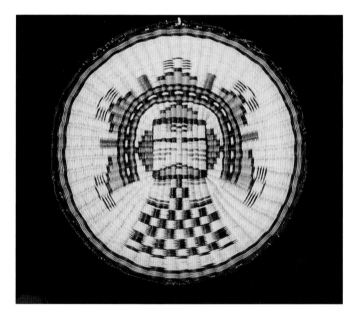

SW-29. Shalako Maiden, with her white face mask, an elaborate tableta, and black and white feathered wedding robe, poses on this Hopi plaque, gifted at a basket dance in 1955, 14.5″ diameter.

SW-30. Hopi women participating in a Lalkont basket dance in the shadow of Dance Rock at Oraibi village on Third Mesa, around 1900, are pictured in this Fred Harvey postcard.

SW-31. Hopi plaited wicker bowl for apricots and peaches, made in 1930 for a school teacher at Moenkopi, 7.5″ diameter.

SW-32. Traditional Hopi *piiki* tray plaited of dunebroom holds *piiki* rolls of wafer-thin blue corn bread, mid-20th century, 15" long.

SW-34. Early "Old Pueblo" basket, 11.5" diameter, preserved as an heirloom by a Zuni trading family.

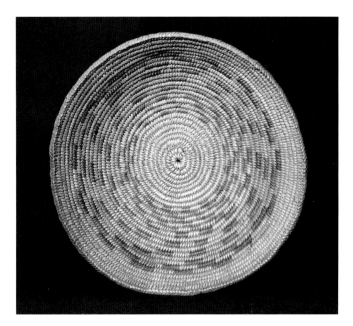

SW-33. "Old Pueblo" basket, possibly late 18th century, 10" diameter. The late Dr. Andrew Hunter Whiteford argued convincingly for an heirloom Zuni Pueblo origin for these scarce, early two-rod-and-bundle coiled baskets with false-braided rims and simple dyed black or dark brown decoration. Such modest-looking baskets can go unrecognized in basketry collections.

SW-35. Early Akimel O'odham (Pima) and Tohono O'odham (Papago) bundle-coiled, willow-stitched baskets, commonly trays or shallow bowls (*left*) used in Native households for winnowing and grinding wheat, gathering cactus fruit, and other chores. Ollas or jars (*right*) especially appealed to outsiders and were made primarily for sale, 9.5" high.

SW-36. False-braid rim finishes edging some Akimel O'odham baskets are fashioned with black devil's claw. False-braid rims appear also on Navajo, Havasupai, and Jicarilla Apache baskets in the Southwest.

SW-37. Devil's claw and willow stitches form this classic, old Akimel O'odham design sometimes called "butterfly wings." This tray is of average size for examples dating to the early 20th century, 15.5" diameter.

SW-38, SW-39. Coiled willow trays featuring "whirlwind" design. Note lighter, more dynamic feel to the Akimel O'odham example (*above*), 16" diameter, in contrast to larger black center and heavier overall use of devil's claw in the Tohono O'odham tray (*below*), 13.25" diameter.

SW-40. Finely stitched early Akimel O'odham tray, c. 1890-1910, 16" diameter. Central scorching may indicate Native use as a parching tray. Added pink and green paint highlights the traditional stitched "whirlwind" design and is only rarely seen.

SW-41, SW-42, SW-43. Stepped fret or vortex designs appear frequently on Akimel O'odham trays, with three interpretations shown here. Four-part fret or ancient swastika motif is also known as "whirling logs," 12.5" diameter.

SW-44. Quadrupeds riding a four-armed fret whirl around this Akimel O'odham tray, early 20th century.

SW-45. Akimel O'odham expanding quatrefoil design in willow and black devil's claw, c. 1900, 15.5" diameter. A false-braid rim finish helps distinguish Akimel O'odham from early Tohono O'odham willow baskets.

SW-46, SW-47, SW-48. Three Akimel O'odham versions of the popular "squash blossom" design of willow and devil's claw made a century apart, c. 1890-1910, 18" diameter (*top*); c. 1995, 12" and 10" diameter (*bottom*).

SW-49. Early Tohono O'odham willow and devil's claw plaque encircles a large raptor or "thunderbird" within an unusual looped rim, c. 1900, 17" diameter.

SW-51. O'odham semi-globular bowl with whirling fret design, coiled watertight for fermenting cactus fruit into *tiswin* wine, c. 1880-1910, 16" diameter.

SW-50. Willow and devil's claw star shines brightly in this small Tohono O'odham tray stitched by Josephine Thomas, 1990, 7" diameter.

SW-52. Fine Akimel O'odham olla or jar with polychrome stitching in willow, black devil's claw, and red yucca root, made for the market, c. 1900-1920, 9.5" high.

SW-53. Akimel O'odham cylindrical bowl or wastepaper basket, c. 1900, 10.5" diameter, created to appeal to tourists traveling by auto and rail to national parks and the greater Southwest. Human figures, kiva ladders, "coyote tracks," and random numbers and letters are common design elements in this period.

SW-55. Small Akimel O'odham willow-stitched bowl, of a type commonly made for the tourist trade, c. 1920-1940, 5.5" rim diameter.

SW-54. Large Akimel O'odham willow-stitched bowl with traditional design but made for sale, c. 1900-1920, 20" rim diameter. Rapidly sewn coils, evident in spaced stitches and visible foundation, accelerated production.

SW-56. Early 20th-century Akimel O'odham willow-stitched bowl attracted buyers with its human "friendship" figures and "coyote tracks" of devil's claw, as well as a dozen blue glass trade beads edging its rim, 7" diameter.

SW-57. O'odham bundle-coiled willow bowl crawls with seven polychrome chuckwallas or lizards. The deep red stitching is not natural red yucca root but, instead, was colored with commercial dye, 9.5" rim diameter.

SW-58. Historical photo, c. 1900, of Tohono O'odham woman unloading her *kiaha*, or pack basket, of firewood.

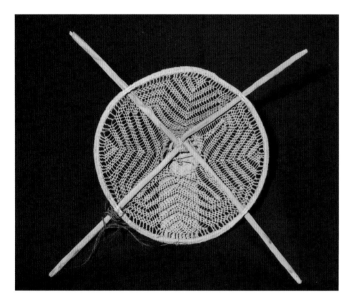

SW-59. O'odham child-sized *kiaha* of the type adults used for gathering wood, cactus fruit, and other necessities. Knotless netting of looped agave fiber, enhanced with red and blue pigments, fastened to a cactus-rib frame, 17″ rim diameter.

SW-61. Tohono O'odham tray with bold polychrome six-pointed design stitched in two natural shades of yucca plus black devil's claw by Virginia Lopez, c. 1970, 10.75″ diameter.

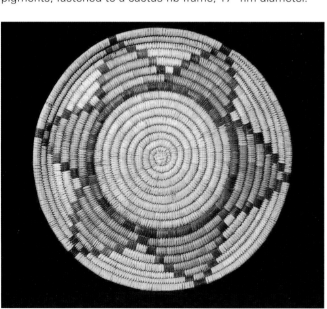

SW-60. By the late 1800s, Tohono O'odham weavers were replacing willow with yucca, more readily available and easily worked, when coiling baskets for a growing tourist trade. Still, souvenir baskets like this bundle-coiled tray stitched in various shades of yucca preserved traditional techniques and designs, c. 1910-1920, about 16″ diameter.

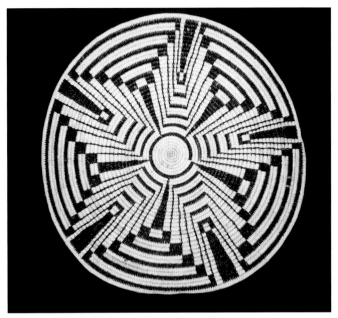

SW-62. Butterflies flit about a central flower or star in Tohono O'odham basketmaker Evelina Juan's yucca-stitched tray, c. 1980, 16.5" diameter.

SW-64, SW-65. Two five-petaled squash blossoms bloom across these large trays, (*upper*) 27" diameter. The polychrome example attributed to Connie Francisco (*lower*) was stitched with yucca, red yucca root, and black devil's claw, c. 1980, 16" diameter.

SW-63. Devil's claw and yucca-stitched tray with the emblem of the Tohono O'odham Nation, by Lolita Manuel, c. 1970, 15" diameter. This popular "Man in the Maze" motif has appeared in basketry since about 1900. The culture hero "Elder Brother" travels life's maze from birth to old age.

SW-66. Polychrome squash blossom pattern with central "Man in the Maze" design in yucca, black devil's claw, and red yucca root adorns this unusually complex Tohono O'odham coiled basket by Marian Cruz, 1997, 13.5" diameter.

SW-67. Yucca-stitched Tohono O'odham olla or jar features an appealing old motif known as "turtle back," early 20th century, 15" high.

SW-69. Yellow snakes with forked tongues and black devil's claw butterflies encircle this polychrome yucca-stitched olla or jar, c. 1930, 14.5" high. Notice the characteristic, obliquely stitched Tohono O'odham rim finish.

SW-68. Designs on this Tohono O'odham olla or jar are sometimes called "juice falling from saguaro fruit" and "coyote tracks," early 20th century, 11" high.

SW-70. Four horned toads or Gila monsters sun themselves around this yucca-stitched Tohono O'odham bowl or tourist wastepaper basket with sewn overstitching that defines the eyes, 1930-1940, 10" deep.

SW-71. Tohono O'odham small yucca-stitched souvenir bowls, c. 1930-1940. Open bowl with devil's claw vortex is 7" diameter.

SW-72. By the mid-20th century, yucca-stitched Tohono O'odham souvenir basketry had expanded to include curios like this turtle effigy basket, 8.5" long.

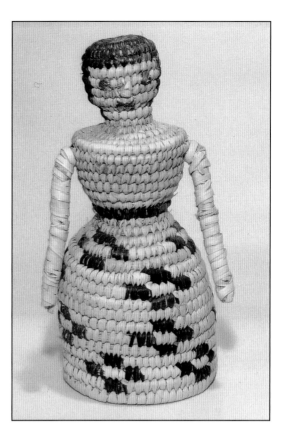

SW-73. Tohono O'odham polychrome doll with overstitched brown eyes of red yucca root by Nancy Antone, mid-20th century, 7" high.

SW-74. Tohono O'odham jar doll with removable olla stopper atop her head by Dalla Cruz, mid-20th century, 12" high.

SW-75. Dorothy Encarsega's tray reinterprets a traditional Tohono O'odham whirlwind design with decorative spaced stitching of yucca on a beargrass foundation to create an airy, motion-filled effect, 1974, 7.5" diameter.

SW-77. Innovative Tohono O'odham work includes wire baskets, coiled from one continuous length of bailing wire, usually by men. The originator of the form, Eugene Lopez of Sells, Arizona, created this handled basket in the early 1980s, 8.5" diameter.

SW-76. Contemporary yucca-stitched trays exhibited by the Tohono O'odham Basketweavers Organization (TOBO) at the Heard Museum's annual Indian Fair and Market, Phoenix, 2004.

SW-78. Miniature Tohono O'odham coiled horsehair trays, c. 1990s, plus miniatures by other Native groups, spill from burden baskets carried by the "Paiute Princess" Carlson doll, 1960s, 7.5" high.

SW-79. Southwest basketry miniatures include an extensive variety of tiny willow, yucca, and horsehair forms, 20th century.

SW-80, SW-81, SW-82, SW-83. Tarahumara twill-plaited baskets, Copper Canyon, northern Mexico, late 20th century: *(lower left)* double-weave lidded basket in two shades of yucca-like sotol, 11" diameter; *(upper left)* ten graduated single-weave sotol baskets, largest 5.5" diameter; *(upper right)* ten nested sotol baskets beside ten graduated single-weave pine needle baskets; *(lower right)* double-weave pine needle jar, 4" high.

SW-84. Western Apache coiled tray, of average size at 13" diameter, has typical black center and vertically stitched self-rim finish with an expanding five-pointed star or net design in black devil's claw, c. 1890-1900.

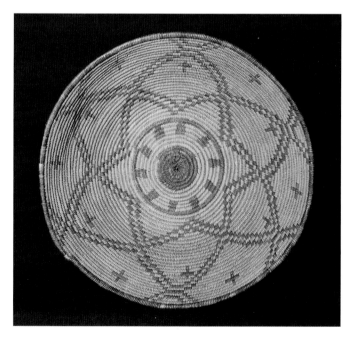

SW-85, SW-86, SW-87. Three Western Apache trays of six-petaled design, c. 1900-1910, embellished with crosses and life forms for market appeal: (upper right) tray with human figures, quadrupeds, and saguaro cacti, 11.75" diameter; (bottom left) tray with triangles and crosses, 9.75" diameter; (bottom right) tray with crosses, 15" diameter.

SW-88. Western Apache tray, generously stitched with black devil's claw to create a bold quatrefoil offset with chevrons, early 20th century, 16.25" diameter.

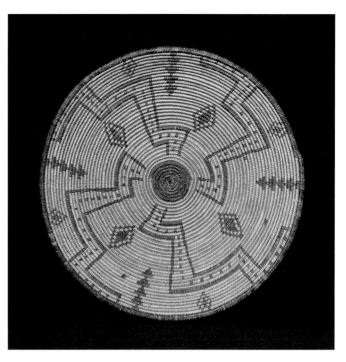

SW-90. Another San Carlos Apache interpretation of "lightning," c. 1890-1910, with red yucca root accents stitched near the tray's rim, 14.5" diameter.

SW-89. Western (San Carlos) Apache tray with dynamic four-armed stepped design, sometimes called "lightning," and added geometrics, c. 1890-1910, 14.5" diameter.

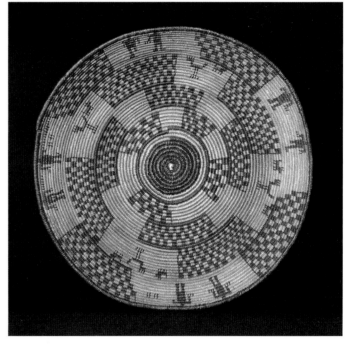

SW-91. Western Apache stepped whirl design becomes a checkered landscape for some unusual birds, small dogs, and eight men missing body parts, c. 1890-1910, 15.25" diameter.

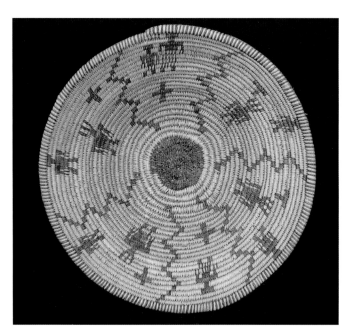

SW-92. Many Western Apache design layouts are slightly skewed, as is this six-part radiating pattern where four polychrome Apache *ghan* dancers dominate other scattered elements. Ticked dark-and-light overcast rim finishes are found less often than solid black on Western Apache baskets, early 20th century, 10.5" diameter.

SW-93. Western Apache coiled tray, stitched with cottonwood and devil's claw, resembles work of San Carlos basketmaker Mary Porter. Cottonwood stitches generally look whiter than willow or sumac, 1960s, 13" diameter.

SW-94. Many collectors covet unusually large trays from the early 20th century. Value increases rapidly with every inch of diameter beyond 16" in trays of excellent condition, because each new coil added to expand the diameter requires considerably more stitches and much extra material. This Western Apache tray is about 24" diameter.

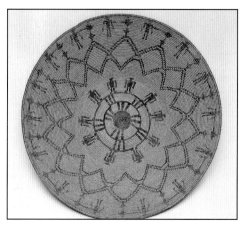

SW-95, SW-96. Evenly stitched trays of an overly large size, each surpassing 24" diameter. Their technical mastery and complexly banded, highly figured designs placed them near the apex of Western Apache basketweaving a century ago, when they were collected.

SW-97. Bands of more than 40 humans and quadrupeds encircle this polychrome tray, over 20" diameter. Adding red yucca root to Western Apache coiled designs, c. 1900-1915, intended to increase sales, backfired commercially when collectors rejected red as non-traditional. Consequently, early 20th-century polychrome is relatively scarce today and, ironically, more highly valued among modern collectors.

SW-98. Finely coiled baskets frame this cradled Western Apache baby in a vintage photo, c. 1900.

SW-99. Western Apache basketmakers began coiling high-shouldered ollas or jars for the market in the late 19th century. This classic narrow-mouthed example is stitched with bands of geometrics, c. 1900, 10" high.

SW-100. Western Apache polychrome pictorial jar combines a generous amount of red banana yucca root with black devil's claw and a dark-and-light ticked rim finish, c. 1900-1915, 17" high.

SW-101. Humans, quadrupeds, geometric forms, and stepped elements on this Western Apache jar with busy horizontal and vertical layout may have appealed to tourists, c.1900-1920.

SW-103. Western Apache diagonally twined jars generally predate coiled examples. This unadorned utilitarian form with globular body and narrow neck would have been used for storage in a Native setting, late 19th century, about 18″ high.

SW-102. Western Apache coiled basketry jar, its flaring neck and broad shoulder heavily embellished with devil's claw quadrupeds, humans, crosses, and geometric bands, is of grand proportions at almost 30″ high.

SW-104. Western Apache diagonally twined seed jar, reinforced with three-strand twining at shoulder and neck, woodsplint lugs, and heavy black rim finish, late 19th century. Twined utility jars may have served as prototypes, inspiring market-driven production of the decorative coiled ollas that became so popular with collectors.

SW-105. Flat-based Western Apache *tus* or water bottle with two twig handles, diagonal twined, then reddened with ochre and mashed juniper leaves before the curious word "Pork"was applied, probably with soot. A coating of melted pinyon pine pitch sealed the interstices and waterproofed the jar, early 20th century, 5" high.

SW-107. Double-bodied Western Apache water jar for carrying on the trail was either held under the arm or suspended on cordage from the waist, like a canteen. The worn pitched surface reveals that the red-ochre-rubbed bottle was overpainted with two lines of black soot or pigment prior to waterproofing, c. 1920-1930, 12.25" high.

SW-106. Flat-based Western Apache water jar with old collection tag, diagonally twined and originally pitch coated, with pitch loss revealing two black lines encircling the ochre-reddened body, early 20th century, 7" high.

SW-108. Western Apache burden basket for women's chores and ceremonies like girls' puberty rites, plain and diagonal twined with three red and black bands, brain-tanned buckskin fringe, and base protected with red cloth-lined cut-work buckskin patch. Native use against an owner's back reshaped the basket, c. 1900, 11" high.

SW-111. Early diagonally twined Mescalero Apache burden basket with metal cones that jangle rhythmically when the basket is in motion, 13" high.

SW-109. Contemporary Western (White Mountain) Apache burden basket, fringed with Native-tanned buckskin and metal tinklers, twined by Theresa Paxson of Cibeque, Arizona. Woven for a traditional White Mountain Apache wedding ceremony, then sold through a Salt River Canyon trading post, c. 1990, 10" rim diameter.

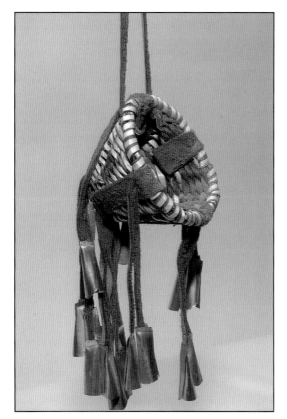

SW-112. Mescalero Apache burden basket, diagonal twined of sumac, c.1920.

SW-110. Hanging from rearview mirrors above vehicle dashboards, small Western Apache burden baskets, about 3" diameter and finished with commercial leather fringe and tin cones, have become both popular and inexpensive cultural mementoes.

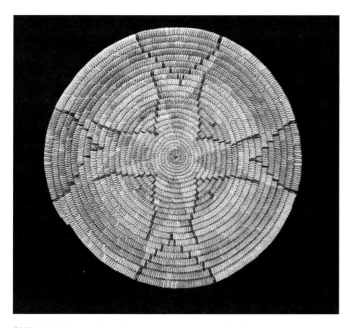

SW-113. Mescalero Apache tray with wide, flat looking yucca-stitched coils, c. 1900-1930, 15.5" diameter. The dominant cross in red yucca root extends from a light-hued, eight-pointed central star.

SW-115. Jicarilla Apache coiled laundry hamper lid (tall, narrow base is missing), with typical bright aniline-dyed sumac stitches, early 20th century, 16" diameter.

SW-114. Mescalero Apache yucca-stitched bowl with slightly flaring walls, a standard commercial form in the early 20th century. Deep red yucca root highlights geometric motifs, 14" diameter.

SW-116. Jicarilla Apache oval basket with loop handles. Its once-vivid design, stitched with commercially dyed sumac strands, has faded almost completely, leaving a plain coiled basket with false-braid rim finish, early 20th century, 9" high, 6.5" x 10" rim diameter.

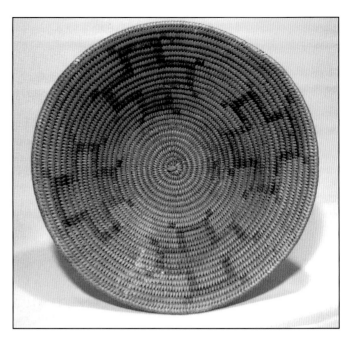

SW-119. Jicarilla Apache call the corner-ticked red and green dyed crosses on this bowl "butterflies," c. 1940, 15" diameter. Found on baskets used only in a four-day Holiness Rite or Bear Dance healing ceremony, "butterflies" resemble black-outlined red "Spider Woman cross" or "rain cross" elements on Navajo and San Juan Paiute baskets.

SW-117. Jicarilla Apache wastepaper basket with two handles, coiled with natural and dyed stitches for commercial sale. Formerly vivid geometric design elements are now faded, early to mid-20th century, 11" high.

SW-120. Two-rod-and-bundle coiled Navajo basket with three corner-ticked and black-outlined red "Spider Woman cross" or "rain cross" motifs, 11.5" diameter. The Navajo consider that Spider Woman, the first weaver, spins the clouds that bring the rain and taught the Navajo to weave.

SW-118. Jicarilla Apache coiled water jar with globular body, straight neck, high shoulder bound with two braided horsehair lugs, and rawhide patch protecting base. Only the interior is pitch coated, as customary with the Jicarilla. Vertical lines of double-course coiling extend from base to false-braid rim, early 20th century, 13" high.

SW-121. Navajo-style "wedding basket" with traditional pathway or break extending from center. Pathway ends at the false-braid rim termination, guiding the medicine man to orient the basket toward the East during weddings and other rituals. Three-rod coiling suggests a Southern Paiute origin for Navajo use, early 20th century, 15.75" diameter.

SW-123. With its 4" depth, this 13" tray of traditional Navajo ceremonial design is deeper and more copious than most early 20th-century examples and may be a basket-drum.

SW-122. Navajo-style "wedding basket" center symbolizes life's beginning, moving outward with coils. Black triangles are rain clouds in red sky band, with outer undyed coils representing the increase of the Navajo people, who emerge along the pathway. Residual corn meal and central cloth plug indicate ceremonial use, mid-20th century, 13" diameter.

SW-124. Reverse of SW-123. Unusual wear on the tray's base suggests basket was "turned down," inverted as a basket-drum in Navajo healing ceremonies, like the nine-night-long Night Chant. Drumming songs drive evil or illness trapped beneath the basket-drum back into the earth. When the basket is turned up again, only good remains, and balance and harmony are restored.

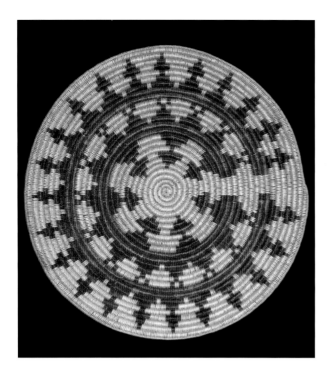

SW-125. Long after forsaking basket weaving, Navajo women–encouraged by an expanding market and guidance from Indian traders–revived the craft in the mid-1970s, moving it in new directions. Made in the Monument Valley, Utah, area, this large tray with double ceremonial design exemplifies this rebirth, c. 1980s, 24" diameter.

SW-127. Navajo basketmaker Nellie Grandson stitched a golden eagle into this tray. Its green and white rim finish recalls a Navajo legend about the false-braid edge origin: green juniper leaf scales inspired a basketmaker to imitate the pattern with a false-braid finish for the margin of her basket, 1970s, 18.5" diameter.

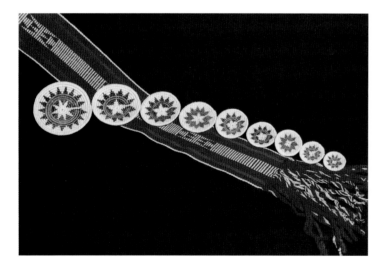

SW-126. At the opposite end of the scale, tiny Navajo-style "wedding baskets," many by Grace Lehi, a San Juan Paiute who specializes in this design, sometimes come in graduated sets, c.1980s, 1" to 4.25" diameter. Grace also makes baskets of "jumbo" size.

SW-128. A 1980s product of the Navajo basketmaking revival, this three-rod coiled tray by Jeannie Rock Begay combines traditional ceremonial design with animals in a black dyed design resembling popular patterns on Western Apache trays. Recent Navajo baskets usually incorporate the traditional spirit break or pathway.

SW-129. Coiled Navajo basket by celebrated weaver Sally Black depicts two yei figures adapted from sandpaintings encircling a central "wedding basket" design, 1990s, 16.5" diameter.

SW-131. Coiled plaque with characteristic Havasupai knotted start, 15" diameter, attributed to Stella Yunosi, or "Corn Eater." In the 1930s and 1940s Stella sold many baskets through Fred Harvey's Hopi House concession at the Grand Canyon. Leaves and lizards were popular motifs with Havasupai basketmakers at that time.

SW-130. Navajo basketmaker Elsie Holiday adapted the elegant O'odham squash blossom design and decorative overstitched type of rim finish to this tray in the 1990s, 17.5" diameter.

SW-132. Havasupai storage jar, diagonal twined with courses of three-strand diagonal twining circumscribing the body to add strength. Two lugs of four braided black horsehair loops and a black devil's claw overcast rim finish accent the warm brown sumac container, which lacks a pinyon pine pitch coating, 1930s, 16" high.

SW-133. Hualapai (Walapai) bowls with simple, aniline-dyed geometric bands diagonal twined for the market. Inexpensively priced, they sold by the hundreds to mid-20th-century travelers visiting the Grand Canyon, Colorado River, and Havasu Canyon, larger bowl 9.75" diameter.

SW-135. Two small Seri bundle-coiled baskets are recent products of a commercially-driven, century-old tradition of basketmaking among the Seri people of coastal northern Mexico.

SW-134. Seri bundle-coiled bowl with six-petaled motif, sewn with natural and dyed reddish brown and black stitches of limberbush, a desert shrub, c. 1995, 4.75" diameter.

SW-136. Yavapai or Western Apache coiled tray with netlike design, early 20th century, 17" diameter. Some experts view this tray as Yavapai; others favor a Western Apache attribution. Co-residents at San Carlos Apache Reservation, 1875-1900, with subsequent interaction and intermarriage, Yavapai and Western Apache weavers produced baskets nearly indistinguishable from one another without further documentation clarifying the weaver's tribal affiliation.

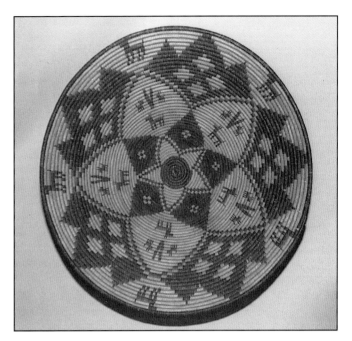

SW-137. Coiled tray, c. 1910, 15.5" diameter. Some might identify this basket as Western Apache given its uneven five-petaled central device and both right and left facing quadrupeds. Others might attribute it to Yavapai based on light-colored elements imposed onto dark design fields, further asserting that Yavapai work "feels" more precise, exacting, and symmetrically balanced than Western Apache. Cultivating a sense of whether a basket is truly well made and aesthetically and artistically appealing may benefit collectors more than assigning attributions solely on style.

SW-139, SW-140. Two additional Yavapai or Western Apache coiled trays, early 20th century, both about 18" diameter. Each somewhat differently interprets an expanding five-pointed allover design accented with positive and negative elements.

SW-138. Coiled tray attributed to Yavapai chieftess and basketmaker Viola Jimulla, who learned how to make baskets while living at San Carlos Apache Reservation before about 1900, 12" diameter.

SW-141. Yavapai or Western Apache coiled tray, early 20th century, generously sized at 22.25" diameter, required considerable amounts of material, patience, and skill during its creation.

SW-142. Yavapai or Western Apache olla or jar, coiled by a recognized but as-yet unnamed woman associated with San Carlos around 1900, has stacked quadrupeds and rows of male and female figures. The 48.5" high masterpiece dwarfs the chorus of trays perched below in this vintage Peabody Museum, Harvard, postcard, c. 1910.

SW-143. Another finely stitched and highly figured masterwork, this Yavapai or Western Apache coiled basketry jar, c. 1900-1910, soars to over 36" in height.

SW-144. Masterful technical and artistic expertise is revealed in the refined form, balanced layout, and overall aesthetics of this coiled Yavapai basketry jar, c. 1900-1915.

Great Basin

Most Great Basin peoples were hunters and gatherers who ranged cyclically through semi-desert expanses in search of scarce foods. These foragers pieced together a varied diet of large and small animals, like bighorns, mule deer, jack rabbits, and mice, along with berries, seeds, pinenuts, birds, and even reptiles and grasshoppers. Durable and lightweight utilitarian baskets were indispensable to families as they moved about, gathering, processing, and storing their hard-gained foods. This lifeway has been but the most recent phase of a Desert Archaic tradition that extends back more than 10,000 years.

Archaeologists have recovered some of the earliest preserved basketry in the Americas from the dry caves of this region. Baskets collected today, however, date from more recent post-contact times, mostly within the past 150 years. Baskets from the Great Basin have long attracted avid collectors, and examples from older collections are eagerly pursued whenever they come into the marketplace.

Of the Native bands who moved seasonally through overlapping Great Basin territories, basketry falls into two sub-regional styles:

- southern Great Basin
- northern Great Basin

Southern Basin baskets represent foragers, like the Southern Paiute, Southern Ute, Panamint Shoshone, and the forager-farmer Chemehuevi, a southern band of Southern Paiute. Northern Basin basketry includes that of Northern Paiute, Washoe, and Western Shoshone groups who, by the late 1700s, were influenced by the equestrian lifestyle of their Plateau and Plains neighbors.

The predominantly Uto-Aztecan speaking foragers who occupied both Great Basin sub-regions twined mostly utilitarian forms: conical burden or pack baskets, jars (some of which were pitch-coated to hold water), fan-shaped seed beaters, winnowing and parching trays, cooking baskets for stone-boiling, bowls, trays, hats, mats, baby carriers, sandals, and bags. These utilitarian wares might be decorated with simple geometric designs, either twined with dark devil's claw or bracken fern root or else overpainted with dyes or pigments.

Southern Great Basin Baskets

Most traditional utilitarian baskets from the southern Basin are twined. Some coiled baskets have been made here as well. In the late 19th and early 20th centuries, Southern Ute and the San Juan Southern Paiute basketmakers coiled well-known Navajo-style "wedding baskets," which they traded or sold to their Navajo neighbors who were no longer weaving them for themselves. At about the same time, basketmakers of three southern Basin groups—the Southern Paiute, Chemehuevi, and Panamint Shoshone—also excelled at coiling baskets for trade or sale to local ranchers and shop keepers.

GB-1. Detail of Paiute diagonal twined woman's hat with overpainted netted design.

Like their forerunners who moved regularly through shared territories, Basin basketmakers often adopted appealing traits of others' baskets into their own, thus coiling baskets that blend attributes of two or more neighboring styles. Southern Paiute, Chemehuevi, and Panamint Shoshone basketmakers generally were all coiling bowls, bottleneck jars, and other forms with three-rod bunched foundations and stitches of willow. Preferences for specific decorative materials, rim finishes, and design layouts differed among them, however, and some major distinctions are summarized here.

For their coiled designs, Southern Paiute groups favored stitching with black devil's claw, then bulrush, as the primary colored material, usually accented secondarily with yellow juncus (and less often with reddish Joshua tree root or aniline-dyed willow or sumac). The Southern Paiute also preferred horizontally oriented designs of geometric elements and

107

compound cross-stitched (XXX) black-on-light rim finishes or alternating dark-on-light overstitching that resembles Panamint self-coiled rim ticking.

Chemehuevi basketmakers—situated as they were at the junction of the Great Basin, southern California desert, and Southwest cultural areas—were eclectic, and their baskets shared enough traits to be misattributed sometimes to other Basin peoples or even Western Apache or Cahuilla makers. The Chemehuevi preferred black devil's claw for spare banded geometric patterns, with some yellow juncus or aniline-dyed willow or sumac as a secondary material, and they usually fashioned solid black- or light-colored self-coiled rim finishes, though some rims may be fully ticked.

The Panamint Shoshone favored natural or black-dyed bulrush, with red Joshua tree root as the secondary and some juncus as the tertiary colored material, for bold vertically or diagonally placed geometric or representational life forms like bighorn sheep, birds, or butterflies. Stitches of pink or white quill also are found. Many Panamint Shoshone baskets have a single-course coiled black line at the junction of the base and wall with a second one placed several courses below the rim to frame the design field. Self-coiled rim finishes on Panamint Shoshone baskets usually are either entirely light colored or consist of sections of dark-and-light ticking alternating with solid light-colored blocks.

Northern Great Basin Baskets

In the northern Great Basin, Northern Paiute, Washoe, and Western Shoshone basketmakers mostly twined utilitarian forms with willow until the late 19th century. The Northern Paiute and Washoe selected from dark bracken fern, golden-brown willow with inner bark intact (also called "sunburned willow"), and dark reddish unpeeled redbud to make simple design elements, while the Western Shoshone occasionally turned to aniline and vegetal dyes for added color.

In the 1910s, after the Mono Lake Paiute near Yosemite, California, began to sell colorful coiled baskets with surfaces overlaid with a netting of tiny glass seed beads, other northern Basin weavers followed their example. Some Washoe, meanwhile, stitched fine cooking and storage baskets, trays, and bowls to appeal directly to the growing curio trade, taking the art of coiling to new heights.

The famous Washoe basketmaker Louisa Keyser (c. 1835–1925), also known as Dat-so-la-lee, introduced innovations in the 1890s that include adding unpeeled redbud to her decorative stitching materials and creating the popular *degikup* form—a fancy, incurving globular bowl. Fine baskets by Dat-so-la-lee and other Washoe makers that are documented as having been sold in the early 20th century through Amy and Abe Cohn's Emporium Store in Carson City, Nevada, can reach ethereal levels in today's collectors' market and are counted among the most prized examples of Native basketry.

GB-2. Chemehuevi basketmaker prepares splints in this vintage postcard view.

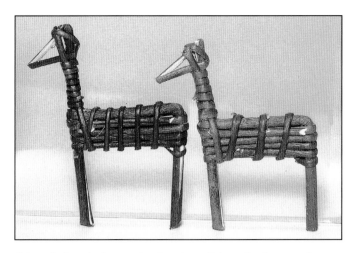

GB-3. Split twig figures by Southern Paiute-Goshute maker Everett Pikyavit in a style fashioned more than 3,000 years ago in the Green River and Grand Canyon areas, 2004, about 3" high.

GB-5. Diagonal twined conical gathering basket, a form used in collecting activities throughout the Great Basin and adjacent regions, c. 1900-1910, 13.5" diameter.

GB-4. Native women throughout the semi-arid regions of the West wielded open twined beaters to knock ripened grass seedheads into wide-mouthed burden baskets, c. 1850.

GB-6. Paiute fan-shaped parching and winnowing tray, open twined of split willow, early 20th century, 16" long, for processing pinenuts, an important staple and principal source of protein harvested from scrubby pinyon trees.

GB-9. Large Paiute jar, waterproofed with a coating of pinyon pine pitch and given lugs to accommodate a carrying strap, was used for storing precious water, late 19th century, 22.5" high. The conical base allowed the bottle to stand upright in soft earth or sand.

GB-7. Paiute winnowing and sifting tray, diagonal twined of willow with three reddish-brown bands of "sunburned willow" showing unpeeled inner bark, early 20th century, 17.5" long. Countless generations of Great Basin foragers have used this multipurpose form to winnow grass seeds, as well as to sift ground pinenuts or acorn meal.

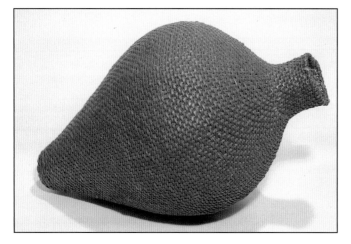

GB-10. Great Basin personal-sized water jar, completely coated with pitch both inside and out, could be carried like a canteen, early 20th century, 6" high.

GB-8. Diagonal twined Paiute jar with a pointed base was probably used for seed storage, c. 1900, 11" high.

GB-11. Southern Paiute diagonal twined seed jar or "treasure" basket embellished with overstitched black devil's claw rim ticking and two encircling bands of partially peeled "sunburned willow," early 20th century, 8.5" high.

GB-13. Owens Valley Paiute woman's hat, diagonal twined willow with a netlike pattern of "sunburned willow" strands overpainted with a dark brown mix of limonite and the desert shrub ephedra, collected c. 1910, 8.4" diameter. Paiute hats are large enough to accommodate a woman's hair while also protecting her forehead from the chafing action of a burden basket's tumpline.

GB-12. Southern Paiute mammiform woman's cap diagonal twined with black devil's claw weft strands to create simple horizontal bands, c. 1900, 6" high.

GB-14. Interior of the Owens Valley Paiute woman's hat, showing the "sunburned willow" decorative bands worked in "full-turn twining," in which the netted design on the exterior appears–like a photographic negative–with a reversed diamond-like pattern on the inner surface.

111

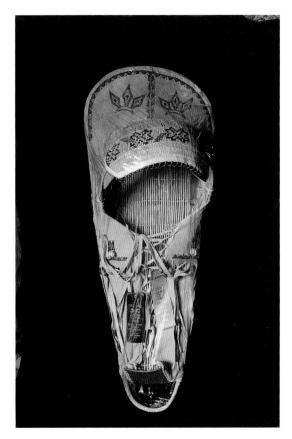

GB-15. Northern (Pyramid Lake) Paiute hooded cradlebasket by Mamie John, open twined of willow with a beaded buckskin cover and embroidered hood, received award ribbons in 1978, 42" high.

GB-16. Four Great Basin flat-bottomed work baskets for daily use; bowl at left collected by Lieutenant John Guilfoyle, Ninth U.S. Cavalry, between 1878-1910, 12" long.

GB-19. Coiled Panamint Shoshone oval bowl with characteristic fine, smooth-looking stitches of willow and bulrush, the design motifs accented with pink quill centers, early 20th century, 8.5" long.

GB-17. Panamint Shoshone-style coiled bottleneck seed jar with five ticked rim segments and snakelike zigzag bands stitched predominantly in dark bulrush plus some red Joshua tree (yucca) root and one short section of white (quill?) stitching, late 19th century, 7.5" shoulder diameter.

GB-18. Three butterflies sewn with red yucca root alight on this Panamint Shoshone bowl attributed to Mamie Gregory, c. 1910-1930, 9" rim diameter.

GB-22. Plant forms were a favorite design element among Paiute and Washoe basketmakers, c. 1910-1930, 11" diameter.

GB-20. Panamint Shoshone gift basket, a style made for sale by several basketmakers near Darwin, California, depicts six black and yellow birds–probably Scott orioles that nested locally–plus a stylized eagle on the base, sewn in willow, bulrush, and yellow juncus, 1930s, 6" diameter.

GB-21. Panamint Shoshone coiled gift basket by Mary Wrinkle appealed to travelers with its enchanting life forms stitched in willow, dark bulrush, yellow juncus, and pink flicker quill, 1930s.

GB-23. Southern (Moapa) Paiute (southern Nevada) bottleneck jar, with diagonally placed designs sewn with yellow juncus and black devil's claw on a coiled willow ground, has a decorative devil's claw rim finish, c. 1930, 6.5" high.

GB-24. Likely Southern (Moapa) Paiute bowl with four-color willow, black devil's claw, red Joshua tree root, and yellow juncus geometric elements and alternating natural and black overstitched rim finish, c. 1930, 10" rim diameter.

GB-26. Coiled Chemehuevi bowl ornamented with two simple black decorative bands and rim finish, finely sewn with fifteen devil's claw and willow stitches per inch, c. 1920, 7.5" diameter.

GB-25. Fine even stitching with black devil's claw and willow typifies Chemehuevi coiling, as does the rounded jar form, elegantly spare horizontal design, and black-edged, self-rim finish, c. 1910, 6" high.

GB-27. California Chemehuevi weaver Mary Snyder stitched twelve black waterbugs, for which she is known, into this large tray that combines variegated juncus with more commonly used Great Basin materials, c. 1920s-1930s.

GB-28. California Chemehuevi weaver Mary Snyder, famous for her trademark bug and rattlesnake designs, coiled two mice and a rattlesnake into this tray, c. 1920, 13.5" diameter.

GB-29. Northern Paiute or Washoe conical burden basket made for sale, diagonal twined with willow, "sunburned willow," and dark bracken fern root, early 20th century, about 20" long.

GB-30. Washoe burden basket by Scees Bryant condenses a standard utilitarian cone into an 8" long miniature with proper proportions, techniques, materials, and design, c. 1910, 6.5" long, 6" rim diameter.

GB-31. Globular basket with decorative beaded netting in four colors of glass seed beads, collected in the 1940s, typical of those made for sale by Washoe, Northern Paiute, and other northern Basin basketmakers as far west as the Mono Lake Paiute near Yosemite, California, 6.5" diameter.

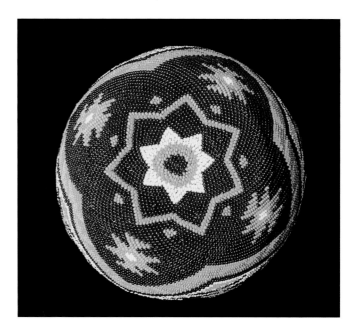

GB-32. View of beaded base.

GB-33. Northern Paiute coiled basket, overlaid with netting of colorful seed beads secured at the inner rim, is a commercial product, mid-20th century, 3.25" diameter.

GB-34. Miniature coiled willow basket by Northern Paiute-Washoe basketmaker Sandra Eagle, decorated with tiny glass and shell beads individually sewn into the coiled stitching–not netted over the surface, was awarded Second Prize ribbon from the Gallup Inter-Tribal Indian Ceremonial, 1998, 0.5" diameter.

GB-35. Washoe basketmaker Louisa Keyser, also known as Dat-so-la-lee (c. 1835-1925), displays outstanding examples of her coiled *degikup* baskets.

GB-36. Washoe coiled *degikup* attributed to Lily James, c. 1908-1910, 11" diameter.

GB-37. Typical examples of the globular *degikup* with vertically oriented geometric elements for which Washoe weavers are known, early 20th century, (*left*) 9.75" diameter.

GB-38. Small Washoe one-rod coiled *degikup* and inset snap-lock lid sewn with willow, reddish unpeeled redbud, and black dyed bracken fern root strands, early to mid-20th century, 4.5" diameter. The gap stitch, or spaced stitch, technique produced baskets comparatively quickly for the market.

GB-39. Four-color Washoe gap-stitch coiled *degikup* and snap-lock lid with a partially faded design of dyed pinkish and yellow willow plus black bracken fern stitches in the style of basketmakers like Maggie Mayo James or Sarah Mayo, c. 1920s, 6.5" diameter.

GB-40. Great Basin diagonal twined covered bottle made for sale, mid-20th century, 7.75" high.

California

Bountiful and varied wild food resources supported a host of Native California groups, most of whom lived in small territories where they fished, hunted, and gathered. Acorns of several species were central to their diets, and virtually all groups made specialized baskets for processing them. Basketry is widely recognized as Native California's most highly developed form of material culture. Before ceramic and metal vessels and cloth arrived with Europeans, basketry served every aspect of Native life, filling roles literally from birth through death.

Men twined rough fish and bird traps, but women have been the primary basketmakers here, as elsewhere. They wove cradle baskets for babies; caps or hats; seed beaters and winnowing and parching trays; acorn gathering, cooking, and storage baskets; hopper or mortar baskets used in grinding acorns; bowls and trays; lidded tobacco baskets; ceremonial dance baskets; and gaming trays. In addition, some like the Pomoans coiled spectacular feathered baskets as gifts for the living or the departed. Epidemics of European-introduced diseases and conflicts over land decimated California's Native populations in the mid- to late 19th century, but the craft of basketmaking persisted among the survivors. Today it remains a vibrant living tradition.

Basketry techniques used throughout California are best considered within three geographic sub-regions:

• southern California
• central California and the San Francisco Bay area
• northern California

Most southern California baskets are bundle coiled and utilize the juncus rush. Both twining and coiling techniques are found further north toward central California, the San Francisco Bay area, and the San Joaquin River drainage. In northern California, twining prevails, to the exclusion of coiling. General differences in basketry of these three regions are discussed below.

Southern California Coiled Baskets

Southwestern California (Mission) baskets include decorative bundle-coiled bowls, trays, and jars, in addition to other utilitarian forms. Most southwestern California coiled examples were stitched with glossy strands of golden or basal red juncus, giving the baskets a dark yellow or reddish appearance that is both distinctive and appealingly warm—and nearly irresistible to collectors. Some strikingly bold designs effectively combined the natural-colored hues of juncus, dark dyed juncus, and natural-colored sumac sewing elements.

Finer technical details are helpful for distinguishing baskets of separate groups—for instance, coastal Mission examples by Chumash versus Luiseño makers—and include specific attributes like work direction, starts, rim finishes, splices, and fag or moving ends of stitching strands. These important diagnostic traits are examined more fully in publications listed in our regional bibliography.

Central California Baskets

Central California baskets are both coiled and twined. Products of the coastal groups differ somewhat from those of the central mountainous region, which in turn are distinct from the southern Sierra products.

To the east, in the rugged Sierra Nevada mountains, the Maidu and Central and Northern Sierra Miwok excelled at three-rod coiling with dynamic, bold designs of either split redbud or dark bracken fern root. The Southern Sierra Miwok, perhaps influenced by neighboring Yokuts and Western Mono (Monache) groups, created similar baskets but with bundle-coiled foundations of deergrass. From 1916 to 1929, Yosemite Miwok basketmakers and their Mono Lake Paiute relatives, from just to the east in the Great Basin, coiled enormous bowls to vie with one another for awards in Yosemite's Indian Field Days competitions.

In the southern Sierras, baskets of the Western Mono (Monache), Yokuts, and Tubatulabal include both twined utilitarian forms and bundle-coiled examples. Western Mono and Foothill Yokuts coiled baskets with deergrass foundations have very thin walls. Western Mono baskets display sedge and black bracken fern stitching elements, often with layouts of horizontal bands that may be interrupted with vertical design elements. Many Yokuts products are stitched with both red and black decorative elements against a neutral ground of sedge. Yokuts bottleneck jars with horizontal banded red and black designs, sometimes edged with quail topknot feathers and red yarn along the shoulder, are especially desirable.

Tubatulabal and Kawaiisu neighbors of the Yokuts coiled bowls and bottleneck baskets that look similar in form and design to Yokuts examples, but they tend to be stitched with willow or sumac rather than sedge, reddish Joshua tree (yucca) root instead of redbud, and/or dark bracken fern root. Occasionally they added decorative red wool, quills from bird feathers, and quail topknots, as well.

Two unusual basket types are unique to this sub-region. At first glance, the Kawaiisu "interrupted stitch" coiled baskets and the "string" baskets of groups like the Sierra Miwok, Yokuts, and Western Mono may be confused with spaced-stitch coiling, which they can resemble, yet both are quite different.

In the former, short sections coiled with several regular stitches repeatedly alternate with blocks of four to twelve stitches that simply wrap around the foundation bundle, thus "interrupting" the coiling process, without engaging adjacent coils or stitches.

"String" basketry bowls and trays are fashioned using an ancient technique that combines aspects of both coiling and twining. Coil-like bundle foundations are bound together in a twining-like way by using many radiating, widely spaced pairs of binding strands, Native cordage, or cotton string.

In the western, San Francisco Bay area of central California, the highly skilled Pomoan peoples and their neighbors, like

the Ohlone (Costanoan), Coast Miwok, Yuki, and others, both twined and coiled a variety of baskets. The basketmakers' highly developed love of decoration is evident in much of this region's basketry. Even utilitarian twined forms like hopper baskets (used with stone mortars) and pack baskets are not only sturdy but also skillfully decorated. Embellishing methods like three-strand twining and lattice twining also add strength. These techniques, enhanced with various well selected decorative materials like reddish unpeeled redbud, have produced baskets that are both finely executed and aesthetically appealing.

Coiled baskets from this central coastal region are stitched on either one-rod or three-rod foundations. One of the most unusual and highly prized of these products was the exquisite feathered basket, or *epica*, by the Pomoans and neighboring groups. The plush surfaces of these beautiful coiled gift baskets may incorporate as many as 30 to 50 tiny colorful bird feathers per lineal inch. In addition to its feathered surface design, an *epica* may have an underlying woven structural design created with natural, dark-colored stitching elements usually of bulrush. Pendants and edge trimmings of clam shell disk beads and abalone or stone drops also add to their opulence. Today, potential collectors of these feathered baskets should take care to familiarize themselves with current federal laws regarding endangered migratory bird species, as discussed on page 60.

Northern California Twined Baskets

While all northern California basketmakers generally twined their baskets to the exclusion of coiling, individual groups decorated them in distinctive ways, many prescribed by cultural traditions. Recognizing these varied techniques and decorative styles may help a collector establish more specific attributions for otherwise poorly documented baskets. For example, northwestern Californians like the Yurok used the half-twist overlay technique in which the design is seldom visible on the interior of the basket.

In contrast, their northeastern California neighbors including the Shasta, Achumawi, and Atsugewi favored full-twist overlay designs that are as fully visible on the interior as on the exterior of a basket. Some Northern California design elements are shared with Klamath and Modoc in the neighboring southern Plateau.

Northern California Basketry Caps

Northern California basketmaking groups also preferred their own styles of basketry caps or hats. Remnant peoples comprising the amalgamated Hupa (Hoopa) group of northwestern California, for example, created fancy dress caps that were low in height when compared to the taller versions of northeastern California and the Plateau further to the north. In these northwestern California caps, color-combination preferences and design element choices also varied, sometimes in ways that may be culturally specific. Some Karuk weavers, for example, criticized caps with "too much" yellow-dyed porcupine quill in them, preferring instead the liberal use of red alder-dyed woodwardia fern with black maidenhair fern for motifs, or red-dyed design fields supporting design elements of light-colored beargrass and black maidenhair fern. Others, along with their Yurok and Hupa (Hoopa) neighbors, favored either black, black and yellow-dyed, or black and red-dyed design elements against light-colored beargrass backgrounds. Today, some basketry collectors focus only on twined northern California women's fancy dress caps for their great variety and interest.

CA-2. Susan, a northwestern California basketmaker, selling baskets, c. 1920.

CA-3. Four bundle-coiled southwestern California (Mission) baskets include (*clockwise, from top*): parching tray, rectangular tray, small bowl, bowl, c. 1900-1920, left bowl 7.5" diameter.

CA-4. Some recall that Valerie Jean Dates near Thermal, California, used to market several pounds of dates in an uncommon rectangular-shaped southwestern California (Mission) tray, similar in form to this example, c. 1930-1950, 14" long.

CA-5. Bundle-coiled globular bowl of mottled natural and black mud-dyed juncus stitching has a six-petaled flower or star motif when viewed from the base. Cahuilla, among other southwestern California (Mission) basketmakers, often added back stitches–in this instance four–at the rim finish terminal, early 20th century, 7.5" diameter.

CA-6. The easy to recognize, diagnostic stitch, called "Mission tuck" or "Bound Under Fag End Stitch" (BUFES) found on most southwestern California (Mission) coiled baskets, appears as a tucked stitch oriented at a 45-degree angle to other vertical stitches. Bundle-coiled bowl sewn with white-looking sumac and variegated natural and black mud-dyed juncus, c. 1900, 5.75" diameter.

CA-7. Bundle-coiled bowl in the Luiseño and Kumeyaay (formerly Diegueño) style, with a sumac-stitched start and a body wall of split natural juncus stitches on a bundled foundation of Coulter pine needles, is still made today, though this example was collected much earlier, c. 1900, 4" high.

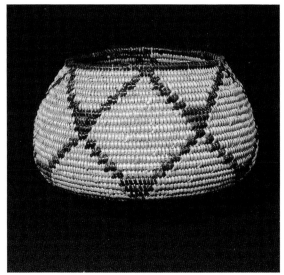

CA-8. Sometimes a basket's ID remains elusive. This small bundle-coiled bowl, technically southwestern California (Mission) in style, even with "Mission tuck" stitching, lacks juncus and uses shiny blackish maidenhair fern and maple strands common to Miwok examples further north, c. 1900-1920, 5.75" diameter. Its full story still waits to be told.

CA-9. Southwestern California (Mission) bundle-coiled basketry bowls and trays come in many forms and sizes, as seen in this image, printed directly from Edward S. Curtis's original 1926 glass plate positive.

CA-10. Bundle-coiled winnowing and parching trays for processing seeds saw daily use among southwestern California (Mission) peoples like the Luiseño. Sumac, more durable than juncus but more tedious to prepare, is the primary stitching material in this tray with two black mud-dyed juncus bands enclosing a variegated juncus stripe, c. 1880-1900, 16" diameter.

CA-12. Expanding six-petal flower or star motif in sumac and variegated natural juncus and black mud-dyed juncus often appears in southwestern California (Mission) basketry, early 20th century.

CA-11. Four repeating motifs ring the light-colored sumac basket start, otherwise stitched almost entirely with black-dyed and mottled natural juncus, on this colorful southwestern California (Mission) tray, c. 1900-1920, 13" diameter.

CA-13. Four-pointed central star stitched in variegated golden juncus against lighter sumac sparkles through the fronds of four dark palm-like plant motifs rendered in dyed juncus on this southwestern California (Mission) tray, c. 1900-1920, 12" diameter.

CA-14. Three design elements representing moths or flowers on this small, strikingly colorful southwestern California (Mission) bundle-coiled tray are stitched almost entirely in natural and black-dyed split juncus, with a few light-colored accents and a small filler element rendered in split sumac, 1900-1920, 8.5" diameter.

CA-16. Chumash lidded treasure basket, a highly collectible and rare masterpiece, is considered one of the finest examples of California and North America Indian basketry, pre-1840, about 12" diameter.

CA-15. Lidded treasure baskets of Chumash peoples who lived on Catalina Island and in coastal Santa Barbara and Ventura counties are almost as scarce as the California condor, early 19th century, 9" diameter.

CA-17. Maidu globular storage bowl with a characteristic three-part geometric design in redbud stitches, typically stopping one course below the top, early 20th century, about 5.5" diameter.

CA-18. Large feast basket, probably Mountain or Foothill Maidu, stitched with buff-colored shoots and reddish unpeeled redbud strands, and three-part geometric pattern ending typically below the rim, c. 1900, about 15" rim diameter, was used for serving acorn soup to numbers of people at ceremonial dances and large community events.

CA-20. Globular coiled bowl with design stitched in both reddish redbud and black bracken fern, by Maidu basketmaker Salena Jackson, 1890.

CA-19. Three-rod coiled winnowing tray with an expanding three-point central design element in typical Maidu style, except for uncommon light and dark rim ticking completely encircling the top coil, c. 1890-1900, 17" diameter.

CA-21. Large three-rod coiled cooking pot for stone-boiling acorn mush, stitched with sedge and black bracken fern root. Its diagonally overstitched rim finish is diagnostic of Sierra Miwok style basketry, c. 1900, 13.5" high, 22.5" diameter.

CA-22. Norman James, nephew of Lucy Telles, Yosemite Miwok-Northern Paiute prize-winning basketweaver, shows off one of her outstanding bowls in a personal way in this 1924 postcard view taken at Camp Curry, Yosemite.

CA-25. Twined fan-shaped trays for acorn flour sifting or winnowing attributed to (*left, center*) Western Mono (Monache) or Yokuts; and a northeastern California conical burden basket embellished with full-twist overlay (*right*), c. 1900, left 23.5" high.

CA-23. Globular coiled bowl by Yosemite Miwok-Northern Paiute basketmaker Lucy Telles with an all-black design of bracken fern and sedge stitched onto a foundation of willow rods, about one foot in diameter, documented to a 1926 Yosemite Field Days photograph featuring Telles holding the basket (see Bates and Lee 1990:103, Fig.199).

CA-24. Open twined Southern Miwok seed beater, with a distinctive form and two-colored peeled and unpeeled elements that are diagnostic of Yosemite Valley work made for sale by a basketmaker known as Indian Mary, c. 1900, 15.25" long.

CA-26. Western Mono (Monache) scoop winnowing tray or seed beater with diagonal-twined openwork almost entirely of unpeeled redbud, with a one-rod willow rim, early to mid-20th century, 10" long.

CA-27. Western Mono (Monache) bundle-coiled bowl sewn with sedge and dark bracken fern and an obliquely overstitched rim finish, early 20th century, 10" diameter.

CA-28. Western Mono open twined cradle basket with a zigzag design worked in redbud on the hood, embellished with three groups of four beaded pendants, mid-20th century, about 15" long.

CA-29. Western Mono open twined hooded cradle basket with a cross design for girls worked in redbud, attributed to Ulysses Goode (Northfork Mono), mid-20th century, about 15" long.

CA-30. Western Mono (Monache) bundle-coiled cooking basket stitched in sedge and black bracken fern on a deergrass foundation, with obliquely overstitched rim and vertical elements punctuating horizontal bands. Small rewoven Native mends, visible along the right rim edge, attest to the stone-boiling basket's daily use, c. 1900, 14.5" diameter.

CA-32. Large Yokuts winnowing tray with "rattlesnake" designs displays the unique "string basket" coil-and-twine technique in which foundation coils are bound together at intervals with radiating paired strands instead of one continuing stitch, c. 1890-1900, 19.5" diameter.

CA-31. Snakes were an ever-present concern for Native hunter-gatherers in southern California and are frequently represented as diamond or zigzag bands on baskets from the interior desert region (*right, center*) and Mission groups (*left*, probably Chumash), late 19th century; left, 9" diameter.

CA-33. Detail of the Y-like joins where additional "strings" were added as the tray's size increased. Occasionally a winnowing tray might stand in for larger coiled gambling trays in a women's counting game, played with eight dice of black walnut halves, each filled with asphaltum and a shell bead.

CA-36. Yokuts bundle-coiled cooking bowl, with six rim-ticked segments and three red and black bands–the lower two representing snakes and the upper a band of ants or flies "to warn the snakes to behave." Interior bears scorch marks from hot stones, c. 1900-1920, 12" rim diameter.

CA-34. Well-used Kawaiisu-style coiled woman's hat protected her head and forehead from the action of a burden basket's tumpline. Design, bordered at top and bottom with a characteristic black course of stitches, is bright inside, but exterior red yucca root stitches show rubbing and wear, c.1890-1900, 7.7" diameter.

CA-35. Three bundle-coiled bowls from the southern Sierras, attributed to Yokuts or Tubatulabal (Kern River) (*left, right*) and Wukchumni Yokuts (*center,* by Katie Garcia), two with horizontal bands representing rattlesnakes and another (*right*) with an X-like butterfly or deerhoof motif, early 20th century; *left,* 21.5" diameter.

CA-37. Coiled Tubatulabal-style "friendship basket" dances with hand-holding humans encircling the rim above four bands of red and black diamondback rattlesnakes, c. 1900, 17.25" diameter.

CA-38. Stylized male and female humans in various poses frequently appear with geometrics on Yokuts-style jars and bowls and were popular with buyers, c. 1900-1920. Bottleneck jar (*left*) has remnant red wool and black quail topknots, 9" diameter.

CA-39. Yokuts bottleneck jar retains original red wool trim and quail topknots, embellishments that many collectors have considered particularly desirable, c. 1900, 5.5" diameter.

CA-40. High-shouldered bottleneck jar with rim ticks typical of southern Foothill Yokuts work seems to spin like a top with diagonally stepped designs ascending the body wall, c. 1900, 8" diameter.

CA-41. Tubatulabal (Kern River) bottleneck treasure jars have lower, somewhat more rounded shoulders and walls that look less angular than comparable Yokuts jars. The "butterfly in flight" design was popular with Kern River basketmakers around 1900, 6.3" diameter.

CA-42. Tubatulabal bottleneck jar with rounded profile, characteristic rim tick groupings, and three "snake" bands, c. 1900.

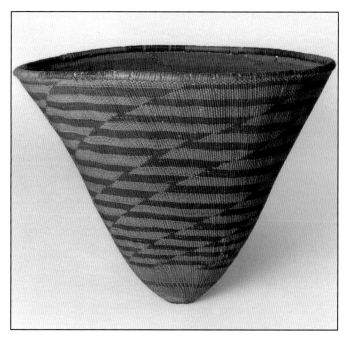

CA-44. Bell-shaped burden basket with twined design balances contrasting shades of sedge and redbud, c. 1900, 20" rim diameter. A large net enveloped this Pomo-style burden basket when used for collecting grass seeds or gathering acorns, bulbs, or other foods. A tumpline around the woman's forehead drew it inward against her back.

CA-43. Cecelia Joaquin, Central Pomo, using a twined seed beater to knock wild grass seeds into her wide-mouthed burden basket in this E. S. Curtis photo, 1924.

CA-45. Winnowing or sifting tray for separating chaff from seed kernels, or coarse from fine acorn flour. Plain twining reinforced with alternating courses of lattice twining strengthened the tray. Design bands consist of sedge and unpeeled redbud strands full-turn twined on willow warps, Eastern Pomo style, early 20th century, 13" diameter.

CA-46. Hopper baskets, like this Pomo example of sedge and redbud on willow, were secured to stone mortars and held firmly with the legs as a woman used her stone pestle to reduce acorns to flour, c. 1890, 20" diameter.

CA-47. Hopper or mortar basket, plain twined with reinforcing courses of lattice twining and a sturdy rim to withstand heavy daily use. Only partially visible here, on the lower left band, is a "dau" mark or break in the pattern, which some Pomo believed would protect the basketmaker from blindness.

CA-48. View of the Pomo hopper basket base with its purposeful hole showing little wear, suggesting that it was collected soon after it was made.

CA-49. Cooking bowl twined of sedge and unpeeled redbud with three decorative bands representing a variant of the design called "deer-back" among Northern Pomo, c. 1910-1920, 13" maximum diameter.

CA-50. Open twined Pomo-style work basket or acorn drying basket, mid-20th century, about 14" diameter.

CA-51. Since the 1960s, Coast Miwok-Kashaya Pomo basketmaker Julia Parker, photographed in 1975, has demonstrated for Yosemite National Park visitors. These miniatures are surely among her smallest creations (*top to bottom*): conical burden basket, pitch-handled basket brush, cradle basket holding infant with cedar berry face, c. 1990, each 1" long.

CA-52. Coiled baskets from the central coastal region of California are either one-rod coiled (*left*) or three-rod coiled (*right*), early 20th century; left, 3" diameter. The whitish blush on surfaces of redbud stitches (*left*), known to botanists as "glaucous bloom," is a wax that forms naturally on plant parts like blueberry skins and bark of young twigs like redbud and cherry. The bloom is not harmful and may be gently wiped off with a soft cotton cloth.

CA-53. Early three-rod coiled basket in a style distinctive to San Francisco Bay area peoples like the Ohlone (Costanoan) and Coast Miwok, ornamented with clamshell disc beads encircling the rim, olivella shell disc and glass bead crisscrosses, and abalone shell and European glass pony bead pendants, 19th century, 10" rim diameter.

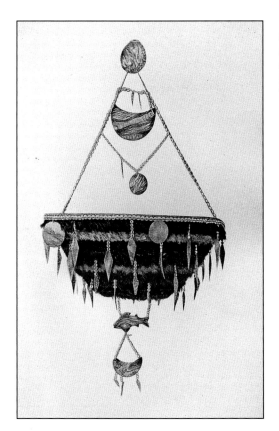

CA-54. Feathered "Yuki sun basket," illustrated in full glory more than a century ago by Otis Mason, embellished with elaborate pendants and suspensions of shaped iridescent abalone drops and white clamshell disc beads as well as countless feathers of green mallard, brown western robin, yellow meadowlark, red woodpecker, and others.

CA-57. Some coiled Pomo baskets rivaling the Yuki sun basket were made for sale and others as gifts for cherished family members or friends. Decorated with delicate little feathers that are susceptible to insect and environmental damage, they demand stable long-term storage and optimal display conditions, c. 1900; *left,* 6.75" diameter.

CA-55. Pomo three-rod coiled gift baskets with primary brown stitched patterns accessorized with clamshell disc beads, glass seed beads, quail topknots, and red feather tufts that can sometimes completely obscure the underlying integral design, c. 1900; left, 11.5" long.

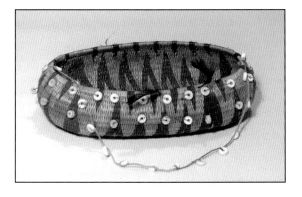

CA-56. Pomo "boat-shaped" oval basket, one-rod coiled sedge and dark bulrush with white clamshell disc beads, quail topknots along the rim, and remnant red woodpecker feathers nipped in around the body, c. 1900, 5" long. Baskets like this, in imperfect condition, pose a dilemma for collectors: keep "as is" or restore to a "prettier" state. With central California feathered baskets, the issue is further complicated. Some, but not all, contain feathers from migratory birds now protected under federal law.

CA-58. Pomo feathered gift basket, probably originally made for sale, ornamented with multicolored nipped-in feathers, clamshell disc beads encircling the rim, and abalone shell and blue glass bead pendants, has some feather loss exposing underlying coils, c. 1900-1920, 4.75" diameter.

CA-60. Designs on fully feathered gift baskets are best viewed from below to appreciate the weaver's intent. The geometric pattern on this Pomo gift basket, called by some a "moon basket" due to its white color, substitutes domesticated duck and goose feathers for those of native song birds. When completing the basket, the maker clipped the feathered surface to an even length, early to mid-20th century, 6" diameter.

CA-59. Topknots rim this jewel-like Pomo feathered bowl, perhaps made as a gift for a special wedding or birth of a child. Green and yellow plumage against a red feather ground replicates a common geometric design that is also sometimes stitched with plant fibers into Pomo coiled baskets without featherwork, c. 1900, 4.25" diameter.

CA-61. Pomo oval beaded basket decorated with yellow and multicolored dark glass seed beads, sewn into the one-rod coiled fabric with split sedge root stitches, early 20th century.

CA-62. Baby in a typical northwestern California sitting-style infant carrier, probably seated on absorbent moss packed into the base, from an early 20th-century photo postcard.

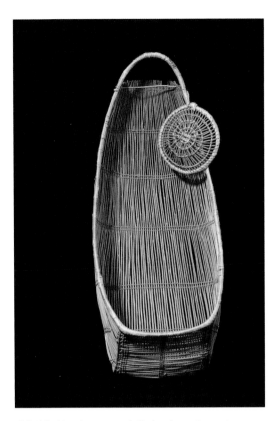

CA-64. Newborn- or doll-sized northwestern California sit-down type of infant carrier has a sun shade for the child's head, open twined of hazel with white beargrass wrapped frame, c. 1900, 21" long.

CA-63. Small northwestern California basketry infant carrier for a newborn or doll, open-twined of hazel shoots with a hazel rod frame wrapped with spruce root, early to mid-20th century, 19" long.

CA-65. Award-winning infant carrier with sun shade by Karuk basketmaker Florence Harrie, ornamented in half-twist overlay of yellow-dyed porcupine quill and white beargrass and black maidenhair fern strands, c. 1978, 29" long.

135

CA-66. Work or gathering basket with wrapped handle, used in acorn drying, shellfish gathering, and other tasks, open twined of hazel shoots in a style found among northwestern California groups like the Tolowa and Karuk, c. 1900, 11.5" diameter.

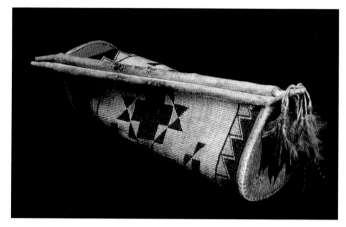

CA-68. Northwestern California Hupa group Jumping Dance basket, twined with half-twist overlay of beargrass, maidenhair fern, and porcupine quills dyed yellow with wolf moss lichen, c. 1900, about 12" long. The Jumping Dance basket, twined flat like a mat by women, is finished by men who bind the basketry fabric to two willow rim rods and enclose each end with a buckskin cap embellished with tassels.

CA-67. Detail of half-twist overlay decorative technique in the interior of a Hupa group woman's cap. This method, typical of northwestern California basketry, produces designs that usually are visible only on the outer surface. Less precise work sometimes results in "ghosts" of the overlay design showing on the interior.

CA-69. Period photo, taken by A. W. Ericson of Arcata, California, shows men and boys holding their special baskets and wearing red-shafted flicker feather headdresses, shell bead necklaces, and deerskins as they participate in the annual Jumping Dance world renewal ceremony, c. 1900.

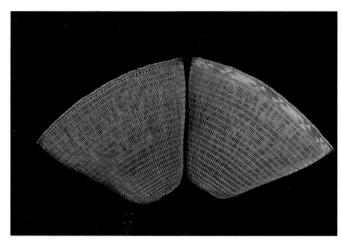

CA-70. Two Hupa group open-twined truncated conical burden baskets for gathering acorns and other foods, one (*right*) with half-twist overlay of beargrass and reddish alder-dyed woodwardia fern root below the rim, attributed to the Karuk, late 19th century, 24.5" diameter.

CA-72. Sturdy twined northwestern California cooking basket with two reinforcing courses of lattice twining encircling the body to support its weight with contents. Imprecisely worked half-twist overlay design called "elk" by Yurok is partly visible on the interior, c. 1900-1920, 14" diameter.

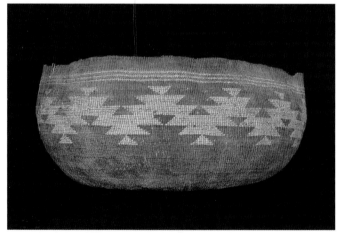

CA-71. Northwestern California everyday cooking basket for stone-boiling food like acorn soup, twined of hazel warp elements and conifer root weft strands, with half-twist overlay of light colored beargrass, c. 1900, 17" diameter.

CA-73. Northwestern California acorn soup bowl for individual use, twined of hazel, spruce root, and decorative half-twist overlay design in beargrass, reinforced with two courses of lattice twining, c. 1900-1910, 9" diameter.

CA-74. When in daily use in northwestern California, individual mush bowls were covered with a basketry plate for holding salmon or deer meat–generally an open twined "stick" version rather than the fancier close twined plate shown.

CA-76. Yurok-Karuk twined miniatures with half-twist overlay in split beargrass, black maidenhair fern stem, and reddish alder bark-dyed woodwardia fern stem: (*left*) woven disc by Yurok basketmaker Lucille McLaughlin, 1970s; (*center*) small mat by Yurok weaver Patsy Hunsucker, 1980s; (*right*) petite tray with a design Karuk call "friendship," attributed to Florence Harrie, mid-20th century, 4.75" diameter.

CA-75. Close twined basket plate with a half-twist overlay design in beargrass that some Karuk call "friendship," c.1900-1910, 11" diameter.

CA-77. Yurok basket becomes a pendant on this necklace ornamented with beads, white dentalia shells, and abalone drops by Lucille McLaughlin. Disc is twined with a triangular "snake nose" design in half-twist overlay of reddish alder-dyed woodwardia fern on beargrass, c. 1985, 2.25" diameter.

CA-80. Northwestern California trinket basket made for the tourist market. Its intricate half-twist overlay design plus the innovative open twined border and extra features like beargrass rim wrapping added desirability to this commercially-driven product, early 20th century, about 7" diameter.

CA-78. Novel six-piece northwestern California basketry-covered tea service represents an accomplished weaver's adaptation of traditional Native basketwork to Euramerican forms and cultural preferences. Despite the non-traditional application, the expert basketwork preserves many standard technological features, materials, and design elements, early 20th century, tray about 16" diameter.

CA-79. Twined gift or trinket basket for holding valuables, decorated in the typical northwestern California way with half-twist overlay visible only on the outer surface, early 20th century, 6.25" diameter.

CA-81. Northwestern California trinket or gift basket, without cover, possibly by Elizabeth Hickox, early 20th century, 5.5" diameter. Expertly twined with half-twist overlay, it departs from convention with a tapered form, a "negative" light-on-dark fabric and design rendered only in black and yellow-dyed elements, and a reinterpreted Yurok-Wiyot-Karuk design motif. In 2004, this distinctive basket sold at auction for over ten times higher than average regional examples.

CA-82. Northwestern California twined gift or trinket basket with an unusually bold design element that weavers considered innovative, probably made for sale, early 20th century, 8.5" diameter.

CA-83. Two Hupa group women's caps with traditional three-banded design layouts, c. 1900-1910. Polychrome dress cap (*left*) has white beargrass and black maidenhair fern half-twist overlay; less finely twined cap for daily wear (*right*) has design alone worked in half-twist overlay, plus two rows of reinforcing beargrass wrapped lattice twining above the brim, 6.75" diameter.

CA-84. Five Hupa group women's caps with varied half-twist overlay designs, c. 1900, average 6.75" diameter.

CA-85. Northwestern California Hupa group, possibly Karuk, twined woman's cap with two courses of lattice twining, ornamented with half-twist overlay. Karuk weavers call the central stepped beargrass design element "flint marks in a diagonal series," edged here with triangular "snake's-noses," c. 1900, 7" rim diameter.

CA-87. Detail of the yellow-dyed porcupine quill-covered "button."

CA-86. Northwestern California woman's dress cap with beargrass, maidenhair fern, yellow-dyed porcupine quill overlay, and yellow quill-covered "button" or start at the top of the cap, twined by an accomplished basketmaker, possibly Elizabeth Hickox, c. 1900-1910, 4" high, 7.5" diameter.

CA-88. Detail of a typical clipped-rim finish found on northwestern California women's caps, with half-twist overlay of beargrass, maidenhair fern, and porcupine quill.

CA-89. Typical of northeastern California work, this Atsugewi twined bowl exhibits the full-twist overlay decorative technique, in which designs are intentionally worked to be clearly visible on both inner and outer surfaces, c. 1900, 8" rim diameter.

CA-91. Wintu twined conical burden basket with chevron-like design called "geese in flight" in beargrass and maidenhair fern using the full-twist overlay method typical of northeastern California, mid-19th century, 15.5" diameter.

CA-90. Northeastern California twined conical burden basket, Atsugewi or Achomawi style, with a popular regional design sometimes called "quail plume," c. 1900.

CA-92. Northeastern California Achumawi style twined hopper basket, with full-twist overlay in beargrass and dark bulrush root and willow rim rod wrapped with unpeeled dark redbud, early 20th century, 16" diameter. Visible wear around the hole indicates heavy use with a stone mortar and pestle to process acorns.

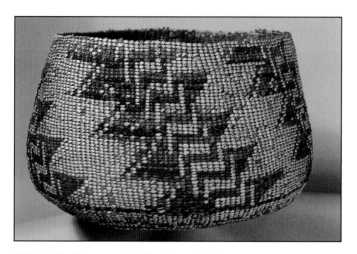

CA-93. Northeastern California, probably Yana, bowl twined of tule with full-turn twining and full-twist overlay of beargrass, late 19th century, 10" diameter.

CA-95. Northeastern California bowl attributed to the Atsugewi, decorated with an elaborate full-twist overlay design, early 20th century.

CA-94. Small northeastern California Achumawi style bowl made for sale, decorated with beargrass and maidenhair fern full-twist overlay, early 20th century, 5.5" diameter.

CA-96. Eastern Atsugewi style child's hat, twined with tule warp elements giving it flexibility like Modoc and Klamath examples of the Plateau, is decorated with full-twist overlay, early 20th century, 4" high.

Plateau

Natives living in the Columbia Plateau region traditionally followed a seasonal round of hunting, gathering, and fishing. Many moved between their villages along major waterways where migrating salmon spawned annually and the surrounding valleys and uplands where roots and tubers like camas (*Quamasia* sp.) and bitterroot (*Lewisia* sp.) grew. The introduction of the horse to the region in the mid-18th to 19th centuries enabled these people to become even more far-ranging. They traveled more readily through the Cascades Mountains to the Pacific in the west and eastward over the Rockies to the Plains, fostering new connections and adaptations. Their basketry adapted and changed accordingly.

Although these groups traditionally fashioned plaited mats, bark buckets, twined rabbitskin robes, and hide bags, coiling with Western redcedar root was once the dominant basketry technique throughout the cultural area. Twined bags were made as well, and today both supple, twined bags as well as hard, coiled baskets with imbrication are considered the characteristic Plateau forms. Basketry from this complex basketmaking region is most simply approached from two cultural subareas:

• southern and eastern Plateau
• western and northern Plateau

The southern and eastern Plateau emphasized twining, and the western and northern Plateau has favored imbricated coiling.

Plateau Twined Baskets

Native inhabitants of the southern and eastern Plateau like the Nez Perce, Yakima, and Umatilla are best known for their flat, flexible, twined carrying bags with geometric design elements. After adopting the horse, these equestrian peoples required new forms of containers suited for carrying on horseback. Most preferred to convert traditional gathering and storage bags—twined of Indian hemp and beargrass—into saddlebags, instead of adopting hide containers like those favored on the nearby Plains.

Somewhat later, but as early as the 1830s, access to cornhusks and wool and also cotton twine became common. These materials replaced beargrass and Indian hemp (or dogbane), respectively, and Plateau bags took on a new look. Plain twining decorated with false embroidery (or external weft wrap) soon surpassed full-turn twining as the dominant basketmaking technique among the predominantly Sahaptian-speaking peoples of the southern and eastern Plateau.

Flexible flat twined pouches and bags proliferated. Very large rectangular bags, some up to three feet long and used for gathering and storing roots and dried salmon, generally are earlier. Smaller, square forms, often brightly colored with commercial dyes and wool yarns after the 1880s, served as women's handbags and are more recent. Design layouts on the front and back sides of these colorful Plateau bags always differ from one another, making them popular with basketry collectors and impressive for display.

Like the Native cultures who made and used them, both older and newer bags and baskets often combine influences from other regions with local indigenous elements. Twined bags frequently shared traits with containers of adjacent peoples. For example, Plateau bags bear geometric patterns and drawstring closures, as do Plains rawhide parfleches. Some design elements that appear on baskets made throughout central and northern California occur as well on these bags. Design devices such as butterfly-like motifs reflect popular Nez Perce elements that were shared with nearby peoples painting on rawhide and doing beadwork.

Tall, fez-shaped twined basketry hats of the Nez Perce, Cayuse, Umatilla, and other southeastern Plateau groups are suggestive of similarly shaped tall, narrow coiled hats of northern and western Plateau peoples like the Klikitat. Again, all these groups interacted extensively, especially after the horse arrived in the region, and this contact is evident in their baskets and other material arts.

The Wasco/Wishxam, Klamath, and Modoc of the western Columbia Plateau use full-turn twining to create somewhat different, flexible twined forms. Since before the days of meeting the explorers Lewis and Clark in 1805 and 1806, the Wasco/Wishxam near The Dalles and the Cascades, for example, have twined hand spun fibers of dogbane into flexible "sally" bags, usually finished with hide-edged rims and loops for attaching the bags to a belt or waistband. These cylindrical bags are less flat than those of the neighboring southeastern Plateau and were used when carrying and storing roots, dried salmon, and other items. Designs include stylized human and animal figures and geometric elements, some of which display influences from the lower Northwest Coast and northern California.

The Klamath and Modoc, whose traditional territory extended geographically into northernmost California, twined flexible hats that, in height, often fall between the shorter twined dress caps of northern California and the taller fez-like examples from the southeastern Plateau. Klamath designs are eclectic, sometimes including elements found elsewhere in the basketry of other Plateau or northern California neighbors. Close examination of some Klamath baskets reveals a distinctive diagnostic trait: Twining elements of tule are sometimes twisted into a double or triple ply like commercial yarn by rolling fibers together between the palm of the hand and the thigh. The Wasco/Wishxam, and also the Shasta of northern California, occasionally used these twisted warp elements, as well.

Plateau Coiled Baskets

Coiling with Western redcedar root prevailed among both the Coast Salish groups straddling the lower Northwest Coast and western Plateau cultural areas and the more insular, predominantly inland Salishan groups of the northern Plateau. Basketry of these peoples shows that it, too, changed with the introduction of the horse. Klikitat basketmakers coiled a hard, truncated conical pack basket that stood up to equestrian travel. Lashings through

PT-1. Detail of coiled and imbricated Klikitat berry basket base by Nettie Jackson, c. 1990.

"ears" or loops along the rim secured the contents. Throughout this western and northern Plateau subarea, watertight cooking baskets for stone boiling and square or rectangular baskets for gathering, transporting, and storing berries and other foods and goods were also common. These stiff coiled baskets generally were embellished with imbrication, a tile-like overlay method that is unique to basketry from this region. Imbricated designs usually are fashioned with materials like mud-dyed beargrass or cedar root skin bark for black, beargrass for white and yellow, and/or wild cherry bark for red. Imbrication may either overlay the entire surface of a basket or form only the design elements against an unadorned coiled background, thus producing the tile-like decorative surface.

Color preferences and design choices vary culturally and regionally. The Lillooet of the western Plateau subdivision, for instance, combined black, white, and red imbrication colors but traditionally divided their design into two distinct horizontal zones with allover or heavier imbrication in the upper band and isolated or short vertical elements below. Fraser River and Thompson River Salish basketmakers, among others in the northern Plateau subdivision, frequently imbricated a free-standing design onto the wall of an otherwise plain coiled surface.

Although coiled, imbricated baskets functioned in similar contexts throughout the region, subtle variations in technology, as well as decoration, help collectors to distinguish among examples from different groups. Western Plateau groups like the Lillooet usually created basketry with flat coils, while the northern Thompson River Salish and their neighbors preferred narrower, rounder coils. More southerly Cascades peoples such as the Klikitat often fashioned false-braid rim finishes, while the northern and western inhabitants like the Thompson River Salish, Chilcotin, and Lillooet favored a whipstitched self-rim finish. Plateau basketmakers have been prolific, offering today's collectors many varieties from which to choose.

PT-2. Wishxam basket maker, photographed in 1909 by Edward S. Curtis.

PT-3. Early twined Plateau root-storage bag designs typically are symmetrical and repetitive, built on a single element like the pattern some call "fish gill," worked in trade yarn on this large 19th-century bag with drawstring closure.

PT-4. Plateau bags characteristically have cornhusk designs that differ on each side by the late 19th century, 17.5" long. Attached "Santa Fe Route/Fred Harvey Agent" green wax seal on a metal-rimmed paper tag dates to the early 20th century. Patched corner supports Native use as a carrying bag.

PT-5. Reverse of Plateau bag bears a common representational motif sometimes called "butterfly," repeated twice on a canvas of inner cornhusk leaves.

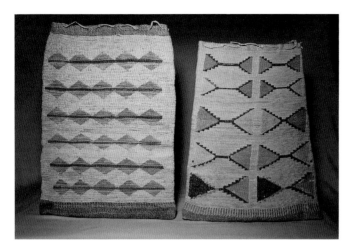

PT-6. Typical repetitive, horizontally banded Plateau bag designs. Boiling cornhusks together with woolen tradecloth likely produced the cornhusk colors (*left*), while commercial worsted yarns supplied material for the replicated "butterfly" motifs (*right*), late 19th century, right bag 18.5" long.

PT-8. Three small Plateau bags (*above*) and two larger root bags (*below*), c. late 19th to early 20th century, 11" to 20" high. All examples at left are decorated with cornhusk strands. The two at right, including one with an intricate "butterfly" variant, use commercial wool.

PT-7. Both Plateau bags retain at least one traditional twined border of knee-spun hemp on upper and/or lower edge, a feature that many collectors prefer. The upper margin (*right*) was worked with more durable white cotton string, which displaced brownish hemp cordage in many later bags.

PT-9, PT-10. Large Plateau bag with vivid geometric design elements, worked in false embroidery with recycled yarns and echoed with undyed "negative-space" motifs, achieves a rhythmic balance of decorated and undecorated spaces on both front (*above*) and back (*below*) surfaces.

PT-11, PT-12 Large Plateau bag with repetitive design organization on both the front (*top*) and back (*bottom*), with motifs worked in natural and dyed cornhusk, is a timeless classic, c. 1900, 19.75" long.

PT-13, PT-14 Complex "butterfly" elements rendered in commercial yarns appear on both sides (*top, bottom*) of this petite Plateau bag, c. 1900, 11.5" high. These smaller bags often lack hemp margins altogether and may be lined with cloth. The buckskin handle replaces the drawstring found on larger root-storage bags, implying a probable role as a handbag. Early 20th-century tourists purchased many such bags, and Natives use them to the present day as part of traditional ceremonial dress celebrating an owner's heritage.

PT-15, PT-16. Representational life forms like these butterfly and deer appear on more recent, smaller Plateau bags, about 11" long. Composing the curvilinear forms can challenge a weaver's ability.

PT-17. Three Plateau twined hats with two typical geometric design layouts: a three-pointed zigzag that local Native people call "mountain peaks" (*left, center*), and a three-pointed undecorated "negative-space" zigzag bordered with repeating colored triangular units (*right*). Hats predating about 1930 are decorated with full-turn twining, using two differently colored weft strands, thus creating a design that is visible in reverse on the inner surface as well. Many hats made more recently are worked with false embroidery (visible only on the outer surface), which uses less material. The hat (*right*) is twined completely of natural and dyed cornhusk and finished at the crown with one feather indicating the single status of the wearer. Another (*left*) is decorated with a yarn design. The third example (*center*) is embellished with valued tusk-like dentalia shells traded from the Northwest Coast.

PT-18. Flexible, cylindrical twined bags, often called "sally" bags and used for storing or carrying possessions, may display plain decorative bands or other simple elements. This Wasco or Wishxam example from the western Columbia plateau has four bands false-embroidered with wool yarn. Designs on other "sally" bags may be full-turn twined or false-embroidered in cornhusk. These serviceable sacks generally have drawstrings and rim bindings of buckskin or heavy cloth, c. 1900, 9" high.

PT-19. Two cylindrical Wasco or Wishxam "sally" bags with designs in full-turn twining. Wishxam consider the repetitive zigzag banded design (*left*) "very old," while stylized faces with diamond-shaped eyes (*right*) may represent the visage of Tsagaglalal, the mythological She-Who-Watches.

PT-21. Flexible Wasco or Wishxam "sally" bag with stylized skeletonized beings and sturgeon, early 20th century. Twined of natural and dyed cornhusk strands on a hemp warp, such designs persist among contemporary Wasco basketmakers.

PT-20. Tsagaglalal or She-Who-Watches endures on this ancient Wishxam petroglyph, resting not far from an ancient village site along the Columbia River at the Dalles near Wishram, Washington.

PT-22. Flexible Klamath or Modoc twined bowl (*left*) and woman's hat (*right*) with knee-spun tule warp elements and simple banded designs punctuated with dark and light tule and cattail weft fibers. Typical rim finish (*left*) shows warp ends folded over and bound to interior weft strands. Two or three yellow-dyed porcupine quill stitches accent the front center of hat (*right*), c. 1900-1920, 6.5" rim diameter.

PT-23. Small soft Klamath or Modoc bowl, twined of tule and cattail weft strands on knee-spun tule warp elements, with full-twist overlay design visible on the interior, early 20th century, almost 4" diameter.

PT-24. Klamath or Modoc flexible bowl or woman's hat of twisted tule warp twined with brown tule and lighter cattail leaf weft strands. Full-twist overlay design was possibly borrowed from northwestern California peoples who call it "friendship." Twined Klamath and Modoc women's hats are angled near their crowns like other Plateau soft hats, but are generally shorter than southeastern Plateau fez-like hats and are somewhat taller than northwestern California women's caps, c. 1900-1920, 4.75" high, 7.75" diameter.

PT-25. Detail of Klamath or Modoc twined rim finish with twisted tule warp strands and tule and lighter colored cattail weft elements.

PT-26. Klamath or Modoc bowl or woman's hat twined with warp and weft elements of two-ply knee-spun tule, lighter colored cattail, and dark mud-dyed tule cordage, c. 1900-1910, 5.25" high.

PT-27. Klamath or Modoc twined bowl or woman's hat with twisted warp and weft elements of knee-spun tule and lighter colored cattail. The design, commonly seen in northern California as well, is better viewed from the basket's start downward, suggesting that the maker's intended use was as a woman's hat, c. 1900-1920, 5.25" high, 7" rim diameter.

PT-28. Modoc or Klamath woman's banded hat of lower height, approaching the dimensions of northwestern California examples, but twined with twisted tule warp elements and weft strands of tule, lighter cattail, and mud-dyed blackish tule, early 20th century, 4" high, 7" rim diameter.

PT-29. Klikitat or Yakima style berry basket coiled of cedar root with tile-like imbricated design. When in use, the looped "ears" along the rim held ties for securing the contents, c. 1900, 12" high.

PT-30. Diminutive Klikitat berry basket, 5.5" high, with imbrication in natural and dyed beargrass, made by contemporary third-generation basketmaker Nettie Jackson, c.1990. Three imbricated beargrass stitches on the basket's base (Figure PT-1) are Jackson's mark.

153

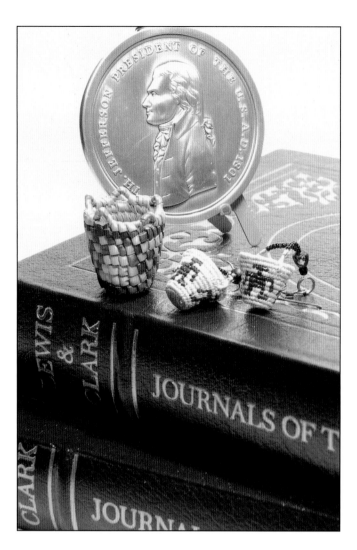

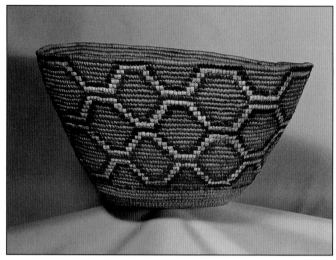

PT-31. Miniature coiled imbricated Klikitat berry basket by Elsie Thomas (*left*), c. 1960-1970, 1" high; pair of Plateau-style coiled raffia "friendship" basket-earrings by Seminole-Arapahoe Carol Emarthle Douglas, c. 2000, 0.5" high.

PT-32. Berry basket, coiled of inner cedar bark and imbricated in white beargrass, red cherry bark, and black bulrush, has an inverted pyramid form typical of the northern Plateau peoples. These attributes plus imbrication overlaying the basket's entire surface conform to a Thompson River Salish style, late 19th century, 9" high, 16.5" maximum diameter.

PT-33. Lillooet Salish-style berry basket, coiled of thin cedar strips in an angular, inverted pyramid form, has decorative elements imbricated across only the upper design field, c. 1900, 6.5" high.

PT-34. Probable Fraser River Salish-style berry basket, coiled of cedar strips and imbricated with white beargrass, red wild cherry bark, and black mud-dyed cherry bark. Vertical columns of a design sometimes named "half arrowhead" extend up the entire wall of the angular, inverted pyramid form. Basket retains original knotted thongs for strapping on a "lid," perhaps of fresh ferns, to protect the berries, late 19th century, 7" high.

PT-35. Small, rectangular lidded storage basket or trunk with imbricated design, a form typical of northern Plateau Salishan groups, is coiled with a foundation of thin cedar sapwood slats that give its courses a wide and flat appearance, c. 1900, 8.5" high, 14" long.

PT-36. Chilcotin coiled pack baskets often are reinforced with a horizontal rod below the rim. Their imbricated designs generally are divided into four horizontal fields, three placed below the rod with a fourth contrasting pattern above. Flattened waterfowl quills edge this rim, c. 1900, about 11" high.

Northwest Coast

The fog-shrouded Northwest Coast supported substantial Native populations. Inhabitants distributed the varied resources of this region's coastal rainforests, rivers, and shores through formal kinship networks, thus maintaining permanent communities without agriculture. Men were highly skilled woodworkers who constructed rectangular plank houses; carved and painted bent-wood boxes, masks, and food dishes; and fashioned large boldly decorated canoes and totem poles. Most Northwest Coast groups have used cedar bark in virtually every aspect of material culture, such as basket and mat making, and even in shredded form for creating clothing. Prehistoric baskets excavated at various sites in this region have been radiocarbon dated, indicating that the same basketry materials and techniques have been used here for several thousand years.

This cultural area may be divided into three major subareas:

• lower Northwest Coast
• middle Northwest Coast
• upper Northwest Coast

Basketmaking by women has figured prominently throughout this region. Men assisted post-production by overpainting some cedar bark basketry objects like mats and hats with totemic emblems that were clearly drawn from the highly developed Northwest Coast woodworking tradition.

Lower Northwest Coast Baskets

Basketmakers used numerous plaiting, twining, and coiling methods in the southernmost subarea, or lower Northwest Coast. They blended their own cultural preferences with styles from neighboring traditions, reflecting the considerable contact and interaction among Native peoples in this and nearby regions. Useful plaited cedar bark or rush bags and open wrapped twined cedar root wares like clam baskets, generally with little or no decoration, accompanied their owners on daily rounds of clamming, fishing, and berrying. Twined and coiled baskets from this area usually have rounded or oval forms. Some of these, too, saw service on a regular or daily basis, but others were preserved as family heirlooms.

An especially lovely twined product from this lower Northwest Coast area was a late 19th-century specialization. Both Native families and collectors consider the distinctive *t'qayas*, the flexible basket of the Skokomish (Twana), to be the finest example of plain twined basketry from this subarea. This slightly rounded form of cattail, cedar, and beargrass is typically decorated with half-twist overlay in an all-over geometric design. Its rim is often edged with loops of cedar bark, and a decorative overlay band generally found below the rim finish may depict a row of quadrupeds or water fowl.

The Quinault, to the southwest of the Skokomish (Twana), twined a similar but stiffer version using spruce root with beargrass overlay. Other southern Coast Salish bands and neighbors like the Quileute also twined and plaited baskets that appeal to collectors. The basketmakers decorated a few baskets with "beading" overlay—most often associated with coiling in this region—in which a decorative ribbonlike strand is placed along the front of a coil or structural weft element and then is bound to the basket with periodic stitches or weaving elements.

Other lower Northwest Coast Salish peoples, like the Cowlitz and Nisqually, stitched split cedar roots into characteristic deep oval coiled baskets, often with buckskin lugs attached to one side, braided rim finishes, and heavily decorated imbricated or beaded overlay designs in attractive combinations of white, yellow, black, and red. Puget Sound Salish examples also display all-over imbrication or beading with a distinctive one- to two-inch wide imbricated band in a contrasting pattern just below the rim.

Some Coast Salish groups made only a few loosely coiled imbricated baskets, using flat foundation slats and cedar root coiling that was not watertight. Instead, when they annually traveled inland to fish for salmon along the Fraser River, they traded with the Thompson and interior Salish groups to acquire better quality baskets suitable for stone-boiling, including rectangular examples that were created by their inland Salish relatives.

Among the Puget Sound Salish, makers of coiled baskets enjoyed great prestige, as did their products, which—though intended for cooking—often were never put into service. In the 20th century, imbricated cedar baskets were reserved for trade or treasured by Native families and passed down through generations.

Middle Northwest Coast Baskets

While cedar plaiting was practiced almost universally throughout the Northwest Coast, the greatest concentration occurred in the middle subarea among the Kwakwaka'wakw (Kwakiutl) and the Nuu-chah-nulth, or West Coast peoples (including the Makah). These groups plaited baskets of Western redcedar, folded lengths of cedar bark into berry baskets or buckets, and made twined baskets. Beyond the traditional, utilitarian, wrapped twined basket forms, other wrapped twined basketry examples are especially decorative and have long been popular with collectors. Enthusiasts seek out low round or oval lidded trinket baskets, small food mats, cedar bark hats, and basketry-covered bottles and abalone shells that were made during the last century primarily for the tourist market. Brightly colored waterfowl, whales, boats, hunting scenes, and even American flags and eagles decorate these coveted little baskets of twined cedar bark and beargrass. Both natural and aniline dyes like purple, orange, green, red, or yellow, when applied to the beargrass weft elements, give baskets like the Makah *piku'u*, or lidded trinket basket, their gay, upbeat appearance.

Upper Northwest Coast Baskets

In the northern subarea, or upper Northwest Coast, plain twined spruce root baskets decorated with false embroidery prevailed among the Tlingit, Haida, and Tsimshian. Most Tlingit

baskets are expertly woven and attractively embellished with either painted elements or colorful false embroidered designs using black maidenhair fern and white or brightly dyed grasses. Before 1870 or 1880, many Tlingit examples were associated with Native activities like berry gathering and processing. Several berry basket sizes were made for specialized tasks. Like modern-day shopping bags, these cylindrical forms could be conveniently collapsed, folded, and flattened for storage when not in use.

Market Economy Influences

After 1880, a developing market economy influenced the production of upper Northwest Coast basketry, with visible results. False embroidery on Tlingit spruce root baskets, for instance, became more colorful, as basketweavers turned increasingly to aniline dyes for tinting their decorative grasses. False embroidery often embellished structural bands of dyed weft strands, which further emphasized the designs.

At the same time, Tlingit basketmakers also began to create smaller forms, and they often omitted the central of three traditional design bands, as well, in an effort to produce baskets more quickly for sale. Open or spaced twining methods, like the decorative crossed warp technique that the Tlingit call *wahk-kus-kaht*, or "eye-holes," were both visually appealing and faster to weave, and so became increasingly popular in the late 19th and early 20th century.

New, non-traditional constructions like compotes with pedestal bases gained acceptance. Rattle-top baskets, or *tu-dar huck*, low cylindrical forms with lids double-woven to enclose loose pebbles or seeds, were purchased in quantity as handiwork baskets for storing sewing notions in Victorian homes. Today, both the berry basket and the rattle-top basket are forms that collectors especially desire.

Haida twined spruce root baskets resemble Tlingit examples but they generally look more plain. Haida basketmakers used little false embroidery, if any, preferring instead to twine bands that alternated natural versus black-dyed spruce root weft strands, thus encircling basket walls with two-color horizontal stripes. In addition, the Haida often gave a basket's surface, particularly below the rim or on the brim of a hat, a decorative pattern by shifting from plain to diagonal or three-strand twining to create structural texture.

The jog in the rim finish on the work surface, or outer side, of a Tlingit or Haida basket helps to differentiate Haida from Tlingit work. Tlingit rims terminate with a left-over-right "jog-down" in the final row of stitches, while Haida rim terminations are a right-over-left "jog-up."

In basket making, the Haida are most widely known for masterfully twined spruce root hats that are overpainted with clan emblems in red, black, and occasionally green. Undecorated covers of cedar bark also were woven to protect the finer hat itself when not in use. Other neighboring peoples like the Tsimshian and Kwakwaka'wakw (Kwakiutl) made some painted hats, too.

Early in the 20th century, Tsimshian living at Metlakatla twined small berry baskets and lidded baskets for sale, using cedar with modest false embroidery designs. These forms resemble Tlingit and Haida spruce root basketwork and come on the market relatively frequently, where they may be confused. The Tsimshians' smaller and more sparingly decorated products, while appealing, generally are not as highly regarded in the marketplace. A basic familiarity with the specific materials used in these baskets is indispensable for collectors in this instance, particularly as a Tsimshian example misidentified as Tlingit or Haida may wear an overvalued price tag.

Enthusiasts may wish to distinguish not only Tlingit, Haida, and Tsimshian examples from each other but also from similar-looking Alutiiq (Pacific Eskimo) twined spruce root baskets, illustrated here but discussed more fully in the Arctic and Subarctic section.

NW-2. Native American woman making a basket, Puget Sound area, Washington state, 1899 postcard view.

NW-3, NW-4. Two flexible Skokomish (Twana) twined baskets, each about one foot high. Quadrupeds encircle both rims, depicted either with half-twist overlay (visible only on the outer surface) or with full-turn twining (seen in reverse colors on the inner surface as well). Some authorities say upturned tails (*above*) represent dogs, and tails turned downward (*below*) signify wolves or horses, c. 1900-1910.

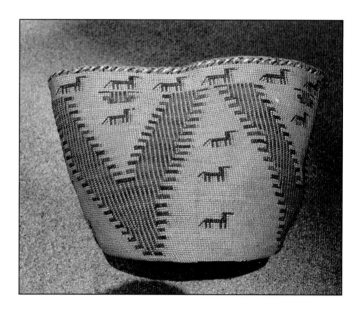

NW-5. Skokomish (Twana) flexible twined *t'qayas* for food gathering and storage depicts a pack of many wolves and lacks the characteristic looped border, which likely wore off with Native use, c. 1900-1910.

NW-6. Six coiled and imbricated baskets for cooking and berry picking, stylistically characteristic of oval-shaped baskets made by Nisqually, Cowlitz, and other neighboring Salishan groups. A narrow band of imbrication or beading overlay encircling the rim, visible on several containers, is a marker of southern Puget Sound baskets, c. 1900-1950, 10" maximum height.

NW-8. Berrying basket or bucket, readily stitched from one folded length of cedar bark as needed by various Northwest Coast and mid-Columbia River groups, c. 1900, 12" long.

NW-7. Nuu-chah-nulth storage basket of natural and dyed cedar bark plaited on the bias represents a form and material used widely throughout the region, c. 1900, 14" high.

NW-9. Nuu-chah-nulth wrapped twined *piku'u*, or trinket baskets, and small mats with bright geometric and representational design elements, c. 1890-1910, largest mat 8.5" diameter.

NW-10, NW-11. Nuu-chah-nulth lidded trinket basket or *piku'u* with geometric design elements (*left*) and detail of lid with five representational birds (*right*). Geometrics slightly precede and overlap the use of life forms in West Coast souvenir basketry, c. 1890-1900, 3.75" diameter.

NW-12. Nuu-chah-nulth groups, known for their prowess as whalers, added whales and other sea creatures to small round and oval lidded baskets by wrapped twining with dyed and undyed beargrass onto a cedar bark warp, c. 1900, 3.25" maximum diameter.

NW-13. Wrapped twined Nuu-chah-nulth *piku'u* emblazoned with red whirling motifs is of relatively large size at 5.5" diameter, c. 1900.

NW-14. Nuu-chah-nulth baskets like these two examples, decorated with elements including (*left*) geometrics, c. 1890, and (*right*) representational whaling scenes and whirlwind, c.1900-1910, are fashioned with wrapped twining over cedar bark starts.

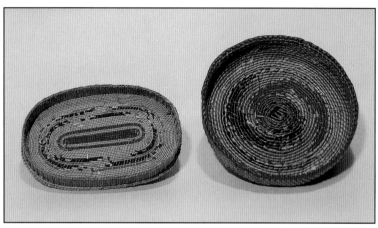

NW-15. Lid interiors have a distinctive appearance that helps identify wrapped twining.

NW-16. Bases reveal the characteristic cedar bark start.

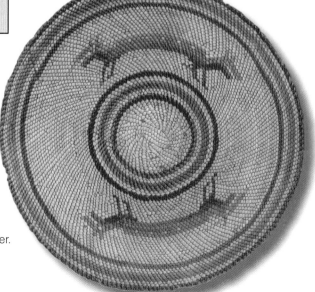

NW-17. Nuu-chah-nulth wrapped twined mat depicts a mythological two-headed sea monster, c. 1900, 8.5" diameter.

NW-18. This design on a colorful Nuu-chah-nulth wrapped twined mat represents four avian forms riding an air current, c. 1900, 6.5" diameter.

NW-20. Six Makah hunters in a long whale boat chase a whale around this wrapped twined bottle, mid-20th century, 3.5" high.

NW-19. Glass bottle covered with basketry fabric in two twining techniques—wrapped twining and crossed-warp open twining—was a souvenir of a visit to the Seattle or Vancouver area in the early 20th century.

NW-21. Nuu-chah-nulth miniature wrapped twined conical hat and covered baskets (*front*) and bottle, mid-20th century, with other regional souvenirs and Edward S. Curtis's 1915 image of a cedar-clad Nakoaktok Kwakwaka'wakw (Kwakiutl) painting a cedar hat.

NW-22. Hat, attributed to the Nuu-chah-nulth, probably of inner cedar bark twined by a woman and painted by a man, about 12" diameter.

NW-24. Small baskets twined by Tsimshian and Quinault basketmakers using inner cedar bark with beargrass false embroidery closely resemble comparable Tlingit and Haida forms twined from spruce root, c. 1900-1920, *back left,* 6" high.

NW-23. Nuu-chah-nulth wrapped twined hat with a knoblike top, featuring two frenzied whaling scenes and an eagle perching atop an arrow, 20th century, 9.5" high.

NW-25. Small Tsimshian or Quinault cedar-bark berry basket featuring central band of beargrass false embroidery, with upper and lower paired courses of cedar plaiting and white beargrass beading overlay, c. 1900-1920, 4.5" high.

NW-26. Detail of base illustrates the "wrinkled" appearance of twined inner cedar bark.

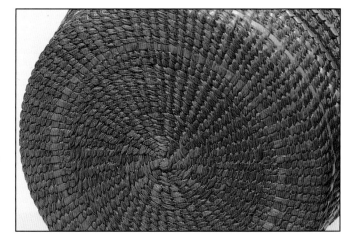

NW-27. Small Tsimshian lidded basket of twined inner cedar bark with undyed and green-dyed beargrass false embroidery. Tsimshian souvenir baskets are more simply decorated than their Tlingit and Haida twined spruce root counterparts, c. 1900-1920, 3" high.

NW-29. The Tlingit rattle-top lidded basket twined with spruce root and decorated with black maidenhair fern and dyed and undyed grass false embroidery remains as popular with today's collectors as it was with Victorian travelers, late 1800s, 9" diameter. The double-woven knob on the lid encloses pebbles that rattle when the basket moves.

NW-28. Small twined cedar bark berry basket with fret bands, "ALASKA," and a whale boat (on reverse) false embroidered with undyed beargrass and black maidenhair fern, probably created at Metlakatla, Alaska, by a Tsimshian basketmaker, early 20th century, 3" high.

NW-30. Rattle-top lidded basket uses false embroidery to interpret Tlingit design elements in bold contrasting colors.

NW-31. Some Tlingit twined baskets are embellished with representational life forms, like the killer whales on this rattle-top lidded basket.

NW-33. Tlingit berry basket, twined of spruce root with false embroidery and textured embellishment using plain and diagonal twining to create a structural pattern in the basketry fabric, c. 1900, 6" high.

NW-32. Tlingit berry basket twined with three rows of colorful false embroidered grass elements that almost seem to float on green and red twined bands of dyed spruce root, c. 1900, 9.5" high.

NW-34. Four upper Northwest Coast twined spruce root forms with designs in false embroidery, c. 1900, include two berry baskets (*left*) and two lidded baskets (*right*).

NW-35. Tlingit double basket used as a pouch for storing lead shot after the introduction of firearms. Twined of spruce root with false embroidery in dyed and undyed grass and black maidenhair fern, both outer and inner baskets are properly decorated with different design elements, late 19th century, about 4" high.

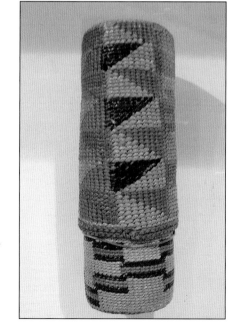

NW-36. Typical rim finish on a Tlingit basket, c. 1900-1920, 5" high. A reliable diagnostic for distinguishing Tlingit from sometimes similar-looking Haida baskets is the "jog-down," or "Tlingit jog," at the termination point on the rim. Tlingit baskets generally are woven right side up, with twined courses progressing counterclockwise from left to right. As seen near top center in this image, this weaving direction produces a stepped "jog-down" terminal point on the finished rim. Haida twined baskets are inverted during weaving and, when completed and set upright, their rims display a "jog-up."

NW-38. Alutiiq (Pacific Eskimo) twined spruce root basket with false embroidery of grass and black maidenhair fern, resembling Tlingit twined spruce root forms, c. 1900, 7" high. Alutiiq twined spruce root baskets, which are often misidentified as Tlingit or Haida due to their similar appearances, can be distinguished by traits absent in baskets from further south, including the presence of both a primary and a secondary design field; design elements differing from usual Tlingit motifs; unpolished dull-looking spruce root wefts unlike shiny spruce root preferred by the Tlingit; and a lower stitch count per inch than found in Tlingit work.

NW-37. Three Haida baskets twined of spruce root lengths with characteristic horizontal dyed bands and textured twined patterns. An upward "Haida jog" is visible at the upper right edge of the basket rim at right, c. 1900, (left) 8.25" high.

NW-39, NW-40. Comparison of Alutiiq and Tlingit twined bases. Alutiiq base (right top) is reinforced with several concentric raised rings of three-strand twining, absent from Tlingit bases. However, as viewed in this Tlingit example (right), early 20th-century Tlingit basketmakers sometimes decorated their bases using a course or two of "between weave" twining-plus-plaiting with dyed spruce root.

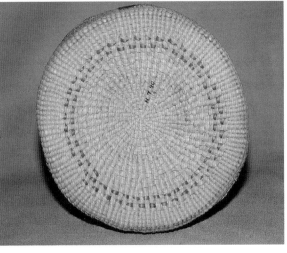

Arctic and Subarctic

Most Arctic and Subarctic groups inhabiting the bleak terrain of the Far North relied primarily on containers of skin, hide, or bark. They created far fewer basketry forms, largely due to a scarcity of suitable basketmaking materials. Across wide parts of this vast region, Native peoples produced no baskets at all. In those specific areas where baskets actually have been made, some vessels served in useful capacities. However, most of those available today were created within the last century specifically for trade or sale to outsiders.

Major vessel styles from this region are found among:

• Aleutian and Alutiiq peoples
• Alaskan Eskimo and Inuit peoples
• Subarctic groups

Twined basketry from the Aleutian Islands and Alutiiq (Pacific Eskimo) peoples, coiled forms of the Yup'ik- and Inupiaq-speaking Eskimo of Alaska and the Labrador Inuit, and birchbark vessels of Subarctic groups are characteristic. Alutiiq (Pacific Eskimo) work, which more closely resembles Tlingit twined forms, is discussed here but illustrated, for comparative purposes, with upper Northwest Coast baskets.

Aleutian and Alutiiq Twined Baskets

Native weavers out on the Aleutian Islands excelled at twining and have made some of the most delicate basketry in North America. Basketmakers utilized the mid-summer growth of beach grass (*Elymus mollis*) that grew close at hand, near Arctic villages situated by the sea. Many baskets are as finely woven as linen cloth. Baglike containers for gathering and storing seeds and fish, hats, cigarette cases, pouches, lidded trinket baskets, covered bottles, and capes, socks, and matting were all twined during the long, dark winter months.

Early twined basketry examples were decorated with materials like feathers, sea mammal gut, or bird skin. After contact with Russian and European explorers, seamen, and fur traders in the 18th and 19th centuries, colorful wool yarns and silk embroidery flosses replaced indigenous decorative materials and embellished new basketry forms intended for sale.

Today, specialists distinguish subtle differences in basketry from each of the Aleutian Islands. They currently proclaim examples from the westernmost Aleutian Islands of Attu and Atka to be the finest, followed by those from the larger inner island of Unalaska. Beach grass stems grow somewhat differently in the microenvironments of each island, and Native villagers, themselves, judged them in the following ways: grass from Attu was thought to be the strongest; Atka's the longest, whitest, and most highly prized; and Unalaska's was long but neither as white as that from Atka nor as strong as grass from Attu.

Other differences in form, weaving technique, and shapes of lid knobs further characterize the twined products from each island. Attu baskets are twined using a third weft strand at junctions in the basketry fabric, thus creating visibly longer stitches. Lid knobs, as well, generally vary in size and height. Attu knobs typically are the squarest and have the shortest stems. Round Atka knobs are greater in circumference and tend to sag on tall, thin stems. Unalaska examples are round but intermediate in height.

The Alutiiq (Pacific Eskimo) peoples of coastal Alaska twined spruce root baskets with decorative false embroidery, setting them apart from other Eskimo, who have been coiling with beach grass for over 100 years. Alutiiq twined basketry closely resembles that of the Tlingit and other coastal Indian populations, who apparently wielded a greater influence on their craft than did their Aleutian Island neighbors.

Due to their similar appearance, Alutiiq twined spruce root baskets are often misidentified as "Tlingit" or "Haida" in collections as well as in the marketplace. Alutiiq examples, however, have several distinctive traits that are absent in those from further south. The extensive research of Molly Lee, who has defined much of what is currently known about Eskimo and Inuit basketry, identifies a number of significant criteria for distinguishing these twined examples.

Alutiiq twined baskets have concentric rings of three-strand twining on their bases; they have unpolished or dull spruce root wefts (unlike shiny spruce root common to Tlingit); they have a lower stitch count per inch than Tlingit; and they exhibit both a primary and a secondary design field comprised of design elements differing from those used by the Tlingit. Typical Tlingit baskets, on the other hand, have no secondary design fields and little or no repetition of design elements. In deference to collectors, for whom this book is primarily written, twined Alutiiq (Pacific Eskimo) examples are illustrated along with Tlingit spruce root baskets in the Northwest Coast section.

Arctic Coiled Baskets

Elsewhere in Alaska, Yup'ik and Inupiaq Eskimo women have fashioned bundle-coiled basketry of beach grass since the late 19th century, well after contact. The large-diameter coils of these baskets may begin on a disk of sea mammal hide, or they can spiral outward from a simple coiled, whipstitched self-start. Collectors find these baskets decorated with a similar range of trade materials as found on post-contact baskets from the Aleutians. Central Yup'ik Eskimo of Alaska continue to coil these attractive baskets for sale today.

By 1920 in northern Alaska, Eskimo *men* at Point Barrow—where males traditionally worked with ivory and whale products—began to coil baleen baskets for sale to tourists. Baleen is the tough, hornlike material comprising mouth plates of plankton-filtering whales like the bowhead. Baleen baskets are started on a pierced ivory disk, and lids on most baleen baskets are decorated with carved ivory knobs or finials. In shape, the bodies of these dark-colored baskets mimic the women's lidded coiled grass baskets, but the baleen examples are one-rod coiled, not bundle coiled. Molly Lee has made a strong case for baleen

AR-1. Detail of twined bag, Aleutian Islands.

basketmaking's connection with the one-rod coiled willow root basket tradition of Alaskan Eskimo in the Point Barrow region, where the earliest coiled willow root examples are documented to the late 19th century. Other neighboring groups, like Northern Athabascans living in interior Alaska and Russian peoples just across the Bering Strait, also coiled similar examples by the beginning of the 20th century.

Similar one-rod coiled baskets from Asia or the Pacific Islands sometimes mislead collectors who believe them to be Eskimo examples from the Point Barrow region. Accurate identification of materials is critically important in this instance. The imports are made with reed, cane, or other non-local materials, and collectors also should closely examine the specific stitches, foundation elements, and shapes of these baskets to help establish origin.

Far to the east, the Labrador Inuit bundle-coiled baskets started with a tight spiral of beach grass. In the late 19th and early 20th centuries, the Grenfell Mission of Newfoundland and Labrador ministered to the economic, emotional, and physical health of local Inuit families. It also encouraged the commercial development of crafts, including hooked rugs and mats and coiled baskets. Some of these bowls have distinctive open, coiled courses or twisted rims. Collectors may find baskets once sold through this venue that will still bear modest string tags identifying their source.

Subarctic Birchbark Vessels

Finally, Subarctic groups living in coniferous forests and along interior waterways, including Northern Athabascans and the Algonquian Cree, folded and sewed birchbark dishes and buckets or *mokuks* for their own use as well as for sale. Birchbark was harvested and prepared in the spring, when it was pliable and could be readily shaped and stitched into various forms.

Many birchbark vessels were minimally decorated. Other containers, like those of the Cree and other groups with access to commercial markets, are boldly etched with the light-colored surface of the bark scraped away to create two-toned designs of life forms or geometric elements. Again, in deference to collectors using this book, the market-driven etched forms are illustrated along with birchbark vessels of the Great Lakes subregion in the Northeast, where an active commercial outlet for these containers persists.

AR-2. Attu, Aleutian Islands, basketmaker twining a basket bottom side up, c. 1900.

AR-3. Open twined bag with wool embroidery, Atka, Aleutian Islands, c. 1900-1920, 8.5" high. The basketmaker used strands split from outer edges of beach grass (*Elymus mollis*) blades, gathered near the village during the long daylight hours of mid-summer. Some accounts say that weaving, itself, generally was done during the dark wintertime.

AR-5. Generously decorated Aleutian twined lidded "trinket basket" made for sale, early 20th century.

AR-6. Two twined lidded "trinket baskets" of different proportions and shades of beach grass, which may reflect variations in styles from two Aleutian islands, were a popular type of tourist item in the early 20th century: (*left*) the short large knob, in the style of Attu, rattles because it contains a pebble; (*right*) the taller knob plus the whiter shade of grass suggest Atka work, 7" high.

AR-4. Open twined bag with braided finish of the type used for collecting fish, berries, and wild plant foods, Aleutian Islands, c. 1900-1905, 7.5" high.

AR-7. Finely proportioned and twined lidded "trinket basket" from Attu, Aleutian Islands, early 20th century.

AR-8. Glass bottles covered with Aleutian Islanders' twined basketry found favor among steamship-traveling tourists docking at port cities in early to mid-20th-century Alaska.

AR-9. Age has mellowed beach grass to a warm golden hue in this ovoid lidded basket, collected almost 100 years ago by a visitor to Alaska. Although this basket in the style of Yup'ik (Nashagak) work is bundle coiled, the distinctive ovoid form also appears in early 20th-century single-rod coiled willow root basketry of Northern Athabascan and Alaskan Eskimo weavers in the Point Barrow region.

AR-10. Covered Inupiaq Eskimo type basket with pendant closure and decorative seal finial and toggles carved of walrus tusk, early 20th century.

AR-11. Lidded beach grass basket from Alaska with brown-dyed diamond-shaped elements and three rows of stitches as well as variegated brownish bird or fish skin overlay, 1930s-1940s, 6" high.

AR-12. Yup'ik Eskimo bundle-coiled covered basket stitched with natural and dyed beach grass to depict geometric and representational figures including flensed seals, c. 1930s, 9" high. Typically knobbed, fitted lids are coiled with a narrower ring attached under their rim that snaps securely into the body of the basket.

AR-13. Yup'ik Eskimo covered "treasure" basket of bundle-coiled beach grass and double-diamond shaped "butterfly" elements in red and purple dyed gut overlay, made by Catherine Dock of Kipnuk on commission from co-author's parents, 1990, 7" high. Colorful dyes were derived from soaking Japanese tissue paper.

AR-14. Two miniature coiled baleen covered baskets, c. 1990s, 1.5" diameter, by Titus Nashoopuk of Point Hope, AK, mounted as a desk set; Yup'ik Eskimo covered basket (*front*), bundle-coiled of beach grass by Tamara Mosier, c. 2000, 1.3" diameter, is the size of some old aluminum trade tokens issued by the Reindeer Commercial Company, Savoonga, Alaska.

AR-15. Large bundle-coiled oval bowl of beach grass, a form made in Alaska from the early 20th century to the present, 10" maximum diameter.

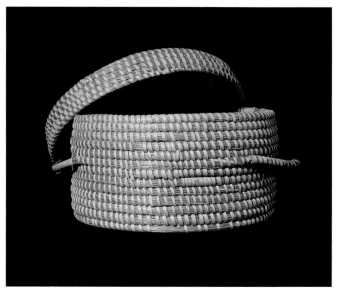

AR-17. Inuit (Canadian Eskimo) style lidded grass basket with side handles, bundle coiled with spaced stitches, probably mid-20th century, 5.5" diameter.

AR-16. Small Labrador Inuit bundle-coiled grass bowl with twisted rim finish (*front*) had original paper string tag: "Labrador Eskimo, Grenfell Labrador Industries," 6" diameter. Medical missionary Wilfred Grenfell brought social services to Labrador Natives in the 1890s. The mission's handicraft division used this label from 1906-1954.

AR-18. Three coiled baleen lidded baskets with carved walrus tusk finials, from the region of Barrow, Alaska, spanning more than 75 years of production, c. 1920-1997. Men, traditionally the workers of baleen and ivory, have made most of the baleen baskets.

AR-19. One-rod coiled baleen basket and lid with carved walrus head finial has the property mark of Kinguktuk incised into the basal starter disk, c. 1920s, 4.5" diameter. Kinguktuk is widely credited with originating the coiled baleen form. From the Eskimo and Inuit viewpoint, the flat lid represents the horizon, with a walrus lifting its head (white) above the surface of the sea (black).

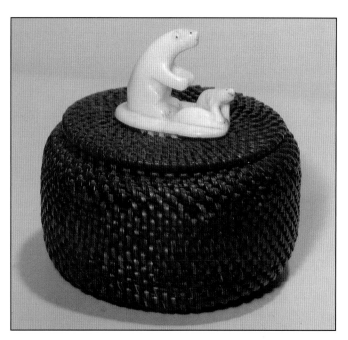

AR-21. Coiled baleen basket and lid with carved narrative finial, for which the maker George Omnik is well known, c. 1950s, 4" diameter. From the Native perspective, an ice floe (white), supporting two polar bears capturing a seal, is adrift on the surface of the sea (black).

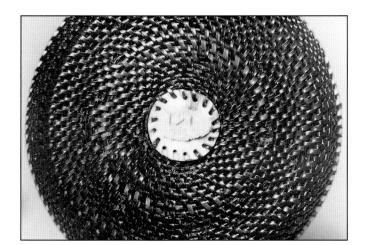

AR-20. Property mark of the basketmaker Kinguktuk, of Barrow, Alaska.

AR-22. Inner surface of the walrus ivory starter disk with maker's signature and basket number, "145/Omnik/Pt. Hope/Alaska."

SA-25. Northern Athabascan (Dene) tray coiled of split willow root by Ellen Savage of Holy Cross, Alaska, 1985, 13" diameter.

AR-23. Contemporary but early-style coiled baleen basket and lid woven by a woman, signed inside on the starter disk "Marilyn/Hank/Otton/Pt. Hope/AK," 1997, 3.5" diameter. Marilyn, a member of a well-known several-generation family of baleen basketmakers, usually prepares all her own materials and carves her own walrus ivory finials, but this polar bear head was carved and signed by "Maurice Nattunguk '97" of Nome.

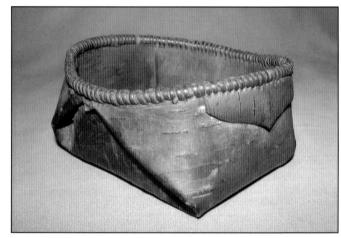

SA-26. Utilitarian folded and stitched birchbark dish of a type made by various Northern Athabascan groups, 6" maximum diameter.

AR-24. Contemporary baleen and walrus ivory desk set, with two miniature coiled baleen baskets, 1.5" diameter, and lids with carved seal head finials, signed under right finial "TN" for Titus Nashookpuk of Pt. Hope, Alaska, c. 1990s, base 6.75" long.

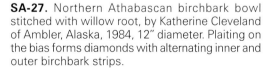

SA-27. Northern Athabascan birchbark bowl stitched with willow root, by Katherine Cleveland of Ambler, Alaska, 1984, 12" diameter. Plaiting on the bias forms diamonds with alternating inner and outer birchbark strips.

Plains

Native peoples inhabiting the vast grasslands of the Plains region during the past 150 years have, for many, come to represent collectively the stereotypical "American Indian." An image of equestrian-mounted buffalo hunters, tipi dwellers, and noble chiefs in eagle-feather war bonnets is well established. Yet the groups living in this area during the post-contact period actually followed two very distinct lifeways.

The popular image of braves on horseback does correspond to certain groups like the Cheyenne, Arapaho, and Teton Sioux. In the 17th and 18th centuries, however, all these peoples were forest-dwelling pedestrians living to the east of the grasslands. Succumbing to increasing pressure, as both white settlers and displaced Natives spread westward, these peoples migrated from the western Great Lakes region onto the Plains. Here, they adopted a horse-based semi-nomadic lifestyle.

These tribes uneasily shared the Plains with others like the Arikara, Mandan, and Hidatsa, who were semi-sedentary agriculturalists already living in compact villages along the upper Missouri River. These maize farmers had inhabited the region for centuries prior to the arrival of the Sioux and others.

During the 19th century, both of these Native lifeways suffered tragic disruptions. In 1837 a smallpox epidemic nearly destroyed the agricultural villagers. Today, many of their descendants occupy the Fort Berthold Reservation in North Dakota. Meanwhile, the nomadic hunters of the Plains endured decades of warfare with U.S. soldiers and the loss of their bison-based economy. By the late 1800s, what most view as traditional Native Plains lifeways were virtually gone, and remnant populations were removed to reservations.

Plains Animal Hide Containers

All the Plains societies fashioned most of their containers like pouches, knife sheaths, and pipe bags from animal hide, particularly that of the bison. Comparatively few plant-fiber baskets were made in this area, and even fewer of these have found their way into museums and private collections.

Plains Mats and Baskets

Rush or cattail mats and twill-plaited burden baskets woven with two-toned dark and light designs of materials like willow and boxelder on a willow frame, characterize examples documented to the farming groups.

Mobile groups like the Cheyenne and Arapaho coiled a few coarse bowls for gambling with dice fashioned from bison bone or from pits of plum, peach, or apricot fruits. Though willow was often used as the material for the one- or two-rod foundation and

PN-1. Cheyenne-style coiled gambling basket, 9″ diameter, with seven decorated fruit pit dice and Plains beadwork backdrop.

stitching elements in these coiled gambling baskets, cottonwood, elm, and even yucca also served. Some coiled gambling baskets have cloth or hide pads sewn onto their bases to minimize the wear and tear of gaming use. Rims also may occasionally be edged with strips of cloth. Useful baskets made by various neighboring groups with whom the Plains peoples interacted were sometimes received through trade and pressed into service as well.

PN-3. The envelope-like parfleche of folded and painted rawhide, made from bison or other animal hides, met most daily needs. It functioned as a saddlebag for transporting possessions and dried foods like pemmican–cakes of pulverized bison meat and dried berries mixed with melted tallow. Mineral and vegetal pigments decorate this classic late 19th-century parfleche, probably once paired with another, 28.5" long.

PN-2. Arikara rush gatherer, photogravure by E. S. Curtis, c. 1908. Plains farming groups used rush mats as floor coverings in their earth lodges.

PN-4. Bicolored twill-plaited burden baskets were used among farming peoples like the Mandan and Hidatsa living along the upper Missouri River. This 1941 North Dakota seed catalog features Scattered Corn, the daughter of the last corn priest of the Mandan, shelling Native-grown corn into her traditional willow-framed basket.

PN-5. Hidatsa burden basket, twill-plaited of willow and boxelder with a rawhide tumpline, probably made by Waheenee (Buffalo Bird Woman), mid- to late 19th century.

PN-6. Cheyenne-style coiled gambling basket with several sets of bone and fruit pit dice for tossing in a women's game of chance. Among the Pawnee, another Plains group, a gambling basket represents the moon and the dice are stars. No particular physical traits distinguish such baskets without cultural context.

Southeast

At the time of first contact with European explorers and traders, many of the Native groups inhabiting the Southeast lived in relatively permanent villages along river bottomlands. They practiced agriculture in the low country and supplemented their crops with fishing; gathering nuts, seeds, and shellfish; and hunting wild game.

By the 18th and early 19th century, a steady stream of Euramerican immigrants to this region threatened traditional Native lifeways. These newcomers felled forests and cleared lands for their extensive plantations and expansive settlements. The United States government reacted to intensified demands for land by forcing entire populations of Native people from their homelands onto reservations in Indian Territory, present-day eastern Oklahoma. The "Trail of Tears," a difficult and tragic 800-mile march that cost many Cherokee lives, is only the best-known of a series of early to mid-19th-century removals. Despite devastating cultural and personal losses, some Southeast peoples remained behind in portions of their ancestral homelands that their descendants occupy even today. Basketmaking is found in both subareas:

• Southeast homeland
• Southeast periphery

In spite of considerable social fragmentation, elements of the rich cultural heritage of these Native peoples, including traditional basketry, endure to the present in both subareas.

Southeast Plain- and Twill-plaited Baskets

Plain- and twill-plaited basketmaking with rivercane (*Arundinaria* sp.) extends back at least 1,000 years into the archaeological record. The technique is still widely practiced throughout the Southeast and, indeed, has been instrumental in reinforcing and maintaining Native identity. For example, this basketmaking tradition played a significant role in the establishment of the Qualla Arts and Crafts Mutual, the cooperative of the North Carolina Eastern Band of Cherokee, in the 1930s and 1940s and contributes substantially to its continuing social and economic success.

Southeastern plain- and twill-plaited basketry is fashioned with lengths of local rivercane to create forms that may feature bold patterns. When decorated, Southeast cane baskets often sport twill-plaited designs of dyed reddish-orange and black elements, highlighted against neutral shades. Other colors like yellow and dark purple appear less frequently. Natural dyes are made with various formulas but have included boiled root of black walnut or butternut for dark brown or black, puccoon or bloodroot for reddish-orange, dock or yellowroot for yellow, and maple for dark purple. Commercial aniline dyes have extended the range of colors to include greens, blues, and other cheerful hues.

Patterns in a design are formed by changing the number of over and under twill-plaited intervals, as well as with contrasting colors. Some basketmakers in groups like the Mississippi Choctaw have alternated both the shiny outer side and the dull inner surface of the rivercane to add texture and interest.

Traditional utilitarian forms, usually woven of undyed cane, include gathering baskets for corn, hominy sieves and sifters, winnowers, storage baskets, and mats. While many groups have produced twill-plaited baskets, the Eastern Band of Cherokee and the Mississippi Choctaw have turned out the greatest number in recent years, creating a wide range of traditional and innovative shapes using both single and double twill-plaiting techniques.

The Chitimacha of Louisiana are regarded by some collectors as the most inspired of the late 19th- to 20th-century Southeast basketmakers. They have created unusually complex designs on finely woven single twill-plaited vessels and on the highly prized "double-weave" twill-plaited baskets. The Chitimacha double-weave basket is double-layered and generally square or rectangular in shape with a matching fitted cover that presses snugly over the basketry base. This form is ancient and traditional, though it is made today primarily for sale to collectors. It commands relatively high prices as well as ribbon awards at major vetted American Indian arts shows.

Although Southeast baskets may share many similarities at first glance, technical variations distinguish the products of specific groups and even individual makers. Collectors should be aware that traits like rim finishes often differ significantly among baskets from various Southeast groups. The Chitimacha, among others, gave their rim bindings a diagonally twisted or false-braid appearance. On the other hand, Cherokee baskets usually are bound obliquely with inner bark of hickory to secure a thin wood hoop along their cane and oak basket rims. Others like the Choctaw and Coushatta generally finished their coiled rims with vertically or obliquely overcast stitches.

Design organization and layout also may vary in meaningful ways. Chitimacha weavers usually prefer colorful bands of angular or curvilinear designs that cover the entire basket, often combined with secondary black and reddish-orange bands that diagonally traverse the main design to create a counterpoint effect. Others, like both the Eastern Band of Cherokee and the Mississippi Choctaw, generally favor simpler patterns of lines or bands of squares, diamonds, and other angled elements, though some recent examples appear to emulate the more complex layouts of vintage Chitimacha baskets.

Cherokee Baskets in Transition

Early Cherokee basketry seems to have been almost exclusively of rivercane, with elements dyed red with bloodroot and black or deep brown with butternut or walnut, or left natural. Later in the 19th century, as canebrakes were depleted, white oak became an additional basketmaking resource. New forms, like oak splint gathering baskets and work baskets with handles, emerged and are evidence of interaction with whites.

SE-1. Detail of Southeast twill plaiting with natural and dyed rivercane and carved hardwood handle.

By the mid-20th century, many groups like the Eastern Band of Cherokee not only plaited traditional rivercane baskets but also were increasingly turning to split white oak, hickory, maple, or other materials in providing woodsplint baskets to an expanding market. Since the 1930s, some Cherokee weavers have adopted local buckbrush and, increasingly, invasive Japanese honeysuckle vine, for making plaited wicker baskets. Today, a few Oklahoma Cherokee wicker basketmakers prefer commercially available reed, substituting it for the honeysuckle or buckbrush that must be gathered and prepared before use. Their compact basketry vases and bowls with aniline-dyed red and black decorative bands or other simple design elements are reasonably priced to sell readily.

Southeast Coiled Tourist Baskets

Several other Southeast groups began coiling by the 1920s, seeking a souvenir market for their decorative baskets and novel animal forms, now popular with collectors of vintage tourist items. The Coushatta (or Koasati) of Louisiana and the Alabama-Coushatta of Texas have used bundles of longleaf pine needles or occasionally Southern sweetgrass (*Muhlenbergia* sp.) to form round baskets with close-stitched oval starts and spaced-stitched, bundle-coiled walls that are usually sewn with raffia. Additions of dyed raffia decorations, such as applied flowers or leaves, highlight many of these souvenir items.

Likewise, by the second quarter of the 20th century, the Seminole of Florida shifted from plaiting mostly undecorated utilitarian shapes of cane or hickory splints to coiling baskets specifically intended for the tourist market. They started their coils on a flat cardboard disk covered with palmetto fiber. Then they sewed bundles of sweetgrass—or sometimes longleaf pine needles—to this disk with decorative spaced stitches, usually of colorful embroidery thread. Fitted lids on some Seminole baskets may have a knob fashioned with a palmetto fiber doll's head representing a traditional Seminole woman. The Oklahoma Seminole continued to plait traditional cane or hickory splint baskets for many decades in the 20th century, using techniques like those of neighboring Creek Indians.

SE-2. North Carolina Cherokee makers Annie Standingdeer and daughter Ollie Toomi plait oak splint baskets, 1934.

SE-3. Thin rivercane splints, twill plaited with a braided rim finish, compose the distinctive scoop-like shape of this traditional Choctaw-style winnowing basket, c. 1900-1920, 19" long.

SE-4. Many Southeast groups have processed corn and rice grains with basket winnowers, sieves, and sifters. Coushatta (Koasati) basketmaker Solomon Batiste twill plaited this rivercane winnowing basket, c. 1950, 16" long.

SE-5, SE-6. Southeast handled carrying baskets, like these Mississippi Choctaw examples, were intended for the non-Native market, early to mid-20th century, (*top*)18.5" long, (*bottom*) 11" diameter.

SE-7. Commercial dyes coloring some of the rivercane splints in this twill-plaited Choctaw fruit basket have faded to a soft hue, early 20th century, 8" rim diameter.

SE-9. Chitimacha double-weave *carba*, or square-cornered covered basket, in rivercane dyed with traditional red and dark brown natural dye formulas by Melissa Darden, 2002, 5.5" high. Chitimacha call the bow-tie-like design element "bottom of basket."

SE-8. Choctaw twill-plaited rivercane forms like this work basket are often woven on the bias, or obliquely, from the base upward and are bound with a compound overcast rim finish, c. 1980, 7" high.

SE-10. Mississippi Choctaw double-weave twill-plaited basket of rivercane colored with red and dark commercial dyes, c. 2005, 5" high.

SE-11, SE-12, SE-13. North Carolina or Eastern band of Cherokee twill-plaited baskets with rivercane strands colored with varying natural dye formulas: low work basket (*top*) by Rowena Bradley with dyed color visible on both sides of weaving strands, "Chief's daughter" design, 1970s, 11.5" long; square-based storage basket (*above right*), c. 1910-1925, 12.5" high; and handled carrying basket (*above*), c. 1910, 9" square base. Double rim-hoops bound obliquely with inner hickory bark are typical.

SE-14. Twill-plaited rivercane basket by Eastern Cherokee basketmaker Rowena Bradley, c. 1980, about 12" high.

SE-15. Chitimacha twill-plaited rivercane basket with characteristic design and braided rim finish, c. 1900, 8" diameter.

SE-17. Chitimacha miniature rivercane basket by Melissa Darden, with braided rim finish and another twill-plaited version of the "blackbirds' eyes" pattern in natural dyes, 2002, 2" rim diameter.

SE-16. Chitimacha twill-plaited rivercane basket with "blackbirds' eyes" design and braided rim finish, c. 1900, 5" diameter.

SE-18. Small so-named "cow nose" basket with rim finish and wrapped handle typical of Mississippi Choctaw work, mid-20th century, 6" high.

SE-19. Narrow boat-shaped basket crafted with dyed rivercane lengths, their dull inner surfaces outward, in a rainbow's range of warm commercial shades by Mississippi Choctaw basketmaker Jeremy McMillan, c. 2010, 12.5" wide.

SE-20, SE-21. White oak splints increasingly replaced rivercane in Cherokee basketmaking. These carrying baskets plaited with natural and dyed reddish orange and dark brown oak splints sold readily, mid-20th century, melon basket (*top left*), about 10" diameter; hemispherical basket (*above right*), 11" rim diameter.

SE-22. Rectangular plaited white oak splint shopping basket with carved wood handle that interlocks at the base without nails or bindings, attributed to Eastern Cherokee basketmaker Agnes Welch, c. 1970, 12.5" long.

SE-23. Eastern Cherokee basketmaker Carol Welch plaited this medley of small white oak splint baskets for sale, c. 1980, to 6" high.

SE-24. Wastepaper basket, plaited of wide and narrow white oak weaving strands that heighten its decorative effect, made for the Qualla Arts & Crafts Mutual shop by North Carolina Cherokee maker Agnes Welch, 1960s, 10" high.

SE-25. Wastepaper basket plaited with oak splints, most dyed either dark brown or orange with natural dye formulas, by Cherokee maker Agnes Welch, c. 1970s, 12" high.

SE-26. Plaited white oak wall basket by Cherokee maker Alyne Driver has three sturdy pockets as a handy catch-all for everything from mail to keys, documented with its original Qualla Arts & Crafts Mutual tag, mid-20th century, 18" high.

SE-27. Available in a wide range of sizes and ever popular with gardeners and decorators, vintage woodsplint flower-gathering baskets made by many craftspersons including Native Americans and Appalachian folks are nearly impossible to distinguish from one another without documentation, mid-20th century, 22" diameter.

SE-28. Southeast groups like the North Carolina Catawba and Cherokee used plaited white oak splint eel traps. Any snake-like fish that swam through the narrow round opening would find itself trapped within the funnel-like basket, early 20th century, 20" long.

SE-29. Plaited wicker honeysuckle vine baskets by Lucy George, marketed through the Qualla Arts & Crafts Mutual in the early 1980s, were modestly priced and small enough for Smoky Mountains visitors to carry home as mementoes of Eastern Cherokee country.

SE-30, SE-31. These baskets represent common types of mid- to late 20th-century Cherokee plaited wicker basketry. Honeysuckle wicker weft elements are plaited over oak or maple splints, often with natural orange and dark brown dyed stripes or bands. Note oblique rim bindings and occasional decorative wickerwork (*top*),10" diameter. Maker's name "Nellie Cucumber" is pencilled in the small basket's cover (*bottom right*), 5" diameter.

SE-32. Four-color honeysuckle mat or tray by Eastern Cherokee maker Helen Smith, known for using natural plant dyes formulated from bloodroot for orange, black walnut for brown, and dock for yellow, c. 1970, 12" diameter.

SE-34. Coushatta (Koasati) basketmaker Lorice Abbott Langley of Elton, Louisiana, produced this lidded pine needle basket in about a week, early 1990s, 7" high.

SE-33. Globular lidded forms of longleaf pine needles stitched with raffia have endured for almost one hundred years as a popular Louisiana souvenir by Coushatta (Koasati) makers. This basket is decorated with embroidered raffia flowers dyed red, yellow, and green, early to mid-20th century, 6" high.

SE-35. Florida Seminole lidded baskets, coiled of Southern sweetgrass (*Muhlenbergia* sp.), stitched with colorful thread, and finished with palm-fiber doll-head knobs, were made for tourists, 1930s-1940s, (*back*) 6.5" high. The pin cushion holds a Seminole perfume-filled glass hatpin decorated with Florida shell art flowers, 1930s.

SE-36. Alligator effigy basket, coiled by the last traditional Chitimacha chief Emile Stouff using longleaf pine needles and pine cone scales with raffia stitches and features, hides an original label within its lidded back, c. 1930s, 9.5" long.

SE-37. Stately swan effigy basket by Coushatta (Koasati) maker Rosaline Medford, c. 1960, 7" long. A non-Indian woman first suggested coiling pine needle figures in the 1930s as a source of added income for the Coushatta.

SE-38. Southeast miniature baskets worked in rivercane, oak splints, honeysuckle, and longleaf pine needles, 20th century, (*front right*) 0.3" diameter. The start of a plaited wicker honeysuckle basket is seen at left.

Northeast

Game animals and wild plant foods sustained prehistoric hunters and gatherers who roamed the broad forests of the Northeast, as well as those who lived near lakes, streams, and coastal waters where fish and shellfish expanded the diet. More than a millennium before Europeans arrived in this region, Native Americans in some temperate areas practiced small-scale horticulture based on local cultivars. Later gardening, augmented by maize, beans, and squash introduced from the south, supported semi-permanent communities in a few places before ships began arriving from the Old World.

Several centuries of exposure to the immigrant populations brought warfare and new diseases, greatly impacting Native groups and severely disrupting traditional lifeways. The Native societies in this area were so reduced by the consequences of European contact that many of the remnant groups merged to improve their chances for survival. Despite generations of upheaval, a number of Native traditions persist. For some, basketmaking continues to be a particularly important marker of cultural and familial identity. It also has served as a vehicle for social and economic adaptation.

Archaeological evidence indicates that Native northeasterners were stitching bark vessels, plaiting rush mats, and twining bags and baskets with flexible materials in pre-contact times. Eventually, twining lost favor in comparison to sewn birchbark and plaited woodsplint work. Birchbark vessels are not true basketry, by technical definition, though they are generally exhibited and curated together with baskets in most museums. A few Northeast twined and bark containers are included in this Collector Showcase section to illustrate regional and tribal styles, though the Showcase emphasizes the more familiar woodsplint basketry plaited usually from pounded splints and dating predominantly to the 19th and early 20th centuries.

Woodsplint Basketmaking

Some scholars, like Ted Brasser, suggest that Native basketmakers throughout the Northeast began making woodsplint baskets only after learning of the technique through early 18th-century Swedish settlers in the Delaware River valley. But not everyone agrees. In any event, American Indian production of woodsplint baskets seems to have spread widely and quickly, and it came to dominate basketmaking throughout the Northeast by the late 1700s to early 1800s.

Plaited woodsplint baskets, usually fashioned of ash (Fraxinus nigra), or of oak, hickory, or other hardwoods, were primarily made for barter or sale and provided an important source of income. Typical early forms were sturdy utilitarian baskets and lidded storage containers that saw service both at Native and non-Native homes and farms. Subsequently, by the mid- to late 1800s, the development of a regional tourist industry opened a new market for a very different range of Indian basketry trinkets and souvenirs.

Even by the early 1800s, basketmakers had devised wooden basketmaking blocks to assist them in weaving standardized shapes. They also used specialized tools like metal "crooked" knives and splint gauges for rapidly shaping the weaving elements, thus streamlining the production of inventory for commercial sale. Decorative techniques, including the application of paints and dyes to woodsplints as well as the structural manipulation of splints to create decorative curlicue weaves, were widely used throughout the region.

At about the same time, the plaiting technique was already developing into several regional styles that shared some general similarities while also differing specifically from one another:

- Eastern Algonquians
- Iroquoians and Mid-Atlantic groups
- Central-Northern Algonquians

Styles include those of the Eastern Algonquians of New England and the Canadian Maritimes, the Iroquoians and other Mid-Atlantic groups, and the Central-Northern Algonquians around the Great Lakes.

Eastern Algonquian Baskets

Within the Eastern Algonquian subarea, some further distinctions may be noted, particularly in the large lidded storage baskets that were common in the early to mid-19th century. Wide woodsplints and spare, hand-painted designs characterized southeastern New England containers. By comparison, southwestern New England baskets featured both wide and narrow splints that often were swabbed with paint on their outer surfaces. Horizontal rows of one or more narrow woodsplints were sometimes introduced to set off several bands of the wider weft splints, which might be additionally decorated with block-stamping. By further comparison, storage baskets in northern New England and the maritime provinces by mid-century had narrower woodsplints that might be swabbed or, later, dyed.

Fancy woodsplint baskets from northern New England and the Canadian Maritimes often dazzled the eye with splints that were brightly dyed in pure aniline colors. After about 1880, Penobscot and Passamaquoddy craftspeople in Maine and Abenaki and Micmac makers in southeastern Canada began interweaving twisted or braided lengths of fragrant sweetgrass (Hierochloe odorata) into their ash splint products. Novel shapes like yarn holders, lidded sewing baskets, handkerchief baskets, fans, bookmarks, and wall pockets gained popularity in late Victorian times and were turned out in quantity.

Iroquoian and Mid-Atlantic Baskets

Some plaited woodsplint baskets in the Iroquoian region closely resemble those from northern New England and the maritime provinces. Crafters in both areas favored ash splints, aniline dyes, decorative curlicue weaves, and braided sweetgrass. Iroquoian basketmakers also commonly plaited the standard

NE-1. Detail of Abenaki plaited ash splint fan, edged with fine splint lace weave, c. 1890s.

utilitarian woodsplint baskets and whimseys but were alone in making distinctive cornhusk products. The Seneca twined the cornhusks into small salt or tobacco containers and into masks for Native ceremonial use or for commercial sale. By contrast, others like the Tuscarora and Onondaga coiled and stitched lengths of braided cornhusk into Husk Face masks and other forms.

In southern New York state, Pennsylvania, and New Jersey, groups like the Delaware (Lenni Lenape) and Nanticoke plaited woodsplint baskets that are similar to Iroquoian types, although white oak or hardwood splints other than ash were often used. These peoples made utilitarian baskets for sifting and washing corn, traps for fish and eels, and containers for berry picking and storage.

Great Lakes Baskets

In the western region of the Northeast, groups living around the Great Lakes more often used weft-twined bags and birchbark vessels than baskets. Wild rice, a primary staple, was gathered, stored, and prepared in bast bags or birchbark containers. Etching and porcupine quillwork were common decorative techniques used on birchbark vessels made for the 19th- and 20th-century tourist market.

Many of the Great Lakes peoples have plaited ash splint baskets, as well. The Oneida and Stockbridge may have initially introduced the plaiting technique to the Ho-Chunk (Winnebago) in the 1820s, when the more easterly groups were being pushed westward from their former homelands. As did groups further to the east, the Great Lakes basketmakers also added dyed splints and curlicue work as decorative elements on plaited woodsplint baskets. However, Great Lakes basket bases are most often twill plaited, and swing handle attachments are steam-bent and looped back on themselves, forming a distinctive "S" or figure-8 shape.

Small bundle-coiled sweetgrass baskets, commonly stitched with black commercial thread, like those by Ojibwa and Potawatomi (Anishinaabe) basketmakers, have been a popular and modestly priced contribution to the western Great Lakes tourist trade.

Northeast Basket Collecting

Basketry from the Northeast provides many collecting opportunities today. Basket lovers who seek examples from this region are able to collect varied examples or to specialize. Some desire only artistic hand-painted or block-stamped 19th-century woodsplint baskets from southeastern New England. For others, Victorian forms and fancy baskets, or colorful early 20th-century kitsch, or perhaps fragrant ash splint and sweetgrass sewing baskets and whimseys from northern New England or New York state hold greater appeal. Etched birchbark examples or woodsplint forms like pack baskets, creels, potato baskets, and eel pots may tempt collectors seeking a campy decorative effect for a country cottage or Adirondack-style cabin. Both vintage and newly made baskets are currently available in the marketplace, and many still may be found at affordable price points.

NE-2. Native Northeast weavers plaited ash splint baskets in many sizes and shapes to sell to seasonal travelers, c. 1900.

NE-3. Covered rectangular storage basket, probably plaited by a southeastern Massachusetts Wampanoag maker, has wide splints handpainted with carbon-like lampblack pigment, c. 1820, 14" long.

NE-5. Small rectangular Mohegan covered storage basket, with very faded brownish black walnut swabbing on surfaces of narrower ash splints as well as painted brown and salmon-colored elements, c. 1850, 12" long.

NE-4. Southeastern Connecticut (probably Mohegan) rectangular plaited ash splint storage basket, missing its cover, with lampblack painted motifs and several brown splints swabbed with black walnut stain, c. 1820, 11" long.

NE-6. Connecticut covered rectangular storage basket with brown swabbed narrow weft splints and stamped decorative elements in Spanish brown—an inexpensive and popular primer in its day—and in a pinkish, salmon-colored mixture of red lead and white lead called "Mohegan pink," c. 1850, 14" long.

NE-7. Few 19th-century baskets are identified to known makers, but this storage basket's folk-art style associates it with the "vase painter" Arnold basketmaking family of Hassanamisco, the Nipmuc "praying Indian" community near Grafton in central Massachusetts. Stylized hearts, one with an urn-shaped vase above, appear in Mohegan pink and Spanish brown on three sides, and floral chains climb each corner, c. 1820-1830, 15.5" rim diameter.

NE-8. Covered storage basket of square boxlike shape, with brown and pinkish elements stamped on all wide splint surfaces, and alternating wide and narrow splints, is the work of a Natick maker in the Massachusett "praying Indian" town, c. 1830s, 12" long.

NE-9. Probable Pennacook or Massachusett round covered storage basket, plaited with alternating wide and narrow ash splints and decorated with handpainted black unit elements so precisely applied that they resemble block-stamping, c. 1830s, 20" rim diameter.

NE-12. Probable Mahican (eastern New York) or Schaghticoke (western Connecticut) covered storage basket with selected splints swabbed with Spanish brown, creating a high-impact pattern of light and dark contrast, c. 1860, 15" long.

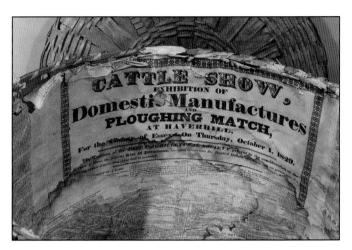

NE-10. Interior of NE-9, lined with newspaper providing clues to origin and age. *Boston Courier* notice promotes the Essex Agricultural Society's October 1829 exhibit at Haverhill, Massachusetts, precursor to current Topsfield Fair–the nation's oldest. The basket's block-like plaited exterior with repetitive unit-painted elements visually approximates the newspaper's handset type, period block-stamped wallpapers, and loom-woven overshot coverlets.

NE-11. Covered storage basket with swabbed narrow weft splints and dotted stamped designs in Spanish brown and faded laundry bluing, 16.5" long. An 1828 newspaper lining mentions Albany and central Massachusetts towns of Enfield, Hadley, and Greenwich Village. Baskets from this region, east of the Christianized "praying town" of Stockbridge, often combine traits attributable to several Native groups.

NE-15. Penobscot or Passamaquoddy (Maine) square-to-round storage basket relies solely on the subtle pattern of wide and narrow weft splints for decorative effect, c. 1850-1860, 8" diameter.

NE-13. Seneca (western New York) high-shouldered storage basket with carved fixed handle, blue swabbed wide and narrow weft splints, and narrow weft splint collar tapering to a rectangular rim, is of an older style but probably 1930s Seneca Arts Project product, 11" long. Iroquois basketmakers favored insertion of one wide colored weaver.

NE-16. Northern New England covered storage basket, probably by an itinerant Western Abenaki basketmaker, with brown swabbed vertical warp splints and characteristic Western Abenaki start–the split, doubly-bound radial splint at lid's center. This sturdy round form likely served as a hatbox or band box, mid-19th century, 18" diameter.

NE-14. Maine covered square-to-round storage basket with some swabbed yellow weft and blue warp splints, likely by a Penobscot maker, 1830-1860, 11.5" diameter.

NE-19. Detail of a handpainted Mohegan "stockade" motif in Mohegan pink and blue dyestuffs on a rectangular work basket with two carved side handles, c. 1820-1830, 19" long.

NE-17. New York Iroquois square-to-round storage basket, lacking its cover, with allover decoration of stamped dotted circular elements and blue and red swabbed splints, c. 1850, 13" rim diameter.

NE-18. Eastern Connecticut (Mohegan or Pequot) ash splint work basket decorated with six painted diamond-shaped "stockade" design elements in Mohegan pink and Spanish brown, c. 1810-1830, 8" rim diameter.

NE-20. Pequot or Mohegan carrying basket, plaited with hickory splints prepared with a drawknife and slightly thinned along the splint edges, has four narrow fitting weft splints where the base meets the body wall, a carved handle, and simple handpainted stockade-like black designs on three sides, c. 1800-1810, 7" rim diameter.

NE-21. Mohegan or Pequot style round-shaped carrying basket with fixed carved handle has traditional three-banded design composition with eight central handpainted "medallions" or rosettes in lampblack infilled with lighter brown swabbing of black walnut stain, c. 1820-1830, 13" rim diameter.

NE-22. Pequot style plaited work basket with handpainted lampblack elements and two set-in side handles, c. 1830, 10.5" long.

NE-26. Eastern Connecticut (Mohegan) open work basket with swabbed Mohegan pink and blue narrow weft splints alternating with pink and blue (aged to green) handpainted wider splints, carved side handle (one missing), and "Clara Levalley" and "1851" in pale blue on base, 10" x 11" long.

NE-23. Eastern Connecticut (Pequot or Niantic) plaited woodsplint work basket with dotted horizontal chain handpainted in lampblack on the front and back panels and a single medallion on each side panel, c. 1830, 11" long.

NE-27. Southern New England rectangular work basket with red swabbed narrow weft splints, missing both side handles, has compound stamped devices of brown dotted circles and X elements that support a western Connecticut provenance with possible Iroquois influence, c. 1860, 11.5" long.

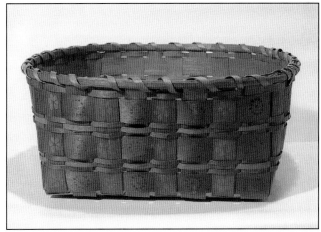

NE-24, NE-25. Plaited western Connecticut-style utility baskets with swabbed horizontal splints and alternating Mohegan pink or brown (*left*) and Mohegan pink or blue (*right*) block-stamped dot-circle and petaled elements, c. 1840, (*left*) 9.5" rim diameter; (*right*) 12" x 13" oval rim diameter.

NE-30. Though faded, this Stockbridge or Schaghticoke style rectangular work basket with ear handles still shows the maker's preference for chrome yellow, or lead chromate (a marker of Stockbridge, some Schaghticoke, and Iroquois), accented with stamped allover elements in more common blue and reddish brown pigments, c. 1860, 12.5" long.

NE-28. Small square-to-round carrying basket plaited with carved fixed handle and wide and narrow gauge-cut ash splints is decorated allover with brown stamped elements, typical of Connecticut weavers exposed to Iroquois basketry, c. 1850-1860, 7.5" x 8.5" rim diameter.

NE-31, NE-32. Sturdy Schaghticoke open utility basket, plaited Yankee-style with white oak splints, a double-wrapped rim finish (above), and domed kickup or demijohn base with two sets of eight carefully shaped basal starting splints (below), all traits diagnostic of baskets made in western Connecticut by Henry Harris, c. 1880-1890, 14" diameter.

NE-29. Stockbridge or Schaghticoke (New York state or western Massachusetts-Connecticut) work basket with narrow gauge-cut splints and yellow, red lead, and blue painted and stamped dotted motifs, c. 1860, 13" x 13.5" rim diameter.

NE-33. Undecorated plaited basket resembles Shaker and Iroquois forms in its kitten-head-like base and slightly bulging walls, but overall proportions, 9-by-9 basal splints, reinforced corners, and double-wrapped rim finish point to the work of Schaghticoke basketmaker Henry Harris, who labored as a farmhand in Kent, Connecticut, c. 1890, 14" diameter.

NE-34. Seneca Iroquois tapered rectangular carrying basket, lacking its handle, with faded blue and reddish brown allover stamped elements and swabbed vertical splints, c. 1870, 9" long.

NE-35. Gay Head Wampanoag basketmakers on Martha's Vineyard (Massachusetts) plaited sturdy utility baskets with their customary rim finish and heavy, wide oak splints with scorched punctate decoration, c. 1890; (front) 4" high without handle. Mineral stains suggest Native potters used baskets when digging colored cliff clays for souvenir Gay Head pottery.

NE-36. As their commercial woodsplint basketry production increased, Native New Englanders relied on standard tools of the trade like splint gauges, crooked knives, splint cutters, and carved stamps.

NE-37. Handmade wooden blocks, like these northern New England Penobscot examples, helped streamline basket production while also standardizing finished forms. Simple blocks, often knocked together from available scrapwood, were used for open shapes like this shopper or purse and covered button basket.

NE-40. In Maine and the Canadian Maritimes plaited woodsplint fishing creels like this Passamaquoddy or Micmac example by Elisée Gaudet could have met Native needs but also sold well to visiting outdoorsmen, early 20th century, 9" high.

NE-41. Plaited ash splint picnic basket with faded purple-dyed wefts, by a Native Maine maker, has been a popular form throughout New England, upper New York state, and eastern Canada for well over a century, 20" long.

NE-38, NE-39. Incurving basket forms like full-height barrel-shaped wastepaper baskets or half-height curved bowls (*above left*) required compound blocks, cleverly assembled of multiple sections that could be pulled apart (*below*) to remove the block from the plaited basket.

NE-42. Sturdy pack baskets have long served like a knapsack to carry heavy loads by foot or by canoe through North Woods country. Micmac, Passamaquoddy, and Penobscot men plaited a range of adult, children's, and miniature sizes from hardwood splints to meet any need, tallest is 19.5" high.

NE-44, NE-45. Passamaquoddy or Penobscot pack basket (*top*) with double-wrapped rim finish and carved handle, 19.5" high, differs somewhat from an Iroquois (likely Oneida) example (*bottom*) with single obliquely-wrapped rim finish, kitten-head-style base, and two openings (at back) for a carrying strap, c. 1880-1900, 15" high.

NE-43. Diminutive Micmac woodsplint potato basket with a nailed rim, made by Eldon Hanning, combines white and brown ash splints, 1980s, 8.5" diameter. Durable Micmac potato baskets in various sizes, finished with either nailed or traditional wrapped rims, were available through L. L. Bean for many years.

NE-46. Uncommon plaited oak splint seed sowing or apple picking basket has concave back (forward in photo), carved peg handle, two set-in openings for a strap, and double-wrapped rim finish, probably Micmac, c. 1880-1900, 10" high without handle.

NE-48. Two additional styles of women's covered work baskets made with blocks and given fixed handles. Wrapped sweetgrass rims and handle on the square-to-round covered basket (*right*) suggest a Maliseet or northern Maine maker, c. 1900, 9" diameter.

NE-47. Covered Penobscot (Maine) or Abenaki (Canada) woman's work or sewing basket with carved fixed handle, plaited over a compound block with narrow gauge-cut splints, some with greenish-blue swabbing, c. 1880, 4" square base. Narrow splints also prevailed in Seneca and Oneida Iroquois territory and in southwestern Connecticut at this time.

NE-49. Penobscot or Micmac open sewing basket with four small basketry holders for notions attached inside and two wrapped ring handles. Many gauge-cut splints, some with faded purple dye, are structurally twisted into curls, c. 1880-1900, 13.5" diameter.

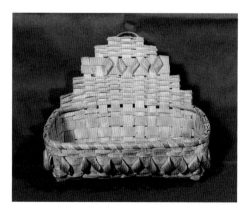

NE-50, NE-51. Plaited splint comb holders or wall pockets by Native makers throughout the Northeast have been useful accessories from the late 19th century (*left*) into the 20th century (*right*). Both are enhanced with twisted splintwork, including sharp, double-turned "porcupine twist" on the example at right, 11" long.

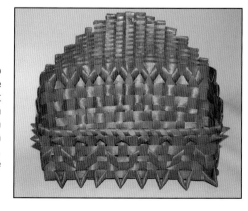

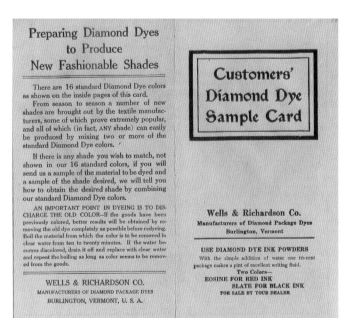

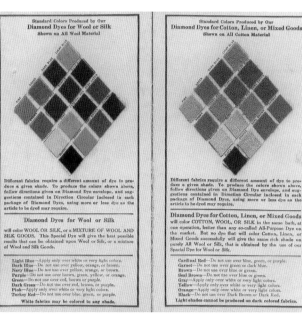

NE-52, NE-53. Brightly colored splints often seen in late 19th- and early 20th-century Native basketry from northern New England and the Canadian Maritimes were dyed with commercial products like Diamond Dyes.

NE-54. Detail of a northern New England plaited basket with fragrant braided sweetgrass, used to embellish splint basketwork after about 1880.

NE-56. Unusual Penobscot or Passamaquoddy covered form, called an "urchin" basket for its resemblance to a small echinoderm found along the Maine seashore, is plaited of sweetgrass and gauge-cut splints in natural and dyed hues, c. 1900-1920, 8.5" diameter.

NE-55. Fancy basketwork helped Natives in New York, Maine, and the Canadian Maritimes meet economic needs. Basketry novelties appealed to Victorian tourists and were readily carried home. Plaited with ash splints and twisted Hong Kong cord, this elaborate, now-faded, loving cup displays ribbon-like splint handles and curly splintwork, c. 1930s, 8.5" high.

NE-57. Akwesasne (St. Regis Mohawk) covered hamper plaited with extensive curly splintwork, looped ribbon-like handles and rings, and a single wide splint accenting its unusually large size, early 20th century, 26" high.

NE-58. Abenaki plaited fans with lace weave edges, dyed splints and sweetgrass wefts, and splint-wrapped handles probably served tourists visiting coastal and lakeside summer resorts, c. 1890, left 14" long.

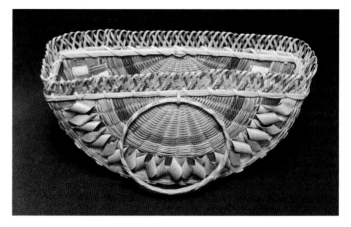

NE-59. Abenaki "half-moon" basket plaited with rainbow-hued splints, an oversized wrapped ring handle, and fancy lace weave edge, c. 1900, 8" long. Sales agent C. N. Saba of Toronto illustrated half-moon-shaped "lunch baskets" for $12.00 per dozen in his wholesale Indian goods mail-order catalog around this time.

NE-60. Abenaki basketmaker Yvonne Robert of Odanak is credited with originating this form of work basket with a bell-shaped cover, early 20th century, 9" high.

NE-61. Other makers of fancy baskets in Maine and New Brunswick elaborated the basic shape with creative splintwork embellishments including lace weave, curly splints, and applied blue-dyed petaled attachments, early 20th century.

NE-62. Maine Indian multi-tiered covered work basket with curly splints resembles a wedding cake decorated with fancy frosting, early 20th century, 11.5" diameter.

NE-63. Low, covered sewing baskets, called "flats" or "flat arm" baskets, could be tucked under the arm or slipped into luggage and were the most popular splint and sweetgrass form, c. 1900, 11" diameter.

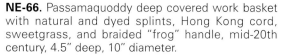

NE-66. Passamaquoddy deep covered work basket with natural and dyed splints, Hong Kong cord, sweetgrass, and braided "frog" handle, mid-20th century, 4.5" deep, 10" diameter.

NE-64. Flats, like this 6"-by-8" oval example, wholesaled through early mail-order catalogs in sizes from 2.25" to 12" for $1.50 to $14 per dozen, respectively. Weavers collected, cleaned, and braided hundreds of yards of sweetgrass for a single average flat.

NE-65. Base and cover of an Abenaki or Penobscot ash splint and sweetgrass work basket or flat with a bound ring and pull on its cover and a dyed blue-green spiral design, c. 1910, 8" diameter.

NE-67, NE-68. Comparison of "frog" handles: braided sweetgrass (*left*), and braided Hong Kong cord (*right*), both covers with sweetgrass centers, c. 1940s.

NE-69. Abenaki covered deep work basket, elevated with a base ring, sports orange dyed splints and Hong Kong cord, c. 1940s, 10" diameter.

NE-70. Colorful covered deep work basket with braided sweetgrass "frog" handle and trim, and natural and dyed splints, c. 1950-1970, 3" deep, 8.5" diameter.

NE-71, NE-72. Passamaquoddy covered work basket by 1994 National Heritage Fellow Mary Gabriel displays her typical wide "frog" (*top*) and dyed splint "half moon" band, visible on the unfaded base (*bottom*) as well as on the cover's faded exterior, c. 1970s, 8" diameter.

NE-73. Clockwise, from lower left: Footed and lidded box likely by Penobscot Leslie Ranco. Passamaquoddy splint and sweetgrass baskets include a wastepaper basket with "diamond" curly splintwork, covered basket, yellow strawberry basket, bell with clapper, and red strawberry basket with "periwinkle" curly splintwork by Clara Keezer; 1980s, yellow strawberry is 7" high.

NE-74. Work baskets might be outfitted with useful accessories, such as this mat-like Abenaki sweetgrass insert for a covered sewing basket with its attached pin cushion, covered holder for notions like a measuring tape or thread, sheath for sewing scissors, and thimble case (*front*), early 20th century, 7" diameter.

NE-75, NE-76. Abenaki (Quebec) boxed "chatelaine" or sewing set on silk ribbons, purchased separately (*left*), 11.5" long, could be custom-fitted to one's favorite sewing basket (*right*), early to mid-20th century, 8.5" diameter. Pelletier (1982) describes French basket makers at Pierreville, Quebec, plaiting many sweetgrass miniatures on blocks for the local Abenaki trade.

NE-77. Some seamstresses loosely housed color-coordinated sets of baskets for small sewing items in their covered splint sewing baskets, Penobscot, early 20th century, needle case (*left,* against basket), 2.5" diameter.

NE-78. Baskets might be creatively modified to increase market appeal, as was this Penobscot covered sewing basket with Hong Kong cord handles added to permit its use as a handbag, c. 1930s, 7" diameter.

NE-79, NE-80. Some Abenaki use the French term "marmite" to describe these kettle-like baskets supported on three miniature basketry feet. Woven on blocks and varying little in overall form, covers are decorated with curly splintwork, early 1900s, both 7.5" diameter. The lower example combines Hong Kong cord with braided sweetgrass.

NE-81, NE-82. Baskets with openings for drawing yarn from a skein have endured from Victorian times to the present. Native northern groups plaited various styles on blocks, sometimes replacing sweetgrass with stronger Hong Kong cord for handles and trim, c.1920-1950, (*far left*) 14" high; (*right*) 11" high.

NE-83. Penobscot covered crochet or tatting basket held supplies like cotton crochet thread and crochet hooks. Plaited with natural and dyed ash splints and fragrant braided sweetgrass, it was given a strong braided Hong Kong cord handle, c. 1920s, 6" high.

NE-84. Penobscot or Passamaquoddy acorn-shaped yarn or string basket was plaited over a wooden block, which sped production and produced an evenly woven, uniform product, c. 1920s, 5.5" high.

NE-85, NE-86, NE-87. Open shopper basket varieties (*left to right*): Abenaki or Micmac splint and braided sweetgrass with swing handles and applied basketry rosettes, c. 1900, 13" wide; Penobscot or Passamaquoddy splint and Hong Kong cord, c. 1940, 13" wide; Abenaki or Maliseet "snowshoe" hexagonal weave, practical for carrying wet beach gear, c. 1940, 12.5" wide.

NE-88, NE-89. Small Penobscot plaited ash splint purse with Hong Kong cord handle and a closure of two wrapped rings is documented to Chief Poolaw's Tepee, Indian Island, Maine, with an attached label on base, c. 1950, 5" wide.

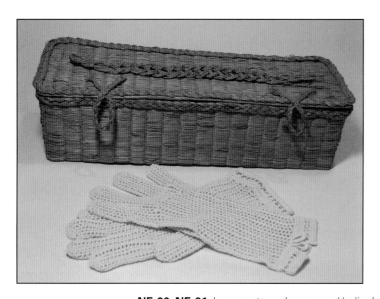
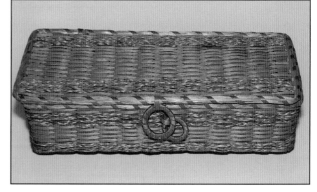

NE-90, NE-91. Long rectangular covered ladies' glove boxes available from Penobscot and Passamaquoddy makers were fashioned using narrow gauge-cut ash splints with sweetgrass trim and closures and a Hong Kong cord "frog" handle (*left*), early 20th century, 13" long.

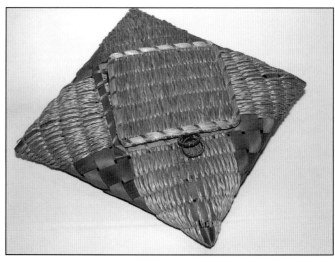

NE-92. Penobscot covered handkerchief basket, plaited on the bias with dyed ash splints and braided sweetgrass, has a pillow shape for packing more easily into trunks or suitcases, c. 1940s, 8.5" square.

NE-93. Similar square covered handkerchief boxes, made in several styles by Native basketmakers of northern New England, Canadian Maritimes, and New York, wholesaled at $5 to $10 per dozen, depending upon size, early 20th century, 5" to 8" square.

NE-95. Footed jewelry box of natural and commercially dyed green ash splints and braided and unbraided sweetgrass, with "diamond" curly splintwork, by Penobscot maker Chief To-me-kin (Leslie Ranco), c. 1970s, 6" square.

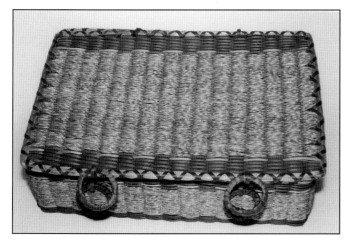

NE-94. Maine Indian (likely Penobscot) rectangular photo or veil basket was kept in a chest and remains as vividly colored as the day it was made, c. 1920, 9" long.

NE-96. Wastepaper basket of dyed ash splints, embellished with "diamond" curly splintwork and Hong Kong cord trim and ring handles, c. 1920-1940, 12" high.

NE-97. Two-handled loving cup, plaited in an urn shape with narrow gauge-cut ash splints and braided sweetgrass, was a popular Penobscot, Passamaquoddy, and Abenaki form, c. 1910, 6" high.

NE-98, NE-99. Urn-shaped vases, plaited with ash splints and sweetgrass or Hong Kong cord over glass jelly jars, sold well in White Mountains, interior lakesides, and coastal resort areas; (*left image*), 8" high; (*right images*), 4.5" and 9.5" high.

NE-100. Stoneware bottle covered by ash splint and sweetgrass basketwork, Nova Scotia (likely Micmac), early 20th century, 7" high.

NE-101, NE-102. Penobscot or Passamaquoddy loop-handled ash splint and sweetgrass flower basket, 1920-1930, 18" high; and two dyed poplar woodsplint flowers made by Micmac basketweaver Madeleine Joe Knockwood, c. 1940, blossom 4.5" diameter.

NE-103. Native basketmakers such as the Penobscot of Maine occasionally created tablewares like this dyed ash splint and sweetgrass tray with reverse painting on glass, c. 1920, 14" long.

NE-105. Probable Penobscot or Passamaquoddy covered square-to-round caddy, perhaps for holding loose tea, was constructed on a compound block with narrow gauge-cut splints, with added sweetgrass-bound lid and handle rings, c. 1900-1920, 5" high.

NE-104. Maliseet-style melon-shaped plaited fruit basket, given four looped splint feet and a "God's-eye" attachment on its distinctive wrapped sweetgrass and splint handle, sold for less than one dollar, early 20th century, 9" long.

NE-106. Covered sweetgrass and ash splint cases for water and shot glasses cushioned these delicate drinking vessels during travels, c. 1900, 3" high.

NE-107. Ash splint and Hong Kong cord table lamp base and shade, c. 1930-1940, 14" high.

NE-108. Micmac "beaver" baskets, heavy-duty yet decorative, plaited with bands of dyed splints and "God's-eye" handle finishes. Marketed in graduated sizes by Canada's Department of Indian Affairs, their bilingual tags explain that the oval beaver-pelt shape symbolizes First Nations industry and harmony with the natural world, c. 1970s, (*left*) 10"-by-11" diameter.

NE-109. Covered ash splint and sweetgrass baskets: Penobscot or Passamaquoddy with curly splintwork (*left*), 1930-1940, 5" diameter; Akwesasne (St. Regis Mohawk) "strawberry" basket with dyed splints and curly splintwork (*right*), 1970s, 5.5" diameter.

NE-110. Small Passamaquoddy covered powder puff box in the shape of a hat, plaited with fragrant braided sweetgrass and green dyed ash splints and displaying Clara Keezer's signature splint bow ribbonwork, 1970s, 5" brim diameter.

NE-111. Ash splint and sweetgrass bookmarks include three Abenaki (Quebec) examples with colorful aniline-dyed splints, and one Akwesasne (St. Regis Mohawk) bookmark (*right*) labeled as the work of Annie Jacobs and priced originally at 10¢, mid-20th century, 8.5" long.

NE-112. Scarce full-sized Indian-used Iroquois (Seneca) child's cradle is plaited with wefts slightly narrower than warp elements and reinforced inside with three rived slats attached with square-headed nails. Eight tulip-like splint overlays ornament the body and hood, and the cradle, with early red paint, rests on carved wooden rockers, 1860, 30" long.

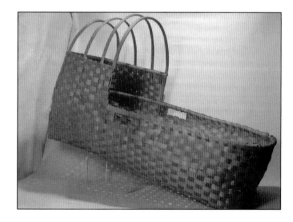

NE-113. Full-sized Abenaki (Quebec or Maine) Indian-used child's cradle, without rockers, plaited with 5/8" wide ash warp splints and slightly narrower wefts, two set-in side handles, and four carved hoops forming an open frame to support a cloth hood covering, early 20th century, 28" long.

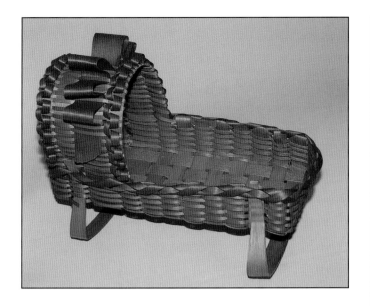

NE-114, NE-115, NE-116. Miniature mid-20th-century doll cradles: hand-trimmed, gauge-cut splint cradle on splint runners in the style of a Passamaquoddy basketmaker (*top left*), 8" long; tiny Passamaquoddy cradle without rockers, with doll impressed "Japan" (*top right*), 4.5" long; two cradles with "diamond" curly splintwork (*left*), one with carved rockers signed "Mary Goo Goo, Mic Mac," 9.5" long.

NE-117. Northeast basketry whimseys include teacups with attached saucers: (*clockwise, from back*) plaited splint and braided sweetgrass with one wide yellow-dyed weft splint, likely Iroquois; two Chippewa or Ojibwa coiled sweetgrass teacups stitched with commercial black thread, one trimmed with black glass beads, all c. 1940-1980, saucers 4" to 4.5" diameter.

NE-118. Nest of four plaited splint swing-handle baskets by Lynn and William Thorp, with ties to the German-Western Abenaki basketmaking Sweetser family of New Hampshire and Vermont, known for distinctive "radial star" basket bases, 1985, 4" to 9" rim diameters.

NE-119. Oneida Iroquois (Ontario) covered ash splint basket with splint-wrapped cover ring, base ring, and handle rings, two bands of wider blue dyed splints, and "diamond" curly splintwork, base signed by Katie Sickles, 1980s, 6" high.

NE-121. Northeast (possibly Great Lakes) long-handled covered basket plaited with natural and dyed ash splints, curly splintwork, and eight splint petals, 1970s, 12" long with handle.

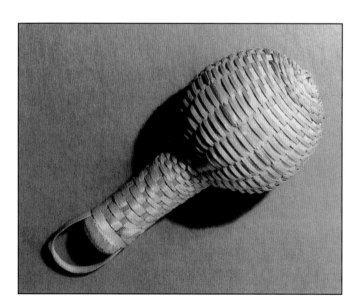

NE-120. Plaited ash splint and sweetgrass baby rattle with handle loop and carved wood stopper, probably Iroquois (Mohawk), 1970s, 5.75" long.

NE-122. New York Iroquois cornhusk salt or tobacco basket, probably by a Tuscarora or Onondaga maker, coiled with braided cornhusk and plugged with a corncob stopper, early to mid-20th century, about 3" high.

NE-123. Iroquois cornhusk masks, or fringed "bushy heads," represent spirits who instructed people to grow maize. Sacred versions, stitched by women but worn by men, have special features and, out of respect, are not displayed. These two examples with original tags were made for sale to travelers, mid-20th century, right 4" high.

NE-124, NE-125. Front and back views *above, below*. Typically stitched with black cotton thread, bundle-coiled sweetgrass and birchbark trays, mats, and inexpensive novelties made around the Great Lakes may be documented to groups like Chippewa or Ojibway through attached labels or back stamps, 20th century, saucer (*center*) 4.5" diameter.

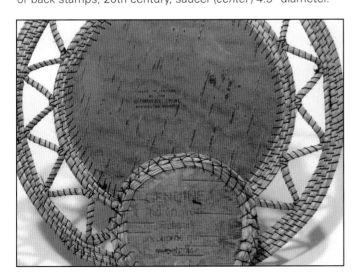

NE-126, NE-127. Ho-Chunk (Winnebago) covered work basket (*above*) plaited in the style of Margaret Decorah, base stamped "Made by Wisconsin Winnebago Indians" (*below*), purchased at Wisconsin Dells, mid-20th century, 10" diameter.

NE-128, NE-129. Ho-Chunk (Winnebago) covered baskets (*left*) plaited with gauge-cut splints on a compound block and given pointed "porcupine twist" ornamentation. So-named "Seneca base" (*right*), signed by maker Velma Marie Lewis, starts with wide radial warp splints that divide to build the wall, late 20th century, 11.5" and 10" diameters.

NE-130. Ho-Chunk (Winnebago) plaited ash splint shopper's basket with characteristic twill-plaited base and two splint-wrapped handles, mid-20th century, 6" square base.

NE-131, NE-132, NE-133. Ho-Chunk (Winnebago) plaited ash splint shopper basket (*above right*) has "diamond" curly splintwork, carved wood swing handle with standard figure-8-shaped, steam-bent attachment (*near right*), and diagnostic Ho-Chunk twill-plaited base (*right*) signed by Alberta White Eagle, Wisconsin Dells, mid-20th century, 10" high.

NE-134. Ho-Chunk (Winnebago) plaited ash splint shopper's basket with usual twill-plaited rectangular base, steam-bent figure-8 handle attachments, "diamond" curly splintwork, and dyed weft splints, made by Margaret Decorah, mid-20th century, 14" long.

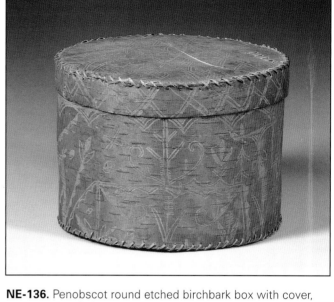

NE-136. Penobscot round etched birchbark box with cover, spruce root stitches, and traditional etched double-curve and foliate design elements, mid-19th century, 15.25" diameter.

NE-135. Some Northeast Indian basketry collectors acquire older birchbark items like this small covered *mokuk,* a folded and stitched container for gathering maple sap or berries or for storing maple sugar, trimmed in sweetgrass and green silk ribbon, c. 1880, 4.75" rim diameter.

NE-137, NE-138. Passamaquoddy wastebasket with etched birchbark walls tacked to wooden base, two birchbark handles, and sweetgrass-edged rim with double-stitched binding. Etched moose, lynx, perched owl, bow and arrows, Indians paddling canoe, "KOLELE MOOK" ("good luck"), cooking kettle, and borders of tipi-shaped wickiups, by Sabattis Tomah, Peter Dana Point, Maine, purchased 1933, 13.5" high.

NE-139. Birchbark lids and boxes contrasting Micmac porcupine quill overlay (*left*) and Huron moose or caribou hair embroidery (*right*) that differ, beyond their geometric or representational floral designs, in the appearance and thickness of the porcupine quills versus the moose or caribou hair embroidery strands, early to mid-19th century.

NE-140. Micmac quilled birchbark lid interior shows patterned insertion holes with quill ends trimmed close to the birchbark.

NE-141. Micmac oval birchbark box with cover, spruce root wrapped lid ring with interwoven quills, porcupine quillwork body design of fir-tree inspired chevron-zigzag element, and cover with geometric pattern of framed eight-pointed star or sun, c. 1850, 11″ maximum diameter.

NE-142. Micmac rectangular porcupine quill decorated birchbark box with vaulted cover, spruce root wrapped lid ring with quill interweave, half-chevron body design, and large central diamond dividing the primary light-colored X design element, mid-19th century, about 10″ long.

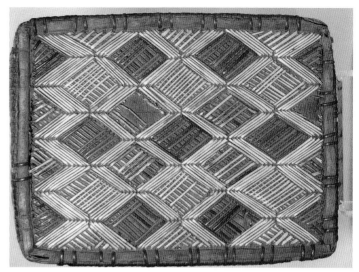

NE-143, NE-144. Micmac rectangular porcupine quill decorated birchbark box (*left*), spruce root stitches and wrapped lid ring without quill interweave, half-chevron body pattern of porcupine quillwork, and repeating diamond design on lid (*right*), late 19th century, 6" long.

NE-146. Huron moose or caribou hair embroidered birchbark, all mid-19th century (*left to right*): needle case, "Niagara Falls 1855;" heart-shaped box, 3.75" wide; tray with four embroidered panels, 8" wide; card case, 3.5" high.

NE-145. Huron round covered birchbark box with moose or caribou hair embroidered floral elements worked in classic French knot and satin stitch embroidery techniques associated with French Ursuline nuns, c. 1830-1860, 4" diameter.

NE-147. Anishinaabe (Michigan Odawa, Ojibwa, Potawatomi) covered rectangular birchbark box, with porcupine quill embroidered floral elements plus sweetgrass closures and thread-bound edging, was a popular souvenir item in the Great Lakes region, 1930s-1940s, 9" long.

NE-148. Small Great Lakes porcupine quill decorated birchbark souvenirs: covered box with allover quillwork (*left*) by Odawa-Ojibway maker Yvonne Walker; and sweetgrass-edged box with isolated central quilled maple leaf element (*right*), c. 1970, 3" diameter.

NE-149. Birchbark *mokuk* and lid with spruce root stitching, etched with simple floral elements, base signed "Max le Gros Huron," mid-20th century, about 6" long.

NE-150. Two Cree covered birchbark *mokuks* with spruce root stitching, etched with moose, bear, and floral elements intended to appeal to visiting hunters and outdoorsmen, c. 1940s-1950s, left 16" long.

NE-151. Northeast ash splint and sweetgrass miniatures represent a wide range of forms and are predominantly made by northern basketmakers, early to mid-20th century.

Section Three

Caution Corner

Indian-style baskets imported from Pakistan
displayed on a Navajo-style rug from Mexico.

chapter 8
"Wannabe," "Maybe," and Other Indian Baskets

The Sincerest Form of Flattery?

Many years ago, in what now seems a much more "innocent" time (the 1970s!), we surveyed the Indian arts field—which was pretty hot then—and mused to ourselves that, of all the Native American craft arts, basketry should be the most immune to deception. We reasoned that, compared to jewelry, fine arts, pottery, and even weavings, the fabrication of basketry products would require a great deal of patience and skill in return for relatively meager compensation. Who, we thought confidently, would go to the trouble of copying or faking Indian baskets?

Today we recognize how naive we were back then. The fact is, people living in marginal conditions in several parts of the globe have been busily churning out baskets. Intentionally or not, some of their work closely resembles the Native American

basket types most favored by collectors. Others, also intentionally or not, take those same imported baskets and pass them along as American Indian examples.

In the 1980s we were at first surprised to come upon little groupings of striking, older looking baskets in unexpected places, like Sunday roadside flea markets. Attractive geometric designs or multiple humans and animals figured some big trays that we saw. The cowboys who had propped the baskets for sale against their pickup truck wheels wouldn't say much about them. But they looked a little odd, and they smelled funny, too. (We mean the baskets, not the cowpokes!) What appeared to be older Apache or Akimel O'odham (Pima) willow and devil's claw treasures eventually proved to be freshly imported Pakistani palm leaf and reed coiled baskets that had been artificially aged with motor oil. So began our growing awareness of a problem that has only become more prevalent since then.

CC-1. Variety of attractive baskets originating from around the globe, some of which may resemble American Indian work. Let's take a closer look at a few, proceeding clockwise from back center.

CC-2. Coiled tray of date palm, 24" diameter, made in Pakistan.

CC-4. Reverse of CC-2. Note untrimmed back surface, not typical of similar-looking American Indian baskets.

CC-3. Detail of CC-2. Basket still bears its import tag.

CC-5. Coiled tray of palm fiber, made in Sonora, Mexico.

CC-6. Coiled longleaf pine needle and raffia purse, made in the 1950s (possibly by North Carolina craftsperson Bessie Mae Hembree), in a style associated with the later American Arts & Crafts Movement.

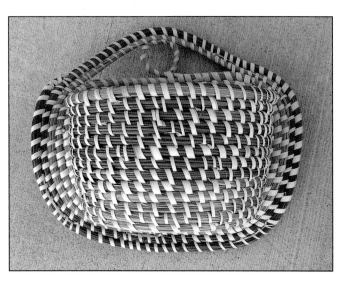

CC-7. Bundle-coiled seagrass and brown longleaf pine straw wall pocket, stitched with palmetto, by a Gullah (African-American) basketmaker living in the coastal lowcountry near Charleston, South Carolina.

CC-9. Handled basket with wooden base and cane and woven straw body dates to early 20th-century Germany.

CC-8. Nigerian bundle-coiled food bowl with dyed, multi-colored palm stitches may be confused with wide-coiled Southwest American Indian baskets, but note the typical untrimmed inner surface of this African example.

CC-10. Vintage paper label confirms European origin of CC-9.

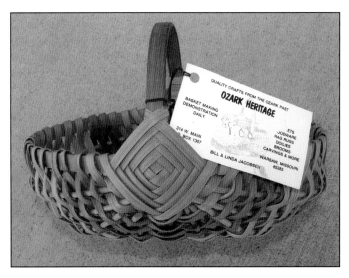

CC-11. Country-style white oak carrying basket from the Ozark craft tradition is American-made but not by American Indians.

CC-12. Carrying basket of similar style, but made of reed, originated in China.

CC-13. Close-up of the CC-12 basket's base reveals reed structure, metal fasteners, and "Made in China" foil label.

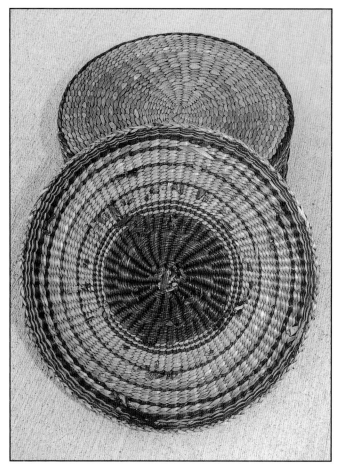

CC-14. Small round and oval grass baskets imported from China. View of round basket lid interior and base displays typical construction details.

In the following pages we will take a close-up look at some of the more common imposters. These non-Native American baskets are very often presented (and priced) as real Indian examples. So often, in fact, that it has become harder to excuse such misattributions as innocent "confusion" on the seller's part. The market in baskets and other Indian products—antique as well as contemporary—financially impacts the collectors, the dealers in the trade, and the Native American community.

The U.S. Department of the Interior's Indian Arts and Crafts Board, in addition to its promotional functions, now has a mandate to deal with these issues. Where deliberate misrepresentation or deception is involved, the American Indian Arts and Crafts Act of 1990 applies. The board's expanded mission includes enforcement of the law by invoking criminal and civil penalties for marketing products as "Indian-made" when, in fact, they were not made by Indians.

Complaints about protected products alleged to be offered or displayed for sale or sold in a manner that falsely suggests they are American Indian-made should be addressed in writing to the Director, Indian Arts and Crafts Board, Room 4004-MIB, U.S. Department of the Interior, 1849 C Street, NW, Washington, DC 20240, or reported through the website (see Appendix A).

Not all the imitation Native American baskets are recent, of course. For example, we have noted several times already (see pages 36-38) that the Arts & Crafts Movement of a hundred years ago was so obsessed with Indian baskets that its devotees commonly exercised the urge to replicate them. Happily, the raffia and reed materials they generally worked with help to distinguish their projects from the Native exemplars.

Commercial Baskets

Even today, modern handcrafters can pay homage to the Indian basket by purchasing kits of prepared materials with instructions at "green" shops, tourist sites, and on the Internet. Here, again, the final product may resemble the pattern, but it will probably be woven from commercially available reed, grass cordage, or raffia provided in the kit.

Baskets of all kinds remain a proven and perennial favorite for decorative and functional purposes. Nearly every general retail chain stocks a variety of woven containers at all times. Most of them look nothing like standard Native American baskets, but some do. Several years ago we opened a catalog issued by Coldwater Creek retailers and were amazed to find what appeared to be Navajo "wedding baskets" presented for sale at a very reasonable price. But we soon recognized that these baskets came from Southwest Asia, not the American Southwest.

Today, we know that many attractive baskets originate in China, although other Asian countries, as well as Africa and Mexico, also provide a steady supply. Baskets, like any other foreign-made products intended for markets in the United States, must be labeled to identify their country of origin for customs purposes. Every basket shipped here once wore a little foil tag, a paper sticker, a string tag, or an ink-stamped mark. Any of those labels are readily detached, and even the stamping can be covered or removed, whether innocently or not.

Basketville

One merchandiser that specializes almost exclusively in imported baskets is Basketville, of Putney, Vermont. As successor to the Gage basket factory founded in 1842 at nearby Bellows Falls, the company once produced all its baskets on-site. Since 1942 it has marketed under the Basketville name and now supplies many nationwide retailers. Today, Basketville promotes itself as "America's oldest basket company," but few if any baskets are still made at the Vermont headquarters. According to the company's website (www.basketville.com):

> Basketville was a pioneer in manufacturing woven products offshore for the home accessories market. We have experienced people on the ground in China who understand how things work–and how to achieve a reliable outcome . . . . Because of our long experience in basket making, we are expert at weaving with a variety of materials, and we know how to tie in with the latest decorating trends. We work with willow, seagrass, paper rope, maize, tropical beech and rush . . . . Our baskets are made entirely by hand following centuries-old methods. We offer the handcrafted look at mass market prices . . . .

Many of their products have come from China, but they now have other international suppliers:

> As basket collectors ourselves, we support the artistry of weavers around the world. Recently we've connected with some amazing basket makers in Africa and Cambodia. Our Fair Trade African baskets are handwoven in mesmerizing, color-rich tribal patterns. They come from Ghana, Kenya, Uganda, Swaziland, Zambia and Botswana. Natural dyes and renewable materials like banana leaf, palm, wild grasses and vines are characteristic.

CC-15. Publications and sample cards of materials available to the Arts & Crafts basketmaker, gathered by the co-author's great grandmother, c. 1900.

CC-16. Raffia baskets made by American Arts & Crafts Movement enthusiasts in the early 20th century can resemble Native American work. If one looks carefully, differences in shape, design elements, and especially materials may help distinguish these products from each other.

CC-17. Modern-day basketmaking kits appeal to the contemporary "on-the-go" craftsperson.

CC-18. American-style "Shaker Collection" baskets made in China from American wood and marketed in the United States under the Basketville label.

CC-19. Basket of typical Shaker-style, kitten-head form, closely copied by Chinese makers and sold at a modest retail price. This example is reed rather than woodsplint.

Basketville has been a source for at least some of the look-a-likes that at one time or another have been confused with or sold as Native American and Country American baskets. For example, certain of their Chinese woodsplint baskets are closely modeled on popular Mohawk and Maine Indian fancywork baskets, in particular those decorated with "ribbon twist" or curlicue projections. Similarly, they offer appealing country-style "egg," "melon," or "buttocks" baskets that mimic those crafted by Appalachian folk and several Southeast Indian groups. However, a noteworthy distinction is that many of Basketville's imported baskets are woven from relatively thick splints *sawn* (cut across the growth rings) from American hardwoods, shipped to China, then returned to the United States as finished baskets.

Longaberger

Sawn hardwood elements are also used in Longaberger and other contemporary non-Indian woodsplint baskets. Eastern American Indians, though, customarily make their splints by *hand-pounding* an ash log to release the individual growth rings, which are then trimmed to a desired width. And 19th-century non-Indian American basketmakers generally plied *riven* splints, which they split with a froe from a length of wood and then thinned with a drawknife.

CC-21. Three typical Longaberger baskets, which come in many sizes and shapes, both with and without handles or lids.

CC-20. Longaberger Basket Company's unique home office building near Newark, Ohio, is a seven-story version of their popular market basket.

CC-22. Longaberger baskets are almost always branded on their bases and occasionally also may be individually hand signed. Note metal fasteners and machine-cut splints.

234

CC-23. Native Americans generally produced splints by pounding a length of ash log to release individual growth rings.

CC-25. American Shaker-made woodsplint basket with finely carved handle.

CC-24. Yankee basketmaker works with riven woodsplints, c. 1900.

CC-26. Taconic or "Bushwacker"-style woodsplint basket with shaved handle.

CC-27. Distinctive swing handle with square openings, among other specific traits, sets this basket apart as the work of Rhode Island maker Rowse Matterson, c. 1900.

CC-29. Contemporary Appalachian woodsplint carrying basket, purchased in 2006, preserves characteristic form but conceals metal fasteners beneath handle wrappings.

CC-28. Yankee basketmaker Rowse Matterson (1853-1936) in his Saunderstown, Rhode Island, home working amid stacks of nearly completed baskets and a supply of prepared materials that include oak splints rived from neighborhood trees and reed brought from Connecticut.

CC-30, CC-31. Modern craftsman starts a traditional Appalachian-style basket using commercially available materials (*left*).

"Country"-style Baskets

Older "country"-style baskets that were actually made in the United States in past generations can be even more challenging to separate from vintage Native American handiwork. At first glance, some of these baskets appear almost identical. As examples, Shaker and Taconic (or "Bushwacker") splint baskets found in western New England and upstate New York closely resemble Native American splint baskets from the surrounding region. In fact, some researchers suspect that all of these people routinely bought and sold each other's products as their own. Likewise, mountain families in the Carolinas fashioned handled carrying baskets of local woodsplints, just as their Cherokee neighbors did. Note, however, that most American craft and commercial baskets have nailed rims and handle attachments that differentiate them from typical Native examples. Authorities can cite other diagnostic rim finishes and construction details when making attributions, but these distinctions are not mutually exclusive.

Take, for example, the familiar "pack" or "trapper" basket, long symbolic of the North woodsman but also useful to earlier Native Americans. Lashed to a person's back with straps, it resembles an oversized grocery sack and as a general carryall it serves just about as many purposes. Plaited from sturdy hardwood splints, a traditional pack basket might have either a wrapped rim or a nailed rim. While nailed rims ordinarily suggest factory production, some Natives like the Sanipass family of Micmac basketmakers have, at least on occasion, turned out both varieties.

CC-33. Pennsylvania German coiled rye straw basket for bread dough is one of many similar forms made worldwide.

CC-32. Northeastern woodsplint "pack" or "trapper" basket with removable canvas strapping.

CC-34. Gullah (African-American) space-stitched coiled baskets from coastal South Carolina take many forms.

CC-35. Base of Tohono O'odham space-stitched coiled tray of beargrass and yucca (*left*), compared to a South Carolina Gullah seagrass and palmetto example (*right*).

CC-36. Bundle-coiled lidded basket with side lugs, from Namibia, Southwest Africa.

To this list we could add many other look-a-likes. Serviceable straw-coiled open baskets and storage containers, their courses expediently sewn with sturdy space-stitching, were a mainstay of farming cultures as far-flung as northern Europe, West Africa, the American Mid-Atlantic states, Mexico, and many other places. Tohono O'odham wheat farmers also made and used seemingly identical baskets in Arizona. African-American Gullah baskets from coastal South Carolina are similarly constructed. Telling them all apart can be a challenge.

International Baskets

African Baskets

Colorful African baskets, including some of the types that originate in countries listed by Basketville, are sometimes misidentified and marketed as Native American. Basketmaking is actively encouraged today as a source of income for indigenous African women and as a reinforcement of their cultural heritage. Cael Chappell founded Baskets of Africa (basketsofafrica.com) in 2002. Today this business, operated from Albuquerque, New Mexico, promotes weavers in more than a half dozen African nations who make baskets that are desirable and collectible in their own right, but some of them can also be confused with those made by American Indians.

CC-37. Rotund basket of palm leaf made by Senufo people, Ivory Coast, West Africa, but labeled "Ojibway" at a western U.S. antiques mall, 8" diameter.

CC-38. Knob-lidded coiled basket and matching coasters from Africa exhibit elemental designs common to many cultures, including American Indian.

CC-39. Many African baskets have thick coils and colors that can resemble American Indian products, but conical lids are more typically an African form.

CC-40, CC-41. Recent Zulu-made South African coiled basket with attached lid. *Detail*: Zulu square-plaited starts can resemble those on some Native American (e.g., O'odham) coiled baskets. Double-checking materials, coiled foundation and stitching, form, and design elements may aid identification.

It is beyond our purpose or means in this book to do more than mention just a few of the most common African basket types represented in today's marketplace that are sometimes mistaken as American Indian. In Botswana, for example, skilled weavers create attractive trays, shallow flaring bowls, and a few lidded baskets. Their bundle-coiling technique, plus their use of colorful starburst or radial geometric designs in rich earthy colors, has allowed Botswana products to be confused with Tohono O'odham yucca wares, among others.

To distinguish many of the African baskets from authentic American Indian examples requires one to pay particular attention to the materials. Uganda basketmakers coil millet, raffia, and banana leaf fiber into large shallow bowls whose bold star-forms and strong geometrics and frets would seem familiar to any Southwest Indian basket collector. Hues range from subtle natural tones that closely resemble American baskets to pure bright colors that do not. Shallow "plateau" baskets made in South Africa and Zambia for international trade have plaited starts and complex geometric motifs that also could be mistaken as southwestern American Indian, except for their being woven of African palm leaf strips.

Compact, pear-shaped or globular forms fitted with knobbed lids characterize South African Zulu baskets that are sometimes found today wherever one might be looking for Indian baskets. Well woven from palm fiber, these baskets have characteristic plaited starts on bases resembling O'odham examples. The Zulu baskets usually exhibit strong zigzag or diamond patterns executed in buff, red, a recognizable grayish-brown, and/or black. They have been a frequent stand-in for baskets sold as "American Indian."

CC-42. Twined grass hats of many types were used in sub-Saharan Africa. This knobbed conical form embellished with interlocking loops somewhat resembles American Northwest Coast twined hats.

CC-45. Bundle-coiled lidded basket, sheathed in rawhide to guard against wear and tear, originated in Nigeria, West Africa.

CC-43. Richly decorated with multiple figures or colorfully dyed geometric designs, Nigerian jar covers of coiled palm are frequently mistaken for Southwest U.S. baskets, but the color combination, materials, design layout, and looped rims are not characteristic of American Indian work.

Older African baskets have also caused confusion. Mat-like basketry lids and trays richly decorated with figures or geometrics in black, green, red, or other colors and made in East Africa by such tribes as the Hausa, as well as similar plaques in different colors originating from Turkey and elsewhere, are routinely offered as "Southwestern Indian." Other African forms have also invaded the American Indian market. A large supply of low coiled-grass baskets, some with worn leather-bound rims and a few completely covered in aged rawhide, showed up in flea markets during the late 1980s. They commonly had old collection numbers penned in white ink on their rims. The claim that these were "Indian baskets" de-accessioned from a major university museum in Pennsylvania gave them a provenance that appealed to collectors and boosted their perceived value. But they originated in Nigeria, where Nupe tribesmen once carried food in them.

CC-44. Brightly colored coiled tray from Turkey, 24" diameter, for carrying bread, resembles some African and American Indian basketry mats and plaques.

CC-46. Stacks of imported Southwest-style baskets from Pakistan are among the arts offered at a western U.S. flea market.

Pakistani Baskets

South Asian baskets frequently masquerade as Native American products. Currently, Zanzibar Trading, operating from Sacramento, California, is a major supplier of baskets from this area. Their products are well made and can be easily mistaken for American Indian wares. Individual Pakistani weavers collect date palm leaves, dry them, and then use natural pigments to dye them in a clay-lined pit. These elements are sewn around coiled bundle foundations of wild river reeds. Finished baskets may be "antiqued" at extra cost, using either a tea dye or a colored wax.

CC-47, CC-48, CC-49. These familiar designs and color combinations are deceptive. The coiled baskets are not what they may appear to be and were made in southern Asia for the American market. Their resemblance to Western Apache, Hopi, and other Southwest American Indian baskets is apparent and can be misleading.

The importer frankly acknowledges the relationship between these Pakistani baskets and those American Indian baskets they so obviously resemble. The following information is quoted verbatim directly from their website (www.zanzibar-trading.com):

The designs are based on both centuries old Pakistan and American Southwest Indian designs and each basket can take weeks to weave. While these baskets feature traditional Zuni, Hopi, Navajo, Ute, Apache and other Native American basket designs and images, they are not produced by Native Americans.

As the story goes, it was a missionary from the American Southwest who introduced a book featuring Native American basket designs (including man in the maze, wedding basket design, dog and horse patterns, etc) to the weavers in Pakistan—and true to this, there are MANY unscrupulous vendors who sell these baskets as Native American Indian baskets. At Zanzibar we pride ourselves in sourcing authentic items from the people who created them. We have deep respect for the inherent pattern and their meanings of Native American basket designs.

We normally do not sell cheap knock-offs or fakes, we would rather sell the real item from the people who originated it/them. In this instance, however, we feel that the Pakistani baskets are dissimilar enough and yet high enough quality and yet at a very affordable price point as to compliment rather than replace Native American baskets. A Pakistan basket priced at under $40 is not going to compete with the real basket that can sell for hundreds or thousands of dollars if crafted by a native American. We do not mean to undermine or belittle the beliefs of the Indigenous people of the Americas by selling these baskets. While some of the designs are Native American, many are designs that are Pakistani and or transcend cultures and borders and are designs that are found in dozens of basket weaving cultures around the world.

CC-50. Not so long ago, imported Pakistani baskets only generally resembled coiled basketry from the American Southwest in technique, form, and design. Unusual bright colors declared their foreign origin.

We have observed these baskets for quite a few years now as they have become more and more difficult to distinguish from their North American counterparts. What began as a general resemblance, based on a shared coiling technique, a similar false-braid or "herringbone" rim finish, and some baskets with a few Native American-inspired design elements (among a majority showing Pakistani motifs), has progressed to a more deliberate and focused replication process. The weaving has gotten better, the design layouts more refined. Some obvious contrasts remain, however, including the materials and dyes employed in making the Pakistani examples and the untidy appearance of their back surfaces. One might also detect that these palm leaf and river reed baskets emit a "green," or tobacco-like scent.

CC-51. Side-by-side comparison of genuine Native American (*left*) versus imported Asian (*right*) products, made half a world apart. Genuine Hopi plaque versus plaque made in Pakistan. Note shared similarities: start, bundle coil size, colors, rim loop, and decorative sewn overstitching.

CC-52. Side-by-side comparison of genuine Native American (*left*) versus imported Asian (*right*) products, made half a world apart. Genuine Tohono O'odham tray with "Elder Brother" or "Man in the Maze" design versus tray made in Pakistan.

CC-53. Side-by-side comparison of genuine Native American (*left*) versus imported Asian (*right*) products, made half a world apart. Genuine Tohono O'odham olla versus small jar made in Pakistan.

The new Pakistani baskets from Zanzibar Trading, Shalimar Trading, and other current suppliers that we know about are truthfully labeled. But, of course, any one of those "MANY unscrupulous vendors" could easily remove the tag, as could any purchaser who might later pass along the basket. One major wholesaler/retailer in West Texas advertises similar products as "Nice Southwest Style Multicolor Baskets" and another Phoenix area merchant offers them as "Hand Made Colorful Southwestern Design Baskets." Neither makes a disclaimer as to origin, and even at retail the prices are low enough to tempt a calculating buyer to resell at a nice profit.

CC-55. Tohono O'odham and Pakistani reverse sides differ noticeably. Untrimmed fibers on the example from Pakistan blur the design.

CC-54. Comparison of two baskets, contrasting an authentic American Indian basket (*left*) and an imported Pakistani imposter (*right*). Genuine Tohono O'odham coiled tray sewn in willow and black devil's claw, versus Pakistani look-alike stitched with natural colored and black-dyed date palm strands.

CC-56, CC-57. Front and back comparison of two baskets, contrasting an authentic Navajo basket (*left*) and an imported Pakistani imposter (*right*). Here, the Pakistani product (*right*) more closely mimics its genuine American Indian counterpart, an older and now faded Navajo-style "wedding basket" (*left*), both front and back. The Pakistani import has date palm fiber stitches over a reed bundle. The Navajo basket, with sumac stitches over woody sumac rods, looks and feels more rigid.

CC-58, CC-59. Front and back comparison of two baskets, contrasting an authentic American Indian basket (*left*) and an imported Pakistani imposter (*right*). Long popular with collectors, Yavapai and Western Apache figural trays inspire imitators. Contemporary Pakistani weavers recently produced the basket stitched with natural colored and black-dyed date palm (*right*), instead of with willow and natural black devil's claw seen in a vintage Native American example (*left*). Reverses expose different finishing techniques.

The reader will want to closely study the side-by-side comparisons we illustrate in this section. Remember, though, basketry remains an evolving craft—and that includes Pakistani baskets. How they look today is not necessarily how they will look (or smell) tomorrow!

Mexican Indian Baskets

Baskets originating recently in Mexico include Hopi-look coiled plaques. Their overly thick coils are somewhat loosely sewn with a fibrous material. Intended as decorative accents, baskets of this type should not fool any but the most inexperienced Indian basket buyer. The same may be said of the Mexican wrap-coiled yucca leaf baskets and bundle-coiled grass baskets, all of which are commonly aniline-dyed with bright magenta, purple, green, and yellow hues (CC-60).

CC-60. *Detail*: Wrap coiling typifies many colorful baskets imported from northern Mexico, southern Asia, and elsewhere, but the technique is not generally seen in North American Indian baskets.

CC-61. Example of a "suspect" Pomo basket with intensely black decoration, including a parade of human figures, and ten quail topknot feathers.

Even more concerning are modern American Indian baskets made expressly to deceive buyers into thinking that they are purchasing a vintage treasure.

A few years back, some fine Pomo-style baskets began circulating through shows and auction houses. These small round or oval, canoe-shaped baskets exhibited very fine workmanship. Some were fully covered with colorful feathers, while others were more simply adorned with quail topknots. A few had human figures woven in black—an uncommon motif for a Pomo basket. The black in the patterns seemed unnatural, as though dyed. Something else seemed not quite right, although it was hard to say exactly what the problem was. The weaving material may have looked slightly more dull and porous than we were used to seeing. But the distinctions were subtle. Some major dealers of antique Indian art suspected that these baskets were recently Indian-made in northern Mexico but were being presented as old Pomo wares.

Similarly, at the present time, contemporary Kumeyaay (Diegueño, or Ipai-Tipai) basketweavers, including several talented women of the Salazar and Silva families of San Jose de la Zorra, Baja California, Mexico, are using natural and dyed juncus rush to sew bundled deergrass coils into traditional "Mission Indian" basket trays and bowls. Figured with rattlesnakes, humans, and stars or flowers, individual baskets of large size and exceptional craftsmanship approach masterwork status on their own merits. Reportedly, however, some lesser examples have been obtained and artificially "antiqued," then resold to unwary collectors for about ten times the original purchase price.

South American Indian Baskets

Single- and double-woven cane plaiting with a red and/or black color preference has characterized much of the historical basketry around the entire circum-Caribbean region. The Baniwa and other peoples living along the upper Rio Negro in the Amazonian rainforest have become known for their graceful twill plaited work. On the other hand, Wounaan and Embera women living in the Darien rainforest on the border between Panama and Colombia make tightly coiled palm fiber baskets. Figured with either angular (often flame-like) designs or naturalistic representations of birds, plants, and insects, the combination of bright colors and classic forms give these baskets great appeal. They have been actively marketed in the United States, where they may resemble Native North American examples.

Other South American Indian cultures have relied on their own basketmaking traditions for millennia, and some continue their production today. The Yekuana of the Venezuelan Amazon region still twine handsome burden baskets. Nearby, the Yanomami select woody vines for twining their sturdy utility baskets. They make large shallow bowls and deep carrying baskets, usually horizontally reinforced inside and at the rim with hoops spaced a few inches apart. They may sparingly decorate their baskets with painted dots, wavy lines, circles, or crosses, using masticated charcoal as pigment. Corresponding somewhat to comparable Western Apache forms, these attractive baskets can be found tagged ambiguously as "American Indian." But the use of applied surface decoration, plus the hoop reinforcements, should help collectors identify a typical South American Yanomami Indian basket.

CC-62. Circum-Caribbean Indian baskets share many characteristics with North American Indian work. Twill-plaited examples include this double-weave twill-plaited bowl with independent interior and exterior designs, made by Waimiri-Atroari people of the upper Amazon region, Brazil.

CC-63. Two additional twill-plaited examples are these graceful baskets, crafted by Baniwa makers, 11" and 12" high.

CC-64. Twill-plaited circum-Caribbean single-weave bowl, made by men of the upper Amazonian Baniwa tribe.

CC-66. Flea market display of Wounaan and Embera coiled jars from Darien province, Panama, 1997.

CC-65. Coiled baskets from the circum-Caribbean region include a Wounaan plaque and jar with butterflies.

CC-67. Yekuana twined burden baskets, Venezuelan Amazon.

CC-68. Examples of Yanomami twined carrying baskets display typical features, such as hoop reinforcements and spare applied decorations painted with masticated charcoal.

More (and More!) Asian and Pacific Baskets

As is the case elsewhere in the world, Asia's many indigenous cultures each have had their own rich basketry heritage. The numerous ethnic groups who occupy those varied lands have created an endless variety of baskets that serve many functions. Perhaps most frequently confused with Native North American examples are the small lidded Chinese grass baskets referenced on pages 44-45. Today, very well made baskets from China, Japan, the Philippines, Southeast Asia, and islands in the Pacific flood the American market. More than a few of these can be—and have been—mistaken for American Indian work. We picture some representative types on these pages, but the reader should be alert for other equally troublesome examples.

CC-71, CC-72. Another comparison, contrasting oval Nuu-chah-nulth (*left*) and Asian (*right*) covered trinket baskets, as well as their differing bases.

CC-69, CC-70. Compare these early 20th-century Nuu-chah-nulth twined *piku'u*, or lidded trinket baskets, of cedar bark and natural and dyed grass (*left*) to the late 20th-century imported Chinese covered grass boxes (*right*). Note especially the customary plaited cedar start on the base of the American Indian example versus the Asian grass start.

CC-73, CC-74. Another comparison, contrasting round Nuu-chah-nulth (*left*) and Asian (*right*) covered trinket baskets, as well as their differing bases, to illustrate the considerable variety that may be encountered.

CC-75. Offered recently at an antique consignment gallery as "American Indian," these three lidded baskets are of unknown, possibly western Pacific or Asian, origin. Though their colors and forms may somewhat resemble baskets of several Native American regions, all are made of split bamboo strands.

CC-77. Carefully compare these colorful baskets. Contemporary Native American example (*left*) is a Mississippi Choctaw double-weave rivercane basket, while the covered basket, or *keben,* of single-weave bamboo strips (*right*) was made in Bali, Indonesia. The Balinese basket, with noticeably thinner and lighter weight fabric, may be one of a "nest" of graduated sizes.

CC-76. This large one-rod coiled bowl of natural undyed rattan has a course of wrapped openwork and a false-braid rim that may remind someone of western Native American basketry, but it was made in Bali, Indonesia.

CC-78. Twill plaited into the fabric of this 5.5" high basket, the words "PITCAIRN" and "ISLAND" declare an origin halfway around the world from Native North America. The lid also is signed inside by its maker, "Daphne Warren/née Christian," descendant of first mate Fletcher Christian of *Mutiny on the Bounty* fame.

CC-79. Variety of common basket types, some of which might possibly confuse a collector on a bad day. Happily, each of these examples is clearly marked with its country of origin, starting clockwise from upper left.

CC-80. Philippines.

CC-82. Taiwan.

CC-81. Mexico.

CC-83. Sewing basket with attached tassels and Chinese coins is marked "China" inside.

CC-84. Occupied Japan basket with coasters for post-World War II export.

CC-85. China.

CC-86. Contemporary basketmakers and others who admire Native American cultures may be inspired to recreate treasures like this historical Northeast Indian plaited woodsplint basket, reproduced here by an anthropologist colleague in commercial, non-traditional reed.

CC-87, CC-88. Making a convincing "Indian" basket requires both will and skill. The co-author attempts to convert fresh withes into a basket with guidance from veteran red-willow basketmaker Bob Allalunis, of Taos, New Mexico. The instructor's appraisal of his student's first willow basket is telling.

Afterword

"Who but they who loved the reed that grew beside still waters, and the damp root of shrub and tree, could save it from seasonal death, and with almost superhuman patience weave it into enduring objects of beauty—into timeless art!"
–Luther Standing Bear (Sioux), 1933

Tohono O'odham coiled tray with black devil's claw and red yucca root "squash blossom" design, c. 1980, 16" diameter.

Appendix A
Useful Internet Resources

GENERAL

Basketmakers
basketmakers.org

A website created by basketmaker Susi Nuss as "a comprehensive informational site for basketmakers, basket artists, vendors of basketmaking materials and all others interested in the art of basket weaving."

Go Native American
gonativeamerican.org

A directory of Native American related websites, a "sort of 'Go To' list to help people interested in a particular topic relating to North American Indians."

Indian Country Today Media Network
indiancountrytodaymedianetwork.com

As "the digital gateway to the world's most comprehensive and innovative online Native news and entertainment site, serving Native and American Indian tribes nationwide," this website covers arts and crafts topics under its "Culture" heading.

NATIVE AMERICAN BASKETMAKER WEBSITES

California Indian Basketweavers Association (CIBA)
www.ciba.org

A Native non-profit organization "to preserve, promote, and perpetuate California Indian basket weaving traditions while providing a healthy physical, social, spiritual, and economic environment for basketweavers."

Maine Indian Basketmakers Alliance (MIBA)
www.maineindianbaskets.org

A Native non-profit organization "to preserve the ancient tradition of ash and sweetgrass basketmaking among the Maliseet, Micmac, Passamaquoddy and Penobscot tribes."

Northwest Native American Basketweavers Association (NNABA)
www.nnaba.org

A Native non-profit organization "to preserve, promote, and perpetuate the traditional and contemporary art of Northwest Native American Basketry."

Tohono O'odham Basketweavers Organization (TOBO)
www.tocaonline.org/Home.html

A Native cooperative "dedicated to revitalizing basketry as a viable economic opportunity and valued cultural practice" in the Tohono O'odham community.

INDIAN ARTS PERIODICALS

American Indian Art Magazine
www.aiamagazine.com

Published quarterly since 1975, this glossy magazine features articles primarily on antique Indian arts, with regular columns on auction highlights and legal matters, as well as current show schedules, gallery listings, museum exhibits, and dealer advertising.

Native Peoples
www.nativepeoples.com

Published bimonthly since 1987, this commercial magazine profiles contemporary Indian artists and their work in all media, including music and film, while also providing notices of current and upcoming events with a focus on Native "living cultures."

INDIAN ARTS TRADE ASSOCIATIONS

Department of the Interior Indian Arts and Crafts Board (IACB)
www.doi.gov/iacb

A federal agency created by Congress "to promote the economic development of American Indians and Alaska Natives through the expansion of the Indian arts and crafts market," the IACB also monitors the market for items misrepresented as Indian-made.

Indian Arts and Crafts Association (IACA)
www.iaca.com

A trade association "representing every link in American Indian arts—Native artists from the U.S. and Canada, along with consumers, retailers, wholesalers, museums, government agencies, suppliers and supporting members."

Antique Tribal Art Dealers Association, Inc. (ATADA)
www.atada.org

A trade association "to promote professional conduct among dealers and to educate the public in the valuable role of tribal art in the wealth of human experience," ATADA includes most major American Indian art dealers among its membership.

Southwestern Association for Indian Arts (SWAIA)
swaia.org

A trade association for "bringing Native arts to the world by inspiring artistic excellence, fostering education, and creating meaningful partnerships," SWAIA stages the Santa Fe Indian Market each August.

AUCTION HOUSES WITH PERIODIC CATALOGUED INDIAN ARTS SALES

Allard Auctions, Inc. (St. Ignatius, Montana, with auctions in Phoenix and Santa Fe)
www.allardauctions.com

Bonhams (San Francisco, Los Angeles, and New York)
www.bonhams.com

Christies (international locations)
www.christies.com

Cowan's Auctions, Inc. (Cincinnati, Ohio)
www.cowanauctions.com

Heritage Auctions (Dallas and New York City)
www.ha.com

Skinner, Inc. (Boston and Marlborough, Massachusetts)
www.skinnerinc.com

Sotheby's (international locations)
www.sothebys.com

FIND A LOCAL AUCTIONEER

AuctionZip Auctioneer Directory
www.auctionzip.com/Auctioneer-Directory/

An alphabetical directory of thousands of auctioneers across the country. Sort by name or by location. Includes upcoming auction listings.

FIND AN APPRAISER

American Society of Appraisers (ASA)
www.appraisers.org/

"One of the leading professional appraising organizations representing all of the disciplines of appraisal specialists."

Appraisers Association of America (AAA)
www.appraisersassoc.org

"The premier national association of personal property appraisers who focus on fine and decorative arts."

The International Society of Appraisers (ISA)
www.isa-appraisers.org

"Provides, supports and educates qualified professional personal property appraisers."

FIND A CONSERVATOR/RESTORER

The American Institute for Conservation of Historic and Artistic Works (AIC)
www.conservation-us.org

As "the national membership organization of conservation professionals, its members include conservators, educators, scientists, students, archivists, art historians, and other conservation enthusiasts in over twenty countries around the world."

Appendix B
100 American Museums with Indian Basketry Collections

This guide to U.S. and Canadian museums with American Indian basket collections grew out of a posting we found on Susi Nuss's wonderful *Basketmakers.org* website (see Appendix A). Surely, even with our expanded list, more than a few worthy public collections have been left out. Bear in mind that collection size and representativeness are often but not always the best gauge of significance. Some museums hold a relatively modest group of baskets, but those examples may be carefully selected or they may document a defined cultural area or even an individual tribe.

It is generally the case with larger museums that only a fraction of the total Native basket collection may be on exhibit at any one time. Duplicates and more ordinary baskets, as well as imperfect examples, may remain forever in storage, available for study but unlikely to be viewed by the general public. Today, though, many museums are opening their entire holdings through on-line access. One may take a virtual tour of the whole collection or even research individual items of special interest with just a few clicks of the mouse. You save on gas and no appointment or white gloves are required!

Gaining on-line access to a museum's collection is generally a simple matter. Visit the institution's homepage, locate the appropriate toolbar heading (usually something like "Collections," "Exhibits and Collections," or "Research") and then follow instructions. It may be as straightforward as entering the term "basket" in a search box. You may be invited to refine your search by tribe or geographic area or even by a specific type of basket.

The alphabetical list below includes the street address of each museum's physical (GPS) location, its mailing address (post office box if separate from the street address), and the primary website location. A summary of the museum's American Indian basketry holdings follows. In addition to their basket exhibits and permanent collections, some museums host periodic basketry demonstrations or workshops. A number of them have museum shops that offer Indian baskets for purchase. Consult individual websites for further information.

Abbe Museum
26 Mount Desert Street
Bar Harbor, Maine 04609
www.abbemuseum.org
Featuring Indian culture, history and art, the Abbe maintains one of the largest collections of Wabanaki ash splint baskets, numbering nearly 1,000 specimens.

Agua Caliente Cultural Museum
Village Green Heritage Center
219 South Palm Canyon Drive
Palm Springs, California 92262
www.accmuseum.org
The museum features a collection of over 400 southern California basket items representing Cahuilla basketweavers and neighboring tribes.

Akwesasne Cultural Center
321 State Route 37
Hogansburg, New York 13655
akwesasneculturalcenter.org/museum
The Akwesasne Museum collection includes over 700 ethnographic objects, including a great variety of baskets made by the Mohawk community of Akwesasne for their own use and for sale.

American Museum of Natural History
Central Park West at 79th Street
New York, New York 10024
www.amnh.org
The museum's North American ethnographic collection is exceptional for its size, scope, and age, as well as for its extensive documentation in museum publications. The American Indian basket holdings represent all cultural regions, with particular strengths in Northwest Coast, California, and Southwest basketry.

Amerind Foundation, Inc.
2100 North Amerind Road
P.O. Box 400
Dragoon, Arizona 85609
www.amerind.org
Set amid the fantastic boulder formations of Texas Canyon, the Foundation's strong archaeological and ethnological collections include exceptional baskets from the Southwest and northern Mexico, California, the Northwest Coast, Plateau, and Great Basin.

Arizona State Museum
1013 East University Boulevard
Tucson, Arizona 85721
www.statemuseum.arizona.edu
Located on the University of Arizona campus, the Arizona State Museum's comprehensive Southwest Indian collection includes more than 25,000 woven items, especially its outstanding baskets, as well as sandals, cradle boards, mats, cordage, and preserved fibers.

Autry National Center
4700 Western Heritage Way
Los Angeles, California 90027
theautry.org
The Autry's Southwest Museum of the American Indian collection of nearly 14,000 baskets has many remarkable examples representing over 100 North American tribes.

Barona Cultural Center and Museum
1095 Barona Road
Lakeside, California 92040
www.baronamuseum.org
Associated with a major Indian casino, the Barona Cultural Center and Museum is the tribal showcase of the local Barona Band of Mission Indians (Kumeyaay, 'Iipay, or Diegueño). Dedicated to preserving the Native American culture and history of San Diego County, the collections include coiled basketry of southern and Baja California from 1900 to the present.

Bowers Museum
2002 North Main Street
Santa Ana, California 92706
www.bowers.org
The city-run museum's Native American collection is its largest department, with 24,000 items representing all regions, but particularly the West and Southwest. The basketry collection was the basis for Charles Rozaire's 1977 book, *Indian Basketry of Western North America*.

Brigham Young University Museum of Peoples and Cultures
105 Allen Hall
700 North 100 East
Provo, Utah 84602
mpc.byu.edu
The Great Basin holdings include prehistoric Fremont Culture material, such as basketry and footwear, and ethnographic Ute material. The Southwest collections include artifacts from ancestral Puebloans such as Anasazi and Basketmaker footwear and basketry, as well as Hopi and Navajo baskets.

Burke Museum of Natural History and Culture
Northeast 45th Street
Seattle, Washington 98195
www.burkemuseum.org
    Located on the University of Washington campus, the Burke Museum is especially known for its collections of Northwest Coast and Alaskan art and artifacts, including numerous basketry items gathered by early ethnographers as well as more recent examples.

California Academy of Sciences
55 Music Concourse Drive
Golden Gate Park
San Francisco California 94118
www.calacademy.org
    The Academy of Sciences collection includes more than 350 native California baskets, many of them from the Fitzhugh-Lowe collection donated in 1916 and installed in a 170-foot-long gallery.

California Indian Heritage Center
2618 K Street
Sacramento, California 95816
www.parks.ca.gov/?page_id=22628
    The California State Indian Museum is transforming into a long-awaited California Indian Heritage Center, to be located along the Sacramento River in West Sacramento. The CIHC will be the home for one of the state's largest collections of American Indian artifacts, including over 3,000 California Indian baskets and priceless regalia.

Canadian Museum of Civilization
100 Laurier Street
Gatineau, Quebec K1A 0M8
www.civilization.ca
    The museum's comprehensive northeastern Indian ethnographic collection numbers more than 2,000 basketry specimens, including hundreds of birchbark examples as well as woodsplint and sweetgrass baskets and the tools (splint gauges, knives, and wooden molds) used in making them.

Carnegie Museum of Natural History
4400 Forbes Avenue
Pittsburgh, Pennsylvania 15213
www.carnegiemnh.org
    The museums's small collection of miscellaneous Indian baskets includes some special examples of Pomo feathered gift baskets and at least one Dat-so-la-lee basket.

Central Washington University Museum of Culture & Environment
400 East University Way
Ellensburg, Washington 98926
www.cwu.edu/~museum
    Plateau and Northwest Coast basketry is well represented in this university museum collection.

Chase Home Museum of Utah Folk Art
600 East 1100 South (Liberty Park)
Salt Lake City, Utah 84102
*www.arts.utah.gov/things_to_do/exhibitions/
        galleries/chase.html*
    The Native American gallery includes contemporary baskets and other crafts by members of Utah's resident tribes–Goshute, Navajo, Paiute, Shoshone and Ute–and by American Indians from elsewhere now residing in Utah.

Choctaw Museum
Mississippi Band of Choctaw Indians
101 Industrial Road
Choctaw, Mississippi 39350
www.choctaw.org/culture/museum.html
    The tribal museum exhibits examples of vintage and contemporary swamp cane basketry. Combining dyed and natural strips of cane, some basketmakers create traditional forms such as the egg basket with traditional patterns like the diamond design, while others experiment with color, pattern and shape.

Clarke Memorial Museum
240 E Street
Eureka, California 95501
www.clarkemuseum.org
    The museum's Native American Wing features the renowned Hover collection of Karuk baskets, along with local ceremonial regalia, stone tools and projectile points, as well as some Alaskan, Plains, and Southwestern Native American artifacts.

Clatsop County Heritage Museum
16th and Exchange Streets
P.O. Box 88
Astoria, Oregon 97103
www.cumtux.org/default.asp?pageid=8&deptid=1
    Among the local history exhibits in this historical society museum are finely crafted 19th-century Chinook and Clatsop Indian baskets.

Columbia Pacific Heritage Museum
115 Lake Street
P.O. Box 153
Ilwaco, Washington 98624
columbiapacificheritagemuseum.org
    The museum displays Chinookan basketry as part of its examination of the region's history.

Colville Confederated Tribes Museum
512 Mead Way
Coulee Dam, Washington 99116
www.spokaneoutdoors.com/colvmu.htm
    Artifacts, including basketry examples, are displayed in a museum established by the Colville Confederated Tribes (Moses/Columbia, Wenatchee, Okanogan, Entiat-Chelan, Methow, Nez Perce, Palus, Nespelem, Colville, San Poil, and Lake).

Del Norte County Historical Society Museum
577 H Street
Crescent City, California 95531
www.delnortehistory.org
    One room of the museum is devoted to artifacts of the local Tolowa and Yurok tribes, including many fine northern California baskets.

Denver Art Museum
100 West 14th Avenue Parkway
Denver, Colorado 80204
www.denverartmuseum.org
    The museum's North Building, levels 2 and 3, houses the American Indian art galleries. Exhibits draw from a collection of more than 18,000 art objects representing the heritage of all cultures and tribes across the United States and Canada, basketry included.

Eiteljorg Museum
500 West Washington Street
Indianapolis, Indiana 46204
www.eiteljorg.org
    Native American art and artifacts from all regions of North America are exhibited, with particular strengths in the Plains and Southwest, including some outstanding baskets.

Favell Museum
125 West Main Street
Klamath Falls, Oregon 97601
www.favellmuseum.org
    The Favell family collection of over 100,000 Native American artifacts and western art includes some very fine examples of Indian basketry, primarily from western tribes.

Fenimore Art Museum
New York State Historical Association
5798 State Highway 80 (Lake Road)
P.O. Box 800
Cooperstown, New York 13326
www.fenimoreartmuseum.org
    The famed Eugene and Clare Thaw Collection of American Indian art includes about 70 well-selected baskets, among them a fancy lidded basket by Elizabeth Hickox.

Field Museum
1400 South Lake Shore Drive
Chicago, Illinois 60605
fieldmuseum.org
The museum's premier collection of baskets, ceremonial objects, medicines, clothing, and games from the Western Apache was mostly gathered on the White Mountain Apache reservation early in the 20th century.

Fowler Museum of Cultural History
308 Charles E. Young Drive North
Los Angeles, California 90095
www.fowler.ucla.edu
The museum's North American cultural history collection includes 19th- and early 20th-century California Indian baskets collected among the Panamint Shoshone, Pomo, Shasta, Hupa, Yurok, and Karuk tribes.

Grace Hudson Museum
431 South Main
Ukiah, California 95482
www.gracehudsonmuseum.org
The art, history, and anthropology museum focuses on the lifeworks of artist Grace Hudson (1865-1937) and her ethnologist husband, Dr. John Hudson (1857-1936). The Hudsons spent decades painting and studying and collecting baskets among their Pomo neighbors. Sun House, their charming 1911 Craftsman redwood bungalow adjacent to the museum, is furnished with the Hudsons' eclectic possessions, including many of their prized Indian baskets.

Hampton University Museum
Hampton University
Hampton, Virginia 23668
museum.hamptonu.edu
Founded in 1868, the oldest African American museum in the United States and one of the oldest museums in the state of Virginia includes a selection of Native American objects (some baskets) collected with the intent of nurturing ethnic pride and developing cross-cultural understanding among students.

Heard Museum
2301 N. Central Avenue
Phoenix, Arizona 85004
www.heard.org
The primary collections focus on Southwestern American Indian cultural art and fine art. Historic and contemporary basketry of regional tribes are featured, including a fine collection of Akimel O'odham (Pima) miniatures. Native baskets from Alaska, the Northwest Coast, and California are also exhibited.

Hoopa Tribal Museum
Highway 96 Hoopa Shopping Center
P.O. Box 1348
Hoopa, California 95546
www.hoopa-nsn.gov/departments/museum.htm
Displays of Hupa, Yurok, and Karuk artifacts from northern California include basketry, ceremonial regalia, redwood dugout canoes, and tools and implements. Most of the artifacts are on loan to the museum by members of the local Indian community and are removed annually to be used in traditional tribal ceremonies.

Hudson Museum
The University of Maine
Collins Center for the Arts
Orono, Maine 04469
www.umaine.edu/hudsonmuseum
The Maine Indian collection houses more than 180 Maliseet, Micmac, Passamaquoddy, and Penobscot baskets from 1870 to present, plus dozens of basketmaking tools—basket molds, splint gauges, crooked knives, awls, and samples of basketmaking material including ash splints, Hong Kong cord, and sweetgrass braids.

Huhugam Ki Museum
10005 E. Osborn Road
Scottsdale, Arizona 85256
www.srpmic-nsn.gov/history_culture/museum.asp
The tribal museum of the Salt River Pima-Maricopa community contains examples of O'odham (Pima) and Piipaash (Maricopa) pottery.

Illinois State Museum
502 South Spring Street
Springfield, Illinois 62756
www.museum.state.il.us
The Illinois State Museum owns most of Thomas Condell's collection of Native American artifacts, including outstanding basket work from the mid-19th century to the early 1920s collected during Condell's time in the Southwest and Far West.

Institute for American Indian Studies
38 Curtis Road
P.O. Box 1260
Washington, Connecticut 06793
www.iaismuseum.org
Although the museum has a broad range of objects representing indigenous peoples of the entire western hemisphere, the collections and programming emphasize Eastern Woodlands Indians, including their basketry.

Iroquois Indian Museum
324 Caverns Road
P.O. Box 7
Howes Cave, New York 12092
www.iroquoismuseum.org
The museum recognizes the significant role Iroquoian peoples had in producing varied tourist items from the mid-1800s through the turn of the 20th century, including the well-known Akwesasne basket whimsies. Today the tourist market remains important to Iroquois craftspeople.

Johnson-Humrickhouse Museum
300 N. Whitewoman Street
Coshocton, Ohio 43812
www.jhmuseum.org
A representative collection of fine Indian baskets, most of which were collected around 1900 by Coshocton residents David and John Johnson, is one of several highlights at this museum.

Karshner Museum
309 Fourth Street NE
Puyallup, Washington 98372
www.karshnermuseum.org
The museum includes among its arts holdings a wide array of Northwest, Plains, and Southwest Indian artifacts, including a large basketry collection assembled by the Karshners in the 1930s and 1940s.

Langley Centennial Museum
9135 King Street
P.O. Box 800
Fort Langley, British Columbia
Canada V1M 2S2
www.langleymuseum.org
The Pearson collection of cedar-coiled baskets of the N'laka'pamux people (formerly Thompson River Salish) includes fine lidded baskets, serving trays, and loop-work baskets that are typical of the innovative forms that appealed to tourists in the late 19th and early 20th century.

Lauren Rogers Museum of Art
565 North Fifth Avenue
P.O. Box 1108
Laurel, Mississippi 39440
lrma.org
Displayed in a modern gallery within a gracious southern edifice, Catherine Marshall Gardiner's turn-of-the-20th-century collection of 500 North American Indian baskets has been expanded to include representative examples from all regions, including many fine baskets from the Southeast.

Leelanau Historical Society Museum
203 East Cedar Street

P.O. Box 246
Leland, Michigan 49654
www.leelanauhistory.org

The museum's Anishnabek Basket and Quillwork Room features a key collection of black ash baskets and quillwork on birch bark, primarily the work of Leelanau Peninsula's Odawa artists.

Lelooska Foundation Museum
165 Merwin Village Road
P.O. Box 526
Ariel, Washington 98603
www.lelooska.org

The Foundation's collection, mostly a bequest from Chief Lelooska (who died in 1996), includes Indian basketry from the Northwest, Midwest, Northeast, Southeast, Southwest, and the Arctic.

Logan Museum of Anthropology
Beloit College
700 College Street
Beloit, Wisconsin 53511
www.beloit.edu/logan

The museum collection includes baskets from Great Lakes tribes such as Ho-Chunk and Potawatomi, as well as Seneca and other Iroquoians and the Micmac and Penobscot peoples of the Northeast. Western baskets originated among the Klamath River tribes, Salish, Shasta, Pomo, Tulare, and Washoe. Southwestern basketry represents Hopi, Akimel O'odham, Tohono O'odham, and Apache. Additional baskets come from the Tlingit and Cherokee.

Lowe Art Museum
University of Miami
1301 Stanford Drive
Coral Gables, Florida 33124
www6.miami.edu/lowe

The Alfred I. Barton Collection of Southwest Indian Art, later enhanced through a 1956 exchange with the Denver Art Museum, includes ceramics, beadwork, sculpture, and basketry.

Makah Cultural and Research Museum
Makah Indian Reservation
P.O. Box 160
Neah Bay, Washington 98357
www.makah.com/mcrchome.html

Nearly 1,000 baskets, mats, and hats have come from the 300-500 year-old Ozette archaeological site at Neah Bay and another 150 from the nearby Hoko River site. Styles and materials match the work done by Neah Bay women in historic times and today.

Marion Steinbach Indian Basket Museum
130 West Lake Boulevard
P.O. Box 6141
Tahoe City, California 96145
www.northtahoemuseums.org

Marion Steinbach collected over 800 baskets from 85 tribes throughout California and western North America, ranging from large burden baskets to tiny miniatures. Steinbach's own technical notes and acquisition records supplement the collection, now preserved by the North Lake Tahoe Historical Society as part of their Gatekeeper's Museum.

Maryhill Museum of Art
35 Maryhill Drive
Goldendale, Washington 98620
www.maryhillmuseum.org

North America's varied indigenous arts and cultures are represented in this wide-ranging collection, with an emphasis on ancient Columbia River petroglyphs, fine baskets, beadwork, and other artifacts from Pacific Northwest tribes.

Mendocino County Museum
400 East Commercial Street
Willits, California 95490
www.mendocinomuseum.org

Exquisite Pomo and Yuki Indian baskets are displayed among other local art and artifacts representing northern California history and culture.

Michigan State University Museum
West Circle Drive
East Lansing, Michigan 48824
museum.msu.edu

The important Frank M. Covert/R. E. Olds collection of vintage Native American baskets has been supplemented with more recent basketry examples. The MSU Museum supports and documents contemporary Native North American basketry traditions through its "Carriers of Culture: Contemporary Native Basket Traditions" project.

Millicent Rogers Museum
1504 Millicent Rogers Road
P.O. Box 1210
Taos, New Mexico 87571
www.millicentrogers.org

The museum's comprehensive collection of textiles, pottery, jewelry, and baskets provides an overview to the Native American and Hispanic cultures of the Southwest.

Mills College Art Museum
5000 MacArthur Boulevard
Oakland, California 94613
mcam.mills.edu

Many of the 150 baskets in the collection represent the Yurok, Karuk, and Hupa tribes of northernmost California and exhibit a range of sizes, functions, weaves, and decoration. The collection also includes baskets of the Cahuilla, Pit River, Mono, Pomo, and other California groups.

Milwaukee Public Museum
800 West Wells Street
Milwaukee, Wisconsin 53233
www.mpm.edu

Well-represented in the museum's basketry collection are Great Lakes, Southwest, California, and Northwest Coast groups. Woodlands basketry and textiles are especially notable. Many Native American cradles and cradleboards are represented, including California basketry examples.

Mitchell Museum of the American Indian
3001 Central Street
Evanston, Illinois 60201
www.mitchellmuseum.org

The museum's exhibition galleries showcase the Native cultures of the Woodlands, Plains, Southwest, Northwest Coast, and Arctic regions of the United States and Canada. American Indian baskets selected from the collection are featured in permanent and temporary exhibits.

Montclair Art Museum
3 South Mountain Avenue
Montclair, New Jersey 07042
www.montclair-art.com

The Native American collection of more than 4,000 objects represents cultural achievements from seven major regions: Northwest Coast, California, Southwest, Plains, Woodlands, Southeast, and Arctic. It has particular strengths in basketry and jewelry.

Mt. Kearsarge Indian Museum
18 Highlawn Road
Warner, New Hampshire 03278
indianmuseum.org

A wide range of basketry is included within the exhibits surveying the primary Native North American culture areas. Northeastern woodsplint and sweetgrass basketry is particularly well-represented, as are examples of Southwestern and California basketweaving.

Museum of Anthropology
University of British Columbia
6393 N.W. Marine Drive
Vancouver, British Columbia

Canada V6T 1Z2
www.moa.ubc.ca

Of the approximately 5,400 objects representing British Columbia's First Nations, some 1,500 are baskets from Northwest Coast tribes. Best-represented are Nuu-cha-nulth, Coast Salish, Interior Salish, Kwakwaka`wakw, Haida, Tsimshian, Makah, and Tlingit.

Museum of Indian Arts and Culture
710 Camino Lejo
Santa Fe, New Mexico 87505
www.indianartsandculture.org

The museum preserves more than 75,000 objects collected from Southwest Native American communities by the Museum of New Mexico at the beginning of the 20th century, as well as materials acquired by the Laboratory of Anthropology since 1931. Included are representative examples of basketry made by tribes in the region.

Museum of Northern Arizona
3101 North Fort Valley Road
Flagstaff, Arizona 86001
www.musnaz.org

The Southwestern anthropology collection contains significant holdings of historic Hopi and Navajo textiles, baskets, katsina dolls, and jewelry, as well as smaller collections of Apache, Zuni, and Pai material. In addition, the prehistoric Puebloan cultures of the Colorado Plateau are represented by baskets, sandals, weapons, pottery, and many other types of artifacts.

Museum of Primitive Art and Culture
1058 Kingstown Road, Suite 5
Peace Dale, Rhode Island 02879
www.primitiveartmuseum.org

Located in the heart of a historic New England mill village, the museum's period gallery exhibits some especially fine North American Indian baskets from California, the Southwest, and Northeast among other regions.

Museum of the Americas
216 Fort Worth Highway
Weatherford, Texas 76086
www.museumoftheamericas.com

The museum celebrates the diverse heritage of Native peoples of all the Americas through a representative collection of late 19th and 20th century artifacts, crafts (including basketry), and folk art.

Museum of the Cherokee Indian
589 Tsali Boulevard
P.O. Box 1599
Cherokee, North Carolina 28719
www.cherokeemuseum.org

The museum records the history and culture of the Eastern Band of Cherokee Indians of North Carolina through archives and artifacts. Featured are many examples of vintage and contemporary single- and double-weave rivercane baskets, as well as examples made from white oak splint and honeysuckle vine.

National Museum of the American Indian
Smithsonian Institution
Fourth Street & Independence Avenue, S.W.
Washington, DC 20560
www.nmai.si.edu

Basketry is well-represented among the museum's 88,000 objects of North American ethnology: New England splint baskets, Southeastern baskets, baskets and cornhusk bags from the Plateau, Klikitat basketry, as well as upper Thompson and Fraser River examples, Ute and Paiute baskets from the Great Basin, and a comprehensive selection of Southwest basketry. The museum's California collections notably include Pomo baskets (some created by Mary and William Benson for the dealer Grace Nicholson), Yurok, Karuk, and Hupa baskets (including masterworks by Elizabeth Hickox), as well as southern California baskets of the Diegueño and Luiseño. A large collection of Aleutian baskets represent the Arctic region, and basketry made after 1930 enriches the Northwest Coast collection. These holdings constitute the U.S. National Museum basket collection so closely associated with curator of ethnology Otis T. Mason.

National Museum of the American Indian
George Gustav Heye Center
Alexander Hamilton U.S. Customs House
One Bowling Green
New York, New York 10004
nmai.si.edu/visit/newyork

The "Infinity of Nations" exhibit in this New York City satellite of the Smithsonian's American Indian Museum features treasures collected from Native societies throughout the western hemisphere. North American Indian basketry figures prominently, including 2,000-year-old duck decoys from Lovelock Cave, Nevada; basketry and birchbark containers of the eastern Woodlands; masterpieces by Dat-so-la-lee, Elizabeth Hickox, and Mary and William Benson; a rare early Chumash basket with designs copied from a Spanish colonial coin; and even a unique Karuk vest of basketry armor.

Natural History Museum of Utah
301 Wakara Way
Salt Lake City, Utah 84108
nhmu.utah.edu

Among the ethnographic collections are baskets made by the Goshute, Navajo, Paiute, Shoshone, and Ute, and neighboring tribes that interacted with them.

Nevada State Museum
600 North Carson Street
Carson City, Nevada 89701
museums.nevadaculture.org

Located in the historic Carson City branch of the former United States Mint, the museum's collections encompass Nevada's natural and cultural history. Included are outstanding baskets by Louisa Keyser (Dat-so-la-lee) and her contemporaries along with other Great Basin basketry.

Northwest Museum of Arts & Culture
2316 West First Avenue
Spokane, Washington 99201
www.northwestmuseum.org

The museum's American Indian collection represents culture groups from throughout the western hemisphere, most notably including an array of vintage and contemporary Plateau native material culture, including numerous twined bags and baskets.

Oakland Museum of California
1000 Oak Street
Oakland, California 94607
http://museumca.org

The Native Californian collection encompasses about 2,500 baskets from more than 50 tribal groups in nearly all geographic and cultural regions of the state. Noteworthy are some amazing feathered baskets from the Pomo and Wintu and fine basket hats from the Hupa and Karuk. Charles Wilcomb began the collection in the early 20th century with a particular focus on the tribes of the Central Valley and northwest and northeast sections of the state.

Oregon Historical Society
1200 Southwest Park Avenue
Portland, Oregon 97205
www.ohs.org

The museum collections and exhibits display the broad range of Native peoples' artistry, both ancient and contemporary. The Nez Perce, Yakama, Walla Walla, and Umatilla tribes all made flat twined bags and round twined bags, while the Klikitat, Yakama, and Nez Perce made coiled baskets decorated with imbrication.

Oregon State Museum of Anthropology
University of Oregon Museum of Natural and Cultural History
1680 East 15th Avenue
Eugene, Oregon 97403
natural-history.uoregon.edu

An extensive collection of twined basketry from the northern Great Basin contains archaeological specimens dating as far back as 8,000 years, as well as twined basketry caps from Hupa, Karuk, Tolowa, Wiyot, Yurok, Shasta, and Klamath peoples of southwest Oregon and northwest California. It also houses more than 200 Klamath baskets in a wide range of forms and designs, flat twined Columbia Plateau bags made by Nez Perce, Yakama, and Umatilla peoples, and woven "sally bags" made by the Wasco and Wishxam and their neighbors.

Peabody Essex Museum
East India Square
161 Essex Street
Salem, Massachusetts 01970
www.pem.org
    Begun in 1799 by Salem sea captains as the East India Marine Society, the museum's current historical and contemporary Native American art collection covers a wide range of time periods, cultures, and object categories. Some rare Indian baskets date to the first half of the 19th century.

Peabody Museum of Archaeology and Ethnology
Harvard University
11 Divinity Avenue
Cambridge, Massachusetts 02138
www.peabody.harvard.edu
    One of the nation's oldest and largest museums, with some 6 million ethnographic items, the Peabody holds approximately 4,000 Native American baskets representing every cultural region.

Penobscot Nation Museum
12 Downstreet Street
Indian Island, Maine 04468
www.penobscotnation.org/museum/Index.htm
    This small museum provides a repository for contemporary Wabanaki art, such as paintings, woodcarvings, and basketry.

Philbrook Museum of Art
2727 South Rockford Road
P.O. Box 52510
Tulsa, Oklahoma 74152
philbrook.org
    Over 1,100 basketry examples within the museum's Native American art holdings represent many tribes.

Phoebe A. Hearst Museum of Anthropology
103 Kroeber Hall
Bancroft Way at College Avenue
University of California
Berkeley, California 94720
hearstmuseum.berkeley.edu
    Numbering more than 9,000 examples, outstanding craft work representing each of California's many basketmaking tribes dominates the Hearst Museum's comprehensive research inventory of more than 12,000 Native North American baskets. Included is the Blair Memorial Collection of 2,000 baskets representing the work of Cahuilla, Chemehuevi, Chumash, Diegueño (Kumeyaay), Hupa, Maidu, Western Mono, Paiute, Pomo, Washoe, and Yokuts weavers.

Pomona Museum of Art
333 N. College Avenue
Claremont, California 91711
www.pomona.edu/museum
    Several hundred baskets, primarily from California and the Southwest, are included within the museum's Native American collection.

Riverside Metropolitan Museum
3580 Mission Inn Avenue
Riverside, California 92501
www.riversideca.gov/museum
    Founded in 1924 as the Cornelius Earle Rumsey Indian Museum, the greatly expanded Riverside Metropolitan Museum houses a nationally-recognized collection of Native American basketry, most of it collected between 1890 and 1910 among southern California's tribes.

Rochester Museum & Science Center
657 East Avenue
Rochester, New York 14607
www.rmsc.org
    The museum collection has some 100 Iroquois/Seneca splint baskets.

Royal British Columbia Museum
675 Belleville Street
Victoria, British Columbia
Canada V8W 9W2
www.royalbcmuseum.bc.ca
    The museum collection holds nearly 2,000 First Nations basketry items, primarily Northwest Coast cedar and spruce root examples.

San Diego Museum of Man
1350 El Prado, Balboa Park
San Diego, California 92101
www.museumofman.org
    The museum's Native American holdings contain thousands of basketry examples from the Aleut, Interior Athabascan, Northwest Coast, and California tribes. The southern California ethnographic collection includes one of the major basketry assemblages from this area of the country, with many carefully documented specimens. There are also prehistoric baskets from dry caves. Klamath/Modoc, Yokuts, Panamint, Chemehuevi, and Pomo baskets (especially feathered and miniature baskets) are also well-represented.

Sanger Depot Museum
1770 7th Street
Sanger, California 93657
www.sangerdepotmuseum.com
    Sanger pharmacist Oscar Brehler bought basketry from the local Yokuts Indians who lived in the foothills around Squaw Valley, Wonder Valley, and Dunlap, California. The collection of cradle baskets, bottleneck baskets, burden baskets, coiled plaques, eating and cooking baskets, and rattlesnake baskets is reputedly one of the finest in the U.S.

Santa Barbara Museum of Natural History
2559 Puesta del Sol
Santa Barbara, California 93105
www.sbnature.org
    Ethnographic collections, representing tribal groups throughout western North America, include basketry, textiles, pottery, woodcarvings, and other materials used for research and exhibition. The anthropology department, a foremost center for Chumash studies, maintains a major collection of rare pre-Gold Rush Chumash basketry.

Santa Rosa Junior College Museum
Bussman Hall
1501 Mendocino Avenue
Santa Rosa, California 95401
www.santarosa.edu/museum
    Pomo, Klamath River, and southern California basketry is well-represented. The museum features the Elsie Allen Collection of documented Pomo baskets, many of them woven by the master basketmaker and teacher Elsie Allen (1899-1990) or her relatives.

Schingoethe Center for Native American Cultures
Aurora University
347 South Gladstone Avenue
Aurora, Illinois 60506
www.aurora.edu/museum/index.html#axzz1pI7PnspF
    The permanent collections include a representative sample of Native basketry from all regions of North America.

Sharlot Hall Museum
415 West Gurley Street
Prescott, Arizona 86301
www.sharlot.org
    More than 400 older Native American baskets, including an 800-year-old Anasazi basket in excellent condition, represent some 25 Arizona tribes. Local Yavapai-Prescott Indian weavers produced some of the more spectacular examples on display.

Sheldon Jackson Museum
104 College Drive
Sitka, Alaska 99835

Dr. Sheldon Jackson founded Protestant missions and schools, established Alaska's public school system, and introduced domestic reindeer in the late 1800s. He traveled to many parts of Alaska, as well as the coast of Siberia, gathering most of the artifacts (including baskets) now preserved in the museum he established in 1888.

Sierra Mono Museum

33103 Road 228

North Fork, California 93643

www.sierramonomuseum.org

Begun in 1966, the Sierra Mono Museum is one of the first to be solely owned and operated by a Native American organization. Though their Native American basket collection holds baskets from many tribes, the primary focus is on Mono cradle baskets *(huup)* made from sourberry shoots, split winter redbud, split sedge roots, chaparral (buckbrush) shoots, yarn, red earth pigments, and leather. Cradle baskets are still used for a newborn up to two years old.

Siletz Tribal Cultural Center

Siletz Indian Reservation

Highway 229

Siletz, Oregon 97380

(no current website)

Confederated Tribes of Siletz Indians is developing a cultural center for storage and eventual display of its collections, consisting mostly of the Coastal Indian artifacts from the Horner Museum, which closed in 1995. A sizable collection of local Indian baskets and distinctive women's basket caps is included.

Simon Fraser University Museum of Archaeology and Ethnology

8888 University Drive

Burnaby, British Columbia

Canada V5A 1S6

www.sfu.ca/archaeology-old/museum

Canadian First Nations basketry from British Columbia is one of the specializations of this museum.

Stark Museum of Art

712 Green Avenue

Orange, Texas 77630

www.starkmuseum.org

This varied collection of Western and decorative arts includes Great Plains, Southwest, Eastern Woodlands, and Northwest Coast Indian objects—among their baskets.

Suquamish Museum

Suquamish Way and Division Street

P.O. Box 498

Suquamish, Washington 98392

www.suquamish.org/Museum.aspx

Opened at a new facility in 2012, the museum exhibits feature the collection of Martha George, Suquamish basket collector and clam basket maker.

Tamástslikt Cultural Institute

47106 Wildhorse Boulevard

Pendleton, Oregon 97801

www.tcimuseum.com

Exhibits celebrate the traditions of the Cayuse, Umatilla, and Walla Walla tribes, including some of their distinctive basketry bags and hats.

Texas Memorial Museum

2400 Trinity Street Stop D1500

Austin, Texas 78712

www.utexas.edu/tmm/visit-tmm

The Texas Memorial Museum, located on The University of Texas campus, is the exhibit hall for the Texas Natural Science Center. The Paul T. Seashore Indian basket collection was acquired by museum associate director Glen Evans before 1950.

Twin Rocks Trading Post Museum

Twin Rocks Trading Post

913 East Navajo Twins Drive

P.O. Box 330

Bluff, Utah 84512

www.twinrocks.com/museum

Located inside the active trading post that figures prominently in the revival of Navajo basketweaving since the 1970s, the museum displays prime examples of modern basket work by members of the Bitsinnie, Black, Johnson, and other prominent basketmaking families.

University of Alaska Museum of the North

907 Yukon Drive

P.O. Box 756960

Fairbanks, Alaska 99775

www.uaf.edu/museum

The ethnology collection includes over 12,000 objects made and used by Alaska Natives (Inupiaq and Yup'ik Eskimos, Northwest Coast and Athabascan Indians, and Aleuts) from the 1800s to the present. Exceptional examples of basketry, beadwork, ivory carvings, masks, dolls, and gear used in subsistence activities highlight the collection.

University of Missouri Museum of Anthropology

100 Swallow Hall

University of Missouri-Columbia

Columbia, Missouri 65211

anthromuseum.missouri.edu

The primary basketry holdings in this collection represent tribes of the Eastern Woodlands (Iroquois, Ojibwa, Potawatomi, Creek, Cherokee), Arctic (Aleut), Northwest Coast (Tlingit, Kwakiutl), and Southwest (Pima, Papago, Chemehuevi, Apache).

University of Pennsylvania Museum of Archaeology and Anthropology

3260 South Street

Philadelphia, PA 19104

www.penn.museum

The world-class university museum, founded in 1887, boasts an extraordinary number of fine Chitimacha double-weave rivercane baskets and also many exceptional examples of northern and southern California and Great Basin Indian basketry, as well as representative examples from elsewhere.

Utah State University Museum of Anthropology

0730 Old Main Hill

Logan, Utah 84322

anthromuseum.usu.edu

Examples of American Indian baskets from the West Coast and Great Basin are included among the wide-ranging collections of this university museum.

Warm Springs Museum

2189 Highway 26

P.O. Box 909

Warm Springs, Oregon 97761

www.museumatwarmsprings.org

Run by the Confederated Tribes of Warm Springs Reservation, the museum contains family heirlooms and trade items from other tribes, including numerous twined baskets and cornhusk bags.

Illustration Credits

The authors prepared the photographs in this book except for those credited below. We gratefully acknowledge the following individuals and institutions for permission to use their provided photographs. Historic images and ephemera included in the illustrations are held in private collections.

Courtesy of the Connecticut Historical Society: Fig. 6;

Courtesy of Charles and Blanche Derby: GB-25, CA-86, CA-87, CA-88, NW-33, NE-141;

Courtesy of Leah Dittmer and Arte Amazonia, *www.arte-amazonia.com*: CC-68;

Courtesy of Merrill Domas: SE-4;

Courtesy of Fruitlands Museum, Harvard, MA, Michael Volmar, curator: SW-28, SW-94, SW-95, SW-96, SW-143, CA-16, CA-39, CA-44;

Courtesy of Fred and Susan Ingham: NW-37;

Courtesy of Colleen James: SW-88, SW-100, SW-101, SW-139, SW-140, SW-141;

Courtesy of Christina Kreps: SA-25;

Courtesy of Natalie Linn: Fig. 109, SW-97, SW-144, GB-21, GB-27, GB-36, CA-20, CA-23, CA-42, CA-61, CA-68, CA-95, PT-3, PT-9, PT-10, PT-11, PT-12, PT-13, PT-14, PT-15, PT-16, PT-17, PT-19, PT-21, PT-36, NW-3, NW-4, NW-30, NW-31, AR-7;

Courtesy of Robert Matterson III: CC-28;

Courtesy of the Minnesota Historical Society: PN-5;

Courtesy of Gay and Kent Morris: Fig.1, Fig. 2, Fig. 105, Fig. 113, Fig. 114, Fig. 115, SW-66, SW-120, SW-129, SW-130, GB-26, GB-30, PT-29, SE-7, SE-16;

Courtesy of Mt. Kearsarge Indian Museum, Warner, NH, Lynn Clark, director, and Nancy Jo Chabot, curator: SW-102, CA-78, NW-35, NE-57, NE-61, NE-122, NE-142, CC-23;

Courtesy of the Museum of Primitive Art and Culture, Peace Dale, RI (WAT/SPT photographs): Fig. 102, SW-11, SW-21, SW-41, SW-46, SW-59, SW-92, SW-115, SW-116, SW-117, GB-5, GB-9, CA-6, CA-8, CA-15, CA-19, CA-21, CA-24, CA-31, CA-32, CA-33, CA-34, CA-64, CA-70, CA-71, CA-73, CA-74, CA-75, CA-82, CA-83, CA-93, PT-4, PT-26, PT-32, PT-33, NW-7, NW-8, NW-36, NW-38, AR-34, SA-26, PN-3, SE-15, NE-9, NE-10, NE-17, NE-18, NE-19, NE-22, NE-26, NE-28;

Courtesy of Old Territorial Shop, Scottsdale, AZ, and Szabo Photography: Fig. 111, GB-28;

Courtesy of the Pennsylvania Historical and Museum Commission, from *Susquehanna's Indians*, by Barry C. Kent, used with permission: Fig. 5;

Courtesy of Schlesinger Library, Radcliffe Institute, Harvard University: Fig. 65;

Courtesy of Skinner, Inc. *www.skinnerinc.com*: Fig. 60, SW-20, GB-19, GB-20, GB-35, GB-37, CA-25, CA-35, CA-37, CA-38, CA-40, CA-41, CA-53, CA-55, CA-57, CA-58, CA-59, CA-65, CA-81, PT-8, NW-6, NW-22, NW-23, NW-32, NW-34, AR-5, AR-6, AR-7, AR-17.

Historic Images:

Edward S. Curtis: Title page, Fig. 10, Fig. 58, CA-9, CA-43, PT-2, NW-21, PN-2;

Otis T. Mason: Fig. 18, Fig. 89, CA-54, AR-2;

Karl Moon: SW-9;

Museum of the American Indian, Heye Foundation, *Indian Notes*: Fig. 23;

Original historic images by anonymous photographers in private collections: Dedication left, Fig. 59, Fig. 63, Fig. 70, Fig. 71, Fig. 72, SW-58, SW-98, CA-2, SE-2, NE-2, CC-24.

Historical postcards in private collections: Fig. 1, Fig. 35, Fig. 36, Fig. 47, Fig. 48, Fig. 50, Fig. 51, Fig. 52, Fig. 53, Fig. 73, Fig. 74, Fig. 90, Fig. 92, Fig. 94, Fig. 119, SW-2, SW-5, SW-30, SW-142, GB-2, CA-22, CA-62, NW-2.

Other historical materials from private collections: Fig. 15, Fig. 17, Fig. 20, Fig. 29, Fig. 44, Fig. 45, Fig. 46, Fig. 54, Fig. 61, Fig. 62, Fig. 66, Fig. 67, Fig. 68, Fig. 69, Fig. 75, Fig. 76, Fig. 78, Fig. 79, Fig. 80, Fig. 81, Fig. 106, Fig. 107, Fig. 108, GB-4, CA-69, PN-4, NE-52, NE-53, CC-15.

Selected Bibliography and Further Reading

GENERAL

Adovasio, James M. 2010. *Basketry Technology: A Guide to Identification and Analysis.* Revised and expanded from 1977 edition. Chicago, IL: Aldine Publishing.

American Indian Art Magazine. Special basketry issues: 4(4), Autumn 1979; 24(3), Summer 1999. Scottsdale, AZ.

American Indian Basketry Magazine. 1979-1985. Whole issues 1-20 [vol. 1(1)–vol. 5(4)]. Portland, OR: John M. Gogol.

The Basket: The Journal of the Basket Fraternity or Lovers of Indian Baskets and Other Good Things. 1903-1904. Vol. 1(1)–vol. 2(4). Pasadena, CA: The Basket Fraternity (George Wharton James).

Bernstein, Bruce. 2003. *The Language of Native American Baskets from the Weavers' View.* Washington, DC: National Museum of the American Indian, Smithsonian Institution.

Chancey, Jill R. (ed.). 2005. *By Native Hands: Woven Treasures from the Lauren Rogers Museum of Art.* Laurel, MS: Lauren Rogers Museum of Art.

Fang, Madeleine W., and Marilyn R. Binder (compilers). 1990. *A Photographic Guide to the Ethnographic North American Indian Basket Collection, Peabody Museum of Archaeology and Ethnology.* Cambridge, MA: Peabody Museum of Archaeology and Ethnology, Harvard University.

Finger, Judith W. 2012. "Woven Identities: The Aesthetics of Native American Basketry." *American Indian Art Magazine* 37(4):66-77.

Gogol, John M. 1985. "1900-1910, The Golden Decade of Collecting Indian Basketry." *American Indian Basketry Magazine* 5(1):12-29.

Haskell, Susan H., and Jessica Wilson (compilers). 2005. *A Photographic Guide to the Ethnographic North American Indian Basket Collection,* vol. 2. Cambridge, MA: Peabody Museum Press.

Hedges, Ken. 1997. *Fibers & Forms: Native American Basketry of the West.* San Diego, CA: San Diego Museum of Man.

James, George Wharton. 1901. *Indian Basketry.* Pasadena, CA: Privately printed.

———. 1903. *Indian Baskets and How to Make Indian and Other Baskets.* Third edition. New York: Henry Malkan.

———. 1904. *How to Make Indian and Other Baskets.* Second edition. Pasadena, CA: George Wharton James.

———. 1916. *Practical Basket Making.* Sixth edition. Cambridge, MA: J. L. Hammett.

———. 1972. *Indian Basketry.* Reprint of 1909 fourth edition. New York, NY: Dover Publications.

Lamb, Frank W. 1972. *Indian Baskets of North America.* N.p.: Rubidoux Publishing.

Mason, Otis Tufton. 1901. "The Technic of Aboriginal American Basketry." Separate reprint from *American Anthropologist* (n.s.), 3(1):109-128. Washington, DC.

———.1904. "Aboriginal American Basketry: Studies in a Textile Art without Machinery." *Report of the U.S. National Museum under the Direction of the Smithsonian Institution, for the Year Ending June 30, 1902,* pp. 171-548. Washington, DC.

———. 1984. *Aboriginal American Basketry: Studies in a Textile Art without Machinery.* Reprint of 1904 edition. Glorieta, NM: Rio Grande Press.

Miles, Charles, and Pierre Bovis. 1969. *American Indian and Eskimo Basketry: A Key to Identification.* San Francisco, CA: Pierre Bovis.

Mowat, Linda, Howard Morphy, and Penny Dransart (eds.). 1992. *Basketmakers: Meaning and Form in Native American Baskets.* Hertford, England: Pitt Rivers Museum.

Odegaard, Nancy. 1999. "Basketry: An Introduction to Materials, Techniques and Conservation." *American Indian Art Magazine* 24(3):36-43.

Ogden, Sherelyn. 2004. *Caring for American Indian Objects: A Practical and Cultural Guide.* St. Paul: Minnesota Historical Society.

Porter, Frank W. III (ed.). 1984. *The Art of Native American Basketry: A Living Legacy.* Westport, CT: Greenwood Press.

———. (compiler). 1988. *Native American Basketry: An Annotated Bibliography.* Westport, CT: Greenwood Press.

Schaaf, Gregory. 2006. *American Indian Baskets I: 1,500 Artist Biographies.* Santa Fe, NM: CIAC Press.

Sentance, Bryan. 2001. *Art of the Basket: Traditional Basketry from around the World.* London: Thames & Hudson.

Shaw, Robert. 2000. *American Baskets.* New York: Clarkson Potter.

Turnbaugh, Sarah Peabody. 1992. *Native American Basketry.* Cambridge, MA: Hurst Gallery.

Turnbaugh, Sarah Peabody, and William A. Turnbaugh. 2004. *Indian Baskets.* Revised 1986 edition. West Chester, PA: Schiffer Publishing.

Turnbaugh, William A., and Sarah Peabody Turnbaugh. 1999. *Basket Tales of the Grandmothers: American Indian Baskets in Myth and Legend.* Peace Dale, RI: Thornbrook Publishing.

Wyckoff, Lydia L. (ed.). 2001. *Woven Worlds: Basketry from the Clark Field Collection at the Philbrook Museum of Art.* Tulsa, OK: The Philbrook Museum of Art.

SOUTHWEST

Arizona Highways. 1975. American Indian basketry collector issue, 61(7).

Bell, Jan. 1988. "Tohono O'odham Wire Baskets." *American Indian Art Magazine* 13(4):48-57.

Breazeale, J. F. 1923. *The Pima and His Basket.* Tucson, AZ: Arizona Archaeological and Historical Society.

Cain, H. Thomas. 1962. *Pima Indian Basketry.* Phoenix, AZ: The Heard Museum of Anthropology and Primitive Arts.

Dalrymple, Larry. 2000. *Indian Basketmakers of the Southwest.* Santa Fe, NM: Museum of New Mexico Press.

Dedera, Don. 1973. "Basket Making in Arizona." *Arizona Highways* 49(6):32-46.

DeWald, Terry. 1979. *The Papago Indians and Their Basketry.* Tucson, AZ: author.

Dittemore, Diane. 1986. "Pima Indian Beaded Baskets in the Arizona State Museum." *American Indian Art Magazine* 12(1):46-53.

Dittemore, Diane, and Cathy Notarnicola. 1999. "Anonymous Was a Weaver: In Search of Turn-of-the-Century Western Apache/Yavapai Basketry Artists." *American Indian Art Magazine* 24(3):54-65.

Dittemore, Diane, and Nancy Odegaard. 1998. "Eccentric Marks on Western Apache Coiled Basketry." *American Indian Art Magazine* 23(2):34-43.

Edison, Carol A. (ed.). 1996. *Willow Stories: Utah Navajo Baskets.* Salt

Lake City, UT: Utah Arts Council.

Farrer, Claire. 1992. "Those Who Lived Before." In, Linda Mowat, et al. (eds.), *Basketmakers: Meaning and Form in Native American Baskets*, pp. 77-90. Hertford, England: Pitt Rivers Museum.

Finger, Judith W., and Andrew D. Finger. 2006. *Circles of Life: Katsina Imagery on Hopi Wicker Basketry*. Ukiah, CA: Grace Hudson Museum & Sun House.

Herold, Joyce. 1979. "Havasupai Basketry: Theme and Variation." *American Indian Art Magazine* 4(4):42-53.

———. 1984. "Basket Weaver Individualists in the Southwest Today." *American Indian Art Magazine* 9(2):46-53.

———. 1999. "Showing the Sun: Mythological-Ceremonial Foundation of Jicarilla Apache Basketry." *American Indian Art Magazine* 24(3):66-79.

———. 2005. "Baskets of the Southwest and Great Basin." In, Jill R. Chancey (ed.), *By Native Hands: Woven Treasures from the Lauren Rogers Museum of Art*, pp. 76-107. Laurel, MS: Lauren Rogers Museum of Art.

Kissell, Mary Lois. 1972. *Basketry of the Papago and Pima Indians*. Reprint of 1916 edition. Glorieta, NM: The Rio Grande Press.

Mauldin, Barbara. 1984. *Traditions in Transition: Contemporary Basket Weaving of the Southwestern Indians*. Santa Fe, NM: Museum of New Mexico Press.

McGreevy, Susan Brown. 1989. "What Makes Sally Weave? Survival and Innovation in Navajo Basketry Trays." *American Indian Art Magazine* 14(3):38-45.

———. 1999. "Embellishing the Spirit: Design Development in Navajo Baskets." *American Indian Art Magazine* 24(3):44-53.

———. 2001. *Indian Basketry Artists of the Southwest*. Santa Fe, NM: School of American Research Press.

McGreevy, Susan Brown, and Andrew Hunter Whiteford. 1985. "Translating Tradition: Basketry Arts of the San Juan Paiutes." *American Indian Art Magazine* 11(1):30-37.

———. 1985. *Translating Tradition: Basketry Arts of the San Juan Paiutes*. Santa Fe, NM: Wheelwright Museum of the American Indian.

McGregor, Roberta. 1992. "Prehistoric Basketry of the Lower Pecos, Texas." *Monographs in World Archaeology* 6. Madison, WI: Prehistory Press.

McKee, Barbara, Edward McKee, and Joyce Herold. 1975. *Havasupai Baskets and Their Makers, 1930-1940*. Flagstaff, AZ: Northland Press.

Miller, Sheryl F. 1989. "Hopi Basketry: Traditional Social Currency and Contemporary Source of Cash." *American Indian Art Magazine* 15(1):62-71.

———. 1999. "Katsina Designs on Hopi Baskets." *American Indian Art Magazine* 25(1):56-65.

Morris, Earl H., and Robert E. Burgh. 1941. "Anasazi Basketry: Basketmaker II through Pueblo III." *Carnegie Institution of Washington, Publications in Anthropology and Archaeology* 533. Washington, DC: Carnegie Institution.

Museum of Northern Arizona. 1982. "The Basket Weavers: Artisans of the Southwest." *Plateau* 53(4):1-32.

Newman, Sandra Corrie. 1974. *Indian Basket Weaving: How to Weave Pomo, Yurok, Pima and Navajo Baskets*. Flagstaff, AZ: Northland Publishing.

Rhodes, Robert W. 2007. *Hopi Wicker Plaques and Baskets*. Atglen, PA: Schiffer Publishing.

Roberts, Helen H. 1972. *Basketry of the San Carlos Apache Indians*. Reprint of 1929 edition. Glorieta, NM: The Rio Grande Press.

Robinson, Bert. 1991. *The Basket Weavers of Arizona*. Reprint of 1954 edition. Albuquerque, NM: University of New Mexico Press.

Simpson, Georgiana Kennedy. 2003. *Navajo Ceremonial Baskets*. Summertown, TN: Native Voices.

Tack, Eric David. 2000. "Reweaving Tradition: New Trends in Contemporary Southwestern Basketry." *Indian Peoples* 9(6):22-27.

Tanner, Clara Lee. 1976. *Prehistoric Southwestern Craft Arts* (Chapter 2, "Baskets"). Tucson, AZ: The University of Arizona Press.

———. 1982. *Apache Indian Baskets*. Tucson, AZ: The University of Arizona Press.

———. 1983. *Indian Baskets of the Southwest*. Tucson, AZ: The University of Arizona Press.

———. 1990. "Southwestern Indian Basketry." In, Frank W. Porter III (ed.), *The Art of Native American Basketry: A Living Legacy*, pp. 187-211. Westport, CT: Greenwood Press.

Teiwes, Helga. 1996. *Hopi Basket Weaving*. Tucson, AZ: The University of Arizona Press.

Whiteford, Andrew Hunter. 1988. *Southwestern Indian Baskets: Their History and Their Makers*. Santa Fe, NM: School of American Research Press.

Whiteford, Andrew Hunter, and Kate McGraw. 1994. "A Guide to Southwest Indian Baskets." *Indian Art Market*, Summer, pp. 33-60. Santa Fe, NM.

Wyckoff, Lydia L. 2001. "Southwest." In, Lydia L. Wyckoff (ed.), *Woven Worlds: Basketry from the Clark Field Collection at the Philbrook Museum of Art*, pp. 31-49. Tulsa, OK: The Philbrook Museum of Art.

VIDEO

From the Inside Out: Navajo Basketry. 2003. Provo, UT: Brigham Young University. (27 min.)

GREAT BASIN

Adovasio, James M. 1986. "Prehistoric Basketry." In, Warren L. D'Azevado (ed.), *Handbook of North American Indians*, vol. 11, Great Basin, pp. 194-205. Washington, DC: Smithsonian Institution.

Bernstein, Bruce. 1979. "Panamint Shoshone Coiled Basketry: A Definition of Style." *American Indian Art Magazine* 4(4):68-74.

———. 1985. "Panamint-Shoshone Basketry, 1890-1960: The Role of Basket Materials in the Development of a New Style." *American Indian Basketry Magazine* 5(3):4-11, 29.

Cohodas, Marvin. 1976. "Dat So La Lee's Basketry Designs." *American Indian Art Magazine* 1(4):22-31.

———. 1979. *Degikup: Washoe Fancy Basketry, 1895-1935*. Vancouver, BC: The Fine Arts Gallery of the University of British Columbia.

———. 1979. "Lena Frank Dick: An Outstanding Washoe Basket Weaver." *American Indian Art Magazine* 4(4):32-41, 90.

———. 1983. "Washoe Basketry." *American Indian Basketry Magazine* 3(4):4-30.

———. 1984. "The Breitholle Collection of Washoe Basketry." *American Indian Art Magazine* 9(4):38-49.

———. 1990. "Washoe Basketweaving: A Historical Outline." In, Frank W. Porter III (ed.), *The Art of Native American Basketry: A Living Legacy*, pp. 153-186. Westport, CT: Greenwood Press.

Collings, Jerold L. 1979. "Profile of a Chemehuevi Weaver." *American Indian Art Magazine* 4(4):60-67.

Dalrymple, Larry. 2000. *Indian Basketmakers of California and the Great Basin*. Santa Fe, NM: Museum of New Mexico Press.

———. 2008. "Southern Paiute Baskets Collected by Isabel T. Kelly." *American Indian Art Magazine* 33(4):46-55, 92.

Fowler, Catherine S., and Lawrence E. Dawson. 1986. "Ethnographic Basketry." In, Warren L. D'Azevado (ed.), *Handbook of North American Indians*, vol. 11, Great Basin, pp. 705-737. Washington, DC: Smithsonian Institution.

Fowler, Catherine S., and Norman R. DeLorme. 2004. "Bound by Tradition: Contemporary Northern Paiute/Washoe Beaded Baskets." *American Indian Art Magazine* 29(2):32-39.

Fowler, Catherine S., and Judith W. Finger. 2011. "Southern Paiute Fine

Coiled Baskets of Southern Nevada: History and Style." *American Indian Art Magazine* 37(1):44-53.

Fulkerson, Mary Lee. 1995. *Weavers of Tradition and Beauty: Basketmakers of the Great Basin.* Reno, NV: University of Nevada Press.

Givens, Stefanie A., and Sara Larson. 2005. *Woven Legacy: A Collection of Dat-so-la-lee Works, 1900-1921.* Tahoe City, CA: Gatekeeper's Museum.

Herold, Joyce. 2005. "Baskets of the Southwest and Great Basin." In, Jill R. Chancey (ed.), *By Native Hands: Woven Treasures from the Lauren Rogers Museum of Art*, pp. 76-107. Laurel, MS: Lauren Rogers Museum of Art.

Kania, John J. 2006. "Chemehuevi Coiled Baskets: Origins and Stylistic Trends." *American Indian Art Magazine* 31(2):66-73, 98.

———. 2007. "Bread for Baskets: The Ammann Collection of Chemehuevi Baskets." *American Indian Art Magazine* 33(1):42-51.

Sennett-Walker, Beth. 1985. "The Panamint Basketry of Scotty's Castle." *American Indian Basketry Magazine* 5(3):12-17.

Slater, Eva. 2000. *Panamint Shoshone Basketry.* Morongo Valley, CA: Sagebrush Press.

Tisdale, Shelby J. 2001. "Intermontane West." In, Lydia L. Wyckoff (ed.), *Woven Worlds: Basketry from the Clark Field Collection at the Philbrook Museum of Art*, pp. 79-105. Tulsa, OK: The Philbrook Museum of Art.

Washoe Tribe of Nevada and California. 1980. *Plain and Fancy Washoe Weavers and Their Baskets.* Gardnerville, NV: Washoe Tribe of Nevada and California.

CALIFORNIA

Abel-Vidor, Suzanne, Dot Brovarney, and Susan Billy. 1996. *Remember Your Relations: The Elsie Allen Baskets, Family and Friends.* Berkeley, CA: Heyday Books.

Allen, Elsie. 1972. *Pomo Basketmaking: A Supreme Art for the Weaver.* Happy Camp, CA: Naturegraph Publishers.

Ames, Tim. 2004. "The Jump Dance Basket of Northwestern California." *American Indian Art Magazine* 29(3):46-53.

Barrett, Samuel A. 1976. *Pomo Indian Basketry*. Reprint of 1908 edition. Enumclaw, WA: MacRae Publications.

Bates, Craig D. 1979. "Miwok-Paiute Basketry 1920-1929: Genesis of an Art Form." *American Indian Art Magazine* 4(4):54-59.

———. 1982. "Coiled Basketry of the Sierra Miwok: A Study of Regional Variation." *San Diego Museum Papers* 15. San Diego, CA.

———. 1982. "Yosemite Miwok/Paiute Basketry: A Study in Cultural Change." *American Indian Basketry Magazine* 2(4):4-22.

———. 1984. "Yosemite Miwok Basketry: The Late 19th Century." *American Indian Basketry Magazine* 4(1):4-14.

Bates, Craig D., and Martha J. Lee. 1990. *Tradition and Innovation: A Basket History of the Indians of the Yosemite-Mono Lake Area.* Yosemite National Park, CA: Yosemite Association.

———. 1993. "Chukchansi Yokuts and Southern Miwok Weavers of Yosemite National Park." *American Indian Art Magazine* 18(3):44-51.

Bernstein, Bruce. 1990. "Weaver's Talk, the Language of Baskets and the Meaning of Aesthetic Judgments: The Patwin of Central California." In, Frank W. Porter III (ed.), *The Art of Native American Basketry: A Living Legacy*, pp. 213-225. Westport, CT: Greenwood Press.

Bibby, Brian. 1996. *The Fine Art of California Indian Basketry.* Sacramento, CA: Crocker Art Museum.

———. 2004. *Precious Cargo: California Indian Cradle Baskets and Childbirth Traditions.* Berkeley, CA: Heyday Books.

Cohodas, Marvin. 1997. *Basket Weavers for the California Curio Trade: Elizabeth and Louise Hickox.* Tucson, AZ: The University of Arizona Press.

Collings, Jerold. 1975. "The Yokuts Gambling Tray." *American Indian Art Magazine* 1(1):10-15.

Dalrymple, Larry. 2000. *Indian Basketmakers of California and the Great Basin.* Santa Fe, NM: Museum of New Mexico Press.

Dawson, Lawrence, and James Deetz. 1965. "A Corpus of Chumash Basketry." *Archaeological Survey Annual Report* 7. Los Angeles, CA: Department of Anthropology, University of California.

Dean, Sharon E., Peggy S. Ratcheson, Judith W. Finger, and Ellen F. Davis. 2004. *Weaving a Legacy: Indian Baskets and the People of Owens Valley, California.* Salt Lake City, UT: The University of Utah Press.

Dick, Linda E., Lorrie Planas, Judy Polanich, Craig D. Bates, and Martha J. Lee. 1988. *Strands of Time: Yokuts, Mono, and Miwok Basketmakers.* Fresno, CA: Fresno Metropolitan Museum of Art, History, and Science.

Dixon, Roland B. 2010. *Basketry Designs of the Indians of Northern California.* Reprint of 1902 American Museum of Natural History Bulletin. Whitefish, MT: Kessinger Publishing.

Eisenhart, Linda Lichliter. 1981. "Karok Basketry: Mrs. Phoebe Maddux and the Johnson Collection." Unpublished M.A. thesis, Department of Anthropology, The George Washington University Graduate School of Arts and Sciences, Washington, DC.

———. 1990. "Hupa, Karok, and Yurok Basketry." In, Frank W. Porter III (ed.), *The Art of Native American Basketry: A Living Legacy*, pp. 241-266. Westport, CT: Greenwood Press.

Elsasser, Albert B. 1978. "Basketry." In, Robert F. Heizer (ed.), *Handbook of North American Indians*, vol. 8, California, pp. 626-641. Washington, DC: Smithsonian Institution.

Expedition. 1998. Special Issue, "Pomo Indian Basket Weavers: Their Baskets and the Art Market." *Expedition, The Magazine of the University of Pennsylvania Museum of Archaeology and Anthropology* 40(1).

Farmer, Justin F. 2004. *Southern California Luiseño Indian Baskets.* Fullerton, CA: The Justin Farmer Foundation.

———. 2010. *Basketry Plants Used by Western American Indians.* Fullerton, CA: The Justin Farmer Foundation.

Fields, Virginia M. 1985. *The Hover Collection of Karuk Baskets.* Eureka, CA: Clarke Memorial Museum.

Finger, Judith. 2003. "Fancy Coiled Caps of Central California." *American Indian Art Magazine* 26(3):56-63, 93.

———. 2003. "Twined Basketry Caps of Eastern California and the Great Basin." *American Indian Art Magazine* 26(2):64-73.

Gilhan, F. M. [c. 1967]. *Pomo Indian Baskets.* Reprint of c. 1915 sales catalog. Reedley, CA: Leo K. Brown.

Gogol, John M. 1983. "Klamath, Modoc, and Shasta Basketry." *American Indian Basketry Magazine* 3(2):4-17.

Griset, Suzanne. 2001. "California." In, Lydia L. Wyckoff (ed.), *Woven Worlds: Basketry from the Clark Field Collection at the Philbrook Museum of Art*, pp. 51-77. Tulsa, OK: The Philbrook Museum of Art.

Guy, Hubert. 1976. "The Rattlesnake Basket." *American Indian Art Magazine* 1(3):66-70, 74, 78.

Herold, Joyce. 1977. "Chumash Baskets from the Malaspina Collection." *American Indian Art Magazine* 3(1):68-75.

———. 2005. "Baskets of California." In, Jill R. Chancey (ed.), *By Native Hands: Woven Treasures from the Lauren Rogers Museum of Art*, pp. 108-165. Laurel, MS: Lauren Rogers Museum of Art.

Kroeber, Alfred L. 1973. *Basket Designs of the Mission Indians of California.* Reprint of 1922 American Museum of Natural History Anthropological Paper. Ramona, CA: Ballena Press.

———. 2009. *Basket Designs of the Indians of Northwestern California.* Reprint of 1905 University of California publication. Whitefish, MT: Kessenger Publishing.

Lindgren-Kurz, Pat. 2011. *Picking Willows: With Daisy and Lilly*

Baker, *Maidu Basket Makers of Lake Almanor*. Bloomington, IN: iUniverse Publishing.

Lopez, Raul A., and Christopher L. Moser (eds.). 1981. *Rods Bundles & Stitches: A Century of Southern California Indian Basketry.* Riverside, CA: Riverside Museum Press.

Mack, Joanne M. 1990. "Changes in Cahuilla Coiled Basketry." In, Frank W. Porter III (ed.), *The Art of Native American Basketry: A Living Legacy*, pp. 227-239. Westport, CT: Greenwood Press.

McLendon, Sally. 1992. "California Baskets and Basketmakers." In, Linda Mowat, et al. (eds.), *Basketmakers: Meaning and Form in Native American Baskets*, pp. 51-75. Hertford, England: Pitt Rivers Museum.

Moser, Christopher L. 1986. *Native American Basketry of Central California.* Riverside, CA: Riverside Museum Press.

———. 1989. *American Indian Basketry of Northern California.* Riverside, CA: Riverside Museum Press.

———. 1993. *Native American Basketry of Southern California.* Riverside, CA: Riverside Museum Press.

Newman, Sandra Corrie. 1974. *Indian Basket Weaving: How to Weave Pomo, Yurok, Pima and Navajo Baskets.* Flagstaff, AZ: Northland Publishing.

O'Neale, Lila M. 1995. *Yurok-Karok Basket Weavers.* Reprint of 1932 edition. Berkeley, CA: Phoebe Hearst Museum of Anthropology, University of California.

Purdy, Carl. 1971. *Pomo Indian Baskets and Their Makers.* Reprint of 1901 and 1902 articles. Ukiah, CA: Mendocino County Historical Society.

Roseberry, Viola M. 1967. *Illustrated History of Indian Baskets and Plates Made by California Indians and Many Other Tribes.* Reprint of 1915 exhibit catalog. Orange Cove, CA: Leo K. Brown.

Shanks, Ralph, and Lisa Woo Shanks. 2006. *Indian Baskets of Central California.* Novato, CA: Costaño Books.

———. 2010. *California Indian Baskets: San Diego to Santa Barbara and Beyond to the San Joaquin Valley, Mountains and Deserts.* Novato, CA: Costaño Books.

Silva, Arthur M., and William C. Cain. 1976. *California Indian Basketry: An Artistic Overview.* Cypress, CA: Cypress College Fine Arts Gallery.

Smith, Lillian. 1982. "Three Inscribed Chumash Baskets with Designs from Spanish Colonial Coins." *American Indian Art Magazine* 7(3):62-68.

Winther, Barbara. 1985. "Pomo Banded Baskets and Their Dau Marks." *American Indian Art Magazine* 10(4):50-57.

———. 2000. "Yuki and Yuki-style Basketry." *American Indian Art Magazine* 25(3):56-69, 86.

Zigmond, Maurice L. 1978. "Kawaiisu Basketry." *The Journal of California Anthropology* 5(2):199-215.

VIDEOS

Pomo Basketweavers: A Tribute to Three Elders. 1994. Berkeley, CA: Berkeley Media. (59 min.)

A Treasury of California Baskets. 1993. Los Angeles, CA: Tree of Life Productions. (49 min.)

PLATEAU

Cheney Cowles Memorial Museum. 1976. *Cornhusk Bags of the Plateau Indians* (text/fiche). Chicago, IL: University of Chicago Press.

Conn, Richard G., and Mary Dodds Schlick. 1998. "Basketry." In, Deward E. Walker, Jr. (ed.), *Handbook of North American Indians,* vol. 12, Plateau, pp. 600-610. Washington, DC: Smithsonian Institution.

Farrand, Livingston. 1900. "Basketry Designs of the Salish Indians." *Memoirs of the American Museum of Natural History* 2(5):391-399. New York, NY.

Fraser, David W. 2009. "Vertically Twined Plateau Bags." *American Indian Art Magazine* 35(1):48-55.

Glinsmann, Dawn. 2005. "Baskets of the Plateau, Northwest Coast, Subarctic, and Arctic." In, Jill R. Chancey (ed.), *By Native Hands: Woven Treasures from the Lauren Rogers Museum of Art*, pp. 168-215. Laurel, MS: Lauren Rogers Museum of Art.

Kuneki, Nettie, Elsie Thomas, and Marie Slockish. 1982. *The Heritage of Klickitat Basketry: A History of Art Preserved.* Portland, OR: Oregon Historical Society.

Linn, Natalie. 1994. *The Plateau Bag.* Overland Park, KS: Johnson County Community College Gallery of Art.

Lobb, Allan. 1990. *Indian Baskets of the Pacific Northwest and Alaska.* Portland, OR: Graphic Arts Center Publishing.

Miller, G. Lynette. 1990. "Basketry of the Northwestern Plateaus." In, Frank W. Porter III (ed.), *The Art of Native American Basketry: A Living Legacy*, pp. 135-151. Westport, CT: Greenwood Press.

Schlick, Mary D. 1980. "Art Treasures of the Columbia Plateau Indians." *American Indian Basketry Magazine* 1(2):12-21.

———. 1985. "Wasco/Wishxam Basketry: Who Were the Weavers?" *American Indian Basketry Magazine* 5(4):21-27.

———. 1994. *Columbia River Basketry.* Seattle, WA: University of Washington Press.

Tisdale, Shelby J. 2001. "Intermontane West." In, Lydia L. Wyckoff (ed.), *Woven Worlds: Basketry from the Clark Field Collection at the Philbrook Museum of Art*, pp. 79-105. Tulsa, OK: The Philbrook Museum of Art.

NORTHWEST COAST

Busby, Sharon. 2003. *Spruce Root Basketry of the Haida and Tlingit.* Seattle, WA: Marquand Books.

Devine, Sue E. 1980. "Nootka Basketry Hats–Two Special Types." *American Indian Basketry Magazine* 1(3):26-31.

———. 1981. "Kwakiutl Spruce Root Hats." *American Indian Basketry Magazine* 1(4):24-27.

———. 1982. "Spruce Root Hats of the Tlingit, Haida and Tsimsian." *American Indian Basketry Magazine* 2(2):20-25.

Emmons, George T. 1993. *The Basketry of the Tlingit and The Chilkat Blanket.* Combined reprint of separate 1903 and 1907 publications. Sitka, AK: Friends of the Sheldon Jackson Museum.

Farrand, Livingston. 1900. "Basketry Designs of the Salish Indians." *Memoirs of the American Museum of Natural History* 2(5):391-399. New York, NY.

Glinsmann, Dawn. 2005. "Baskets of the Plateau, Northwest Coast, Subarctic, and Arctic." In, Jill R. Chancey (ed.), *By Native Hands: Woven Treasures from the Lauren Rogers Museum of Art*, pp. 168-215. Laurel, MS: Lauren Rogers Museum of Art.

Gogol, John M. 1980. "The Twined Basketry of Western Washington and Vancouver Island." *American Indian Basketry Magazine* 1(3):4-11.

———. 1981. "Nootka/Makah Twined Fancy Baskets." *American Indian Basketry Magazine* 1(4):4-11.

———. 1985. "Cowlitz Indian Basketry." *American Indian Basketry Magazine* 5(4):4-20.

Laforet, Andrea. 1984. "Tsimshian Basketry." In, Margaret Seguin (ed.), *The Tsimshian: Images of the Past, Views for the Present*, pp. 215-280. Vancouver, BC: University of British Columbia Press.

———. 1990. "Regional and Personal Style in Northwest Coast Basketry." In, Frank W. Porter III (ed.), *The Art of Native American Basketry: A Living Legacy*, pp. 281-297. Westport, CT: Greenwood Press.

———. 1992. "Windows on Display: Northwest Coast Baskets in the Pitt Rivers Collection." In, Linda Mowat, et al. (eds.), *Basketmakers: Meaning and Form in Native American Baskets*, pp. 37-49. Hertford, England: Pitt Rivers Museum.

Lobb, Allan. 1990. *Indian Baskets of the Pacific Northwest and Alaska.* Portland, OR: Graphic Arts Center Publishing.

Marr, Carolyn J. 1984. "Salish Baskets from the Wilkes Expedition." *American Indian Art Magazine* 9(3):44-51, 71.

———. 1988. "Wrapped Twined Baskets of the Southern Northwest Coast: A New Form with an Ancient Past." *American Indian Art Magazine* 13(3):54-63.

———. 1990. "Continuity and Change in the Basketry of Western Washington." In, Frank W. Porter III (ed.), *The Art of Native American Basketry: A Living Legacy*, pp. 267-279. Westport, CT: Greenwood Press.

———. 1991. "Basketry Regions of Washington State." *American Indian Art Magazine* 16(2):40-49.

Marr, Carolyn J., and Nile Thompson. 1981. "Suquamish Indian Basketry." *American Indian Basketry Magazine* 1(4):28-31.

Nordquist, D. L., and G. E. Nordquist. 1983. *Twana Twined Basketry.* Ramona, CA: Acoma Books.

Ostapkowicz, Joanna. 2010. "Nuu-chah-nulth and Makah Black-brimmed Hats: Chronology and Style." *American Indian Art Magazine* 35(3):52-67, 84.

Paul, Frances. 1970. *Spruce Root Basketry of the Alaska Tlingit.* Reprint of 1944 edition. Washington, DC: US Department of the Interior, Bureau of Indian Affairs.

Shortridge, Louis. 1984. *Tlingit Woman's Root Basket.* Sitka, AK: Sheldon Jackson Museum.

Thompson, Nile, and Carolyn Marr. 1983. *Crow's Shells: Artistic Basketry of Puget Sound.* Seattle, WA: Dushuyay Publications.

Thompson, Nile, Carolyn Marr, and Janda Volkmer. 1980. "Twined Basketry of the Twana, Chehalis and Quinault." *American Indian Basketry Magazine* 1(3):12-19.

Weber, Ronald L. 1982. "Tsimshian Twined Basketry: Stylistic and Cultural Relationships." *American Indian Basketry Magazine* 2(2):26-30.

———. "Tlingit Basketry, 1750-1950." In, Frank W. Porter III (ed.), *The Art of Native American Basketry: A Living Legacy*, pp. 299-317. Westport, CT: Greenwood Press.

Webster, Gloria Cranmer, and Shelby J. Tisdale. 2001. "Northwest Coast." In, Lydia L. Wyckoff (ed.), *Woven Worlds: Basketry from the Clark Field Collection at the Philbrook Museum of Art*, pp. 107-123. Tulsa, OK: The Philbrook Museum of Art.

Winther, Barbara. 2011. "Pacific Northwest Onion-Domed Whalers' Hats." *American Indian Art Magazine* 36(3):46-53.

Wray, Jacilee. 2012. *From the Hands of a Weaver: Olympic Peninsula Basketry through Time.* Norman, OK: University of Oklahoma Press.

VIDEO

Baskets of the Northwest People: Gifts from the Grandmothers, Parts 1 and 2. 1995. Los Angeles, CA: Mimbres Fever. (76 min.)

ARCTIC and SUBARCTIC

Glinsmann, Dawn. 2005. "Baskets of the Plateau, Northwest Coast, Subarctic, and Arctic." In, Jill R. Chancey (ed.), *By Native Hands: Woven Treasures from the Lauren Rogers Museum of Art*, pp. 168-215. Laurel, MS: Lauren Rogers Museum of Art.

Gogol, John M. 1982. "Indian, Eskimo, and Aleut Basketry of Alaska." *American Indian Basketry Magazine* 2(2):4-10.

Hudson, Raymond L. 1990. "The Influence of Attu Weavers on Aleut Basketry." In, Frank W. Porter III (ed.), *The Art of Native American Basketry: A Living Legacy*, pp. 335-343. Westport, CT: Greenwood Press.

Lee, Molly. 1981. "Pacific Eskimo Spruce Root Baskets." *American Indian Art Magazine* 6(2):66-73.

———. 1990. "Objects of Knowledge: The Communicative Aspect of Baleen Baskets." In, Frank W. Porter III (ed.), *The Art of Native American Basketry: A Living Legacy*, pp. 319-333. Westport, CT: Greenwood Press.

———. 1995. "Siberian Sources of Alaskan Eskimo Coiled Basketry." *American Indian Art Magazine* 20(4):56-69.

———. 1998. *Baleen Basketry of the North Alaskan Eskimo.* Reprint of 1983 edition. Seattle, WA: University of Washington Press.

———. 2002. "Nushagak Baskets: A Case Study in Artistic Fusion." *American Indian Art Magazine* 27(2):48-53, 86.

Lobb, Allan. 1990. *Indian Baskets of the Pacific Northwest and Alaska.* Portland, OR: Graphic Arts Center Publishing.

Marie, Suzan, and Judy Thompson. 2002. *Dene Spruce Root Basketry: Revival of a Tradition.* Hull, QC: Canadian Museum of Civilization.

McMullen, Ann. 2001. "Arctic and Subarctic." In, Lydia L. Wyckoff (ed.), *Woven Worlds: Basketry from the Clark Field Collection at the Philbrook Museum of Art*, pp. 125-137. Tulsa, OK: The Philbrook Museum of Art.

Meany, Edmond S. 1982. "Attu and Yakutat Basketry," Reprint of 1903 article. *American Indian Basketry Magazine* 2(2):11-19.

PLAINS

Jolie, Edward A. 2006. "The Technomechanics of Plains Indian Coiled Gambling Baskets." *Plains Anthropologist* 51:17-50.

Schneider, Mary Jane. 1984. "An Investigation into the Origin of Arikara, Hidatsa, and Mandan Twilled Basketry." *Plains Anthropologist* 29:265-276.

———. 1990. "Plains Indian Basketry: Techniques and Uses." In, Frank W. Porter III (ed.), *The Art of Native American Basketry: A Living Legacy*, pp. 107-134. Westport, CT: Greenwood Press.

Wyckoff, Lydia L. 2001. "Prairie and Plains." In, Lydia L. Wyckoff (ed.), *Woven Worlds: Basketry from the Clark Field Collection at the Philbrook Museum of Art*, pp. 139-147. Tulsa, OK: The Philbrook Museum of Art.

SOUTHEAST

Downs, Dorothy. 1990. "Contemporary Florida Indian Patchwork and Baskets." *American Indian Art Magazine* 15(4):56-63.

Duggan, Betty J. 2005. "Baskets of the Southeast." In, Jill R. Chancey (ed.), *By Native Hands: Woven Treasures from the Lauren Rogers Museum of Art*, pp. 26-73. Laurel, MS: Lauren Rogers Museum of Art.

Duggan, Betty J., and Brett H. Riggs. 1991. "Studies in Cherokee Basketry." *The Frank H. McClung Museum Occasional Paper* 9. Knoxville, TN: The University of Tennessee.

Fariello, M. Anna. 2009. *Cherokee Basketry: From the Hands of Our Elders.* Charleston, SC: The History Press.

Gettys, J. Marshall. 2001. "Southeast." In, Lydia L. Wyckoff (ed.), *Woven Worlds: Basketry from the Clark Field Collection at the Philbrook Museum of Art*, pp. 173-191. Tulsa, OK: The Philbrook Museum of Art.

———. (ed.). 1984. *Basketry of Southeastern Indians.* Idabel, OK: Museum of the Red River.

Green, Rayna. 1992. "Red Earth People and Southeastern Basketry." In, Linda Mowat, et al. (eds.), *Basketmakers: Meaning and Form in Native American Baskets*, pp. 11-17. Hertford, England: Pitt Rivers Museum.

Hill, Sarah H. 1997. *Weaving New Worlds: Southeastern Cherokee Women and Their Basketry.* Chapel Hill, NC: The University of North Carolina Press.

Jackson, Jason Baird. 2000. "Southeastern Indian Basketry in the Gilcrease Museum Collection." *American Indian Art Magazine* 25(4):46-55.

Leftwich, Rodney L. 1970. *Arts and Crafts of the Cherokee.* Cherokee, NC: Cherokee Publications.

Medford, Claude, Jr. 1977. "Chitimacha Split Cane Basketry: Weaves and Designs." *American Indian Art Magazine* 3(1):56-61, 101.

Porter, Frank W., III. 1990. "Basketry of the Middle Atlantic and Southeast." In, Frank W. Porter III (ed.), *The Art of Native American Basketry: A Living Legacy*, pp. 79-105. Westport, CT: Greenwood Press.

Qualla Arts and Crafts Mutual, Inc. 1987. *Contemporary Artists and Craftsmen of the Eastern Band of Cherokee Indians.* Cherokee, NC: Qualla Arts and Crafts Mutual, Inc.

Speck, Frank G. 1920. "Decorative Art and Basketry of the Cherokee." *Bulletin of the Public Museum of the City of Milwaukee* 2(2):53-86. Milwaukee, WI.

Young, Stephen Flinn (ed.). 1983. *Mississippi Choctaw Crafts.* Jackson, MS: Craftsmen's Guild of Mississippi.

VIDEOS

Cherokee Artists, Vol. 1: The Basketweavers. 1994. Cherokee, NC: Qualla Arts and Crafts Mutual. (35 min.)

Ella Mae Blackbear: Cherokee Basketmaker. 1982. Tulsa, OK: Full Circle Communications. (24 min.)

NORTHEAST

Artifacts. 1985. Northeast Basketry Issue, 12(3). Washington, CT: American Indian Archaeological Institute.

Benedict, Salli. 1983. "Mohawk Basketmakers of Akwesasne." *American Indian Basketry Magazine* 3(1):10-16.

Brasser, Ted J. 1975. "A Basketful of Indian Culture Change." *National Museum of Man Mercury Series, Canadian Ethnology Service Paper* 22. Ottawa, ON: National Museums of Canada.

Butler, Eva L. 1947. "Some Early Indian Basket Makers of Southern New England." Addendum to Frank G. Speck, *Eastern Algonkian Block-Stamp Decoration: A New World Original or an Acculturated Art*, pp. 35-54. Trenton, NJ: The Archaeological Society of New Jersey.

Cole-Will, Rebecca. 2006. "'Delicate Sweet Dishes Too They Make:' Birchbark Art in the Abbe Museum's Collections." *American Indian Art Magazine* 31(3):58-65.

Cook, Stephen W. 2005. "Baskets of the Northeastern Woodlands." In, Jill R. Chancey (ed.), *By Native Hands: Woven Treasures from the Lauren Rogers Museum of Art*, pp. 218-237. Laurel, MS: Lauren Rogers Museum of Art.

Faulkner, Gretchen Fearon. 2010. "Tree and Tradition: Maine Indian Brown Ash Basketry." *American Indian Art Magazine* 35(2):36-45.

Gordon, Joleen. 1990. "Micmac Indian Basketry." In, Frank W. Porter III (ed.), *The Art of Native American Basketry: A Living Legacy*, pp. 17-43. Westport, CT: Greenwood Press.

Green, Adriana Greci. 2012. "'Many Gifted Workers:' Odawa Quill Artists Participating in the Works Progress Administration." *American Indian Art Magazine* 37(3):48-59.

Handsman, Russell G., and Ann McMullen. 1987. "An Introduction to Woodsplint Basketry and Its Interpretation." In, Ann McMullen and Russell G. Handsman (eds.), *A Key into the Language of Woodsplint Baskets*, pp. 16-35. Washington, CT: American Indian Archaeological Institute.

Hood Museum of Art. 2008. *Spirit of the Basket Tree: Wabanaki Ash Splint Baskets from Maine.* Hanover, NH: Dartmouth College.

Lester, Joan. 1987. "'We Didn't Make Fancy Baskets Until We Were Discovered:' Fancy-Basket Making in Maine." In, Ann McMullen and Russell G. Handsman (eds.), *A Key into the Language of Woodsplint Baskets*, pp. 38-59. Washington, CT: American Indian Archaeological Institute.

———. 1993. *History on Birchbark: The Art of Tomah Joseph, Passamaquoddy.* Bristol, RI: Haffenreffer Museum of Anthropology.

Lismer, Marjorie. 1982. *Seneca Splint Basketry.* Reprint of 1941 edition. Ohsweken, ON: Irocrafts.

MacDowell, Marsha (ed.). 1999. *Gatherings: Great Lakes Native Basket and Box Makers.* East Lansing, MI: Michigan State University Museum.

McBride, Bunny. 1990. *Our Lives in Our Hands: Micmac Indian Basketmakers.* Gardiner, ME: Tilbury House.

McMullen, Ann. 1982. "Woodsplint Basketry of the Eastern Algonkian." *Artifacts* 10(5):1-9. Washington, CT: American Indian Archaeological Institute.

———. 1983. "Tribal Style in Woodsplint Basketry: Early Paugusset Influence." *Artifacts* 11(4):1-4. Washington, CT: American Indian Archaeological Institute.

———. 1987. "Looking for People in Woodsplint Basketry Decoration." In, Ann McMullen and Russell G. Handsman (eds.), *A Key into the Language of Woodsplint Baskets*, pp. 102-123. Washington, CT: American Indian Archaeological Institute.

———. 1990. "Many Motives: Change in Northeastern Native Basket Making." In, Frank W. Porter III (ed.), *The Art of Native American Basketry: A Living Legacy*, pp. 45-78. Westport, CT: Greenwood Press.

———. 1992. "Talking through Baskets: Meaning, Production and Identity in the Northeast Woodlands." In, Linda Mowat, et al. (eds.), *Basketmakers: Meaning and Form in Native American Baskets*, pp. 19-35. Hertford, England: Pitt Rivers Museum.

———. 2001. "Eastern Woodlands." Lydia L. Wyckoff (ed.), *Woven Worlds: Basketry from the Clark Field Collection at the Philbrook Museum of Art*, pp. 149-171. Tulsa, OK: The Philbrook Museum of Art.

McMullen, Ann, and Russell G. Handsman (eds.). 1987. *A Key into the Language of Woodsplint Baskets.* Washington, CT: American Indian Archaeological Institute.

Mundell, Kathleen. 2008. *North by Northeast: Wabanaki, Akwesasne Mohawk, and Tuscarora Traditional Arts.* Gardiner, ME: Tilbury House.

Nicholas, Joseph A. (ed.). 1980. *Baskets of the Dawnland People.* Calais, ME: Project Indian PRIDE.

Paxson, Barbara. 1985. "Potawatomi Indian Black Ash Basketry." *American Indian Basketry Magazine* 5(1):6-11.

Pelletier, Gaby. 1982. "Abenaki Basketry." *National Museum of Man Mercury Series, Canadian Ethnology Service Paper* 85. Ottawa, ON: National Museums of Canada.

Richmond, Trudie Lamb. 1987. "Spirituality and Survival in Schaghticoke Basket-Making." In, Ann McMullen and Russell G. Handsman (eds.), *A Key into the Language of Woodsplint Baskets*, pp. 126-143. Washington, CT: American Indian Archaeological Institute.

Speck, Frank G. 1915. "Decorative Art of Indian Tribes of Connecticut." *Canadian Geological Survey, Memoir 75, Anthropological Series* 10. Ottawa, ON: Government Printing Bureau.

———. 1947. *Eastern Algonkian Block-Stamp Decoration: A New World Original or an Acculturated Art.* Trenton, NJ: The Archaeological Society of New Jersey.

Tantaquidgeon, Gladys, and Jayne G. Fawcett. 1987. "Symbolic Motifs on Painted Baskets of the Mohegan-Pequot." In, Ann McMullen and Russell G. Handsman (eds.), *A Key into the Language of Woodsplint Baskets*, pp. 94-101. Washington, CT: American Indian Archaeological Institute.

Turnbaugh, Sarah Peabody, and William A. Turnbaugh. 1987. "Weaving the Woods: Tradition and Response in Southern New England Splint Basketry." In, Ann McMullen and Russell G. Handsman (eds.), *A Key into the Language of Woodsplint Baskets*, pp. 76-93. Washington, CT: American Indian Archaeological Institute.

Webber, Alika. 1978. "Wigwamatew: Old Birch Bark Containers." *American Indian Art Magazine* 4(1):56-61.

Whiteford, Andrew Hunter. 1977. "Fiber Bags of the Great Lakes Indians." *American Indian Art Magazine* 2(3):52-64.

———. 1977. "Fiber Bags of the Great Lakes Indians, Part II." *American Indian Art Magazine* 3(1):40-47, 90.

———. 1978. "Tapestry-Twined Bags, Osage Bags and Others." *American Indian Art Magazine* 3(2):32-39.

Whiteford, Andrew Hunter, and Nora Rogers. 1994. "Woven Mats of the Western Great Lakes." *American Indian Art Magazine* 19(4):58-65.

Whitehead, Ruth Holmes. 1982. *Micmac Quillwork.* Halifax, NS: The Nova Scotia Museum.

VIDEOS

Gabriel Women: Passamaquoddy Basketmakers. 1999. Gorham, ME: University of Southern Maine Center for the Study of Lives. (28 min.)

Mohawk Basketmaking: A Cultural Profile. 1980. University Park, PA: Penn State University. (28 min.)

Our Lives in Our Hands. 1986. Watertown, MA: Documentary Educational Resources. (50 min.)

Penobscot Basketmaker–Barbara Francis. 2003. Brunswick, ME: folkfilms.com. (52 min.)

Acknowledgments

The authors thank those who provided review comments on portions of our previous research, many of which have benefitted this volume:

Craig D. Bates
William C. Cain
Marvin Cohodas
Peter L. Corey
Terry DeWald
Betty J. Duggan
Ed A. Jolie

Molly Lee
Carolyn Marr
Ann McMullen
Christopher L. Moser
Nancy Odegaard
Brett H. Riggs
Mary Dodds Schlick

We likewise appreciate our family, plus these additional friends and colleagues, both the present and the departed, who through their generosity and helpfulness toward us over the decades have demonstrated that the spirit of George Wharton James's "basket fraternity" lives on:

Doug Allard and Stephen Allard
Alexander Anthony, Jr.
Jack Antle
George and Jackie Bernheimer
Lynn Bullock
Jay Custer
Mary Dahl
Charles Derby
Merrill Domas
Lisa Fiore
John Gogol
Byron Harvey III
Harlan Henson
Norman Hurst
Ned Jalbert
Colleen James
John Kania
Robert and Marianne Kapoun
Susan Kutzleb
Natalie Linn

Rob Lucas
Bill Malone
Gay and Kent Morris
Alston and Deborah Neal
Steven Pickelner
Steve Pickle
Susan Pourian
Gene Quintana
John Rauzy
Pat Reese and John Rice
Chick and Jane Schell
Barry, Steve, and Georgiana Simpson
Jack Slaughter
Henry Stamm IV
Dianne Stanton
Clara Lee Tanner
Elaine Tucker
Micky and Dolly VanderWagen
Andrew Hunter Whiteford
Stephen Williams

For institutional and individual support of various kinds we gratefully acknowledge:

The Museum of Primitive Art and Culture and its staff and trustees; David Maslyn and Margaret "Mimi" Keefe at the University of Rhode Island library; Robert Bauver and Alice Kaufman of ATADA; Douglas Deihl and staff at Skinner Inc.; faculty and staff of the University of Rhode Island anthropology and textiles programs; Nancy Schiffer and the team at Schiffer Publishing.

Index